"The vivid realism displayed invites us right into Julia's trials and tribulations, and acts as a springboard to let us know that God was always there, even in the midst of chaos and imperfection. The powerful dialog and arresting content confront issues that many have experienced but never wanted to look back upon. As you read the book you will fall in love with the protagonist and begin to see a little bit of yourself in her. I feel that this action-packed adventure has the ability to evoke change in the heart of the reader."

—*Andrew D. Batistich, Reverend, Servant of the Lord*

"'Many Scars' was a nightmare out of my past. The candor that Julia expressed was true and unreal. It reminds me of the seven-year disaster of my C & P exam."

—*Brian Cianella, Captain, USMC (Ret.)*

"Julia articulates so clearly the emotional, the spiritual and the physical trauma associated with abuse. Furthermore she describes how one can get out of the situation despite the conflict and the ambivalence. Congratulations for being a true survivor in every way and an inspiration to us all."

—*Andiea Harris, Ph.D., CCHP, Mental Health Deputy Director, Rikers Island Correctional Facility*

"For the cop and civilian reader alike, Julia's exploits in various roles as an undercover will keep you flipping the pages in suspense. Every time Julia puts on her façade, she placed herself in danger. No gun, often alone with backup hopefully close by, you get the raw feeling that disaster lurks in every moment of the life of an undercover. Julia learned well her 'lesson to adapt in the blink of an eye.' After years crossing the globe with various local, county, and federal agencies, taking down bad operators, she was constantly reminded of some sage advice: 'The most important part of the job is to go home. Remember that.' This story will have you on the edge of your seat, wondering how she'll manage to get home, asking yourself, 'How can she get herself out of this one?'"

—*Leo McGuire, MBA, Sheriff, Bergen County, NJ (Ret.)*

"A great insight into the shadow world of working Undercover through the eyes of a female Undercover who has maintained her moral compass after several years of UC work."

—*Joseph Pistone, Retired FBI agent who spent twenty years working Undercover as Donnie Brasco*

"Julia's writing is such an honest view into the thoughts, fears, and raw emotional roller coaster of an abused woman fighting to not lose herself. She was blessed to have had her daughter to be brave for and to fight for, and because of her, Julia's triumph was a certainty. At a time when she couldn't justify fighting for herself, Julia fought for her daughter, thereby finding the inner strength and resolve to survive. Her story will confirm to other women that their victimization is not their fault and there is a safe way out."

—*Maria Turco-Gulyas, Esq.*

"In her piece on law enforcement, Torres points out, oftentimes with accurate humor, the trials and tribulations encountered by any of those men and women who have strapped on a gun and badge and placed themselves into harm's way. In many of the fictional pieces today, whether in print or on film, the portrayals of law enforcement at any level range from superhero to arch villain, both of which 'never seem to run out of bullets' in a crisis. Torres does a fine job providing insights into a career officer who places herself into the line of fire over a period of time and perfectly depicts the true nature of investigative work. From desk assignments to undercover work, the piece paints a true picture of how such work can go from boring and routine to Mach-3 in an instant. It is a wonderfully written piece of work."

—*Gazmen Xhudo, Ph.D., Professor,*
Fairleigh Dickinson University

BOLDER AND BRAVER

ALSO BY JULIA TORRES
Still Standing: The Story of My Wars

BOLDER AND BRAVER

My Undercover Life

JULIA TORRES

Full Court Press
Englewood Cliffs, New Jersey

First Edition

Copyright © 2015 by Julia Torres

All rights reserved. Some names have been changed to protect individual privacy. No part of this book may be reproduced or transmitted in any form or by any means electronic or mechanical, including by photocopying, by recording, or by any information storage and retrieval system, without the express permission of the author and publisher, except where permitted by law.

Published in the United States of America
by Full Court Press, 601 Palisade Avenue
Englewood Cliffs, NJ 07632
www.fullcourtpressnj.com

Contact the author at JuliaTorresStillStanding@gmail.com
visit us at www.juliatorresstillstanding.com
and www.julias-story.over-blog.com

ISBN 978-1-938812-51-4
Library of Congress Control No. 2015935588

Book Design by Barry Sheinkopf for Bookshapers (www.bookshapers.com)
Cover art and photo enhancements by Rolando E. Corujo
Colophon by Liz Sedlack

To my daughter
My baby bear, my sugar plum

For the silent and for the survivors

In memory
*of all the veterans, cops, family,
and friends who went before me*

Author's Note and Acknowledgments

Here's the part I really like: talking without being edited. Thank you for reading this personal account of my life, and being that I believe we're always learning, I hope it'll teach you something that you can share with others. I gotta say that, as I wrote and sometimes read it back as if it wasn't me, two things came to mind: holy cow, how could so many things happen to one person; and this kid gets out of one thing and then gets into another without even asking for it. It seemed someone was always singling me out, whether for good or bad.

Now I know, without a doubt, that everything happened to get me to this point. God won't waste teachable moments, and most of us know that we seem to learn more from the hard knocks of life. That's what He's doing now, teaching us.

Above all else, though often ignored, and not always given credit, one factor has been a constant presence in my life: God. He allowed me successes that I had attributed mostly to myself (though I was thankful). Despite my recalcitrant and independent ways, He favored me with His grace, sending messages, prophesying, protecting, and cheering me on. I thank Him for not giving up on me. It is my desire that, regardless of the nature of this book, the change in me is obvious in the end, and that He is glorified by it.

My life took on a different light after I retired, and when Marissa Barrios, my old bud, said, "It takes a village, Jules." She was referring to child-rearing, but I realized it applied to other areas in my life, as well as the collective effort it took to accomplish them and live through them. I thought of my self-reliance and concluded that I really hadn't done things on my own. Someone had made a suggestion, a recommendation, a phone call. . . .

During this two-book process, which took longer than I expected, people have encouraged my vision, believing in it. I'd like to thank the village of friends, family, cops, and soldiers, who assisted me in all my past and present endeavors. Special thanks to the professionals who took time from their busy schedules to write blurbs, and offer advice and well-wishes, from Joseph Pistone, the Godfather of undercover work, to the late Dr. Maya Angelou, woman extraordinaire; to my awesome former partner, Jerry Burgos, who contributed police pictures; and to my *old school* friend Paula Frenes, who came up with the perfect title for this book without even trying.

Thank you to those with elephant brains who helped me add forgotten content to my chapters, agreed to be videoed, gave me photographs, and allowed me to use their real names. Thank you also to those who wished to remain private, yet whose stories I shared.

A humongous thanks goes to Jamie Quattrochi, the man who planted the seed. Film director and producer, casting director and actor, Jamie believed in the value of my story when we first met at an audition in Southern Cal in 2009. He spun the reels of this grand task, motivating me to write the book he envisioned as a film and remaining in touch with me until it was finished.

Several months after meeting Jamie, my friend Rolando Corujo became involved, encouraging me, dispensing personal advice, providing technical assistance (which hurt my head) and artistic talent. His ability to put together blogs, websites, and book covers only scratches the surface of his multiple talents. When we discovered that I could actually write my own book

(I hadn't thought about it) rather than pay forty thousand dollars to a ghost writer, I went full steam ahead. Then sometime in 2011, Rolando recommended our high school classmate, Maria-Arriola Fernandez, to help me edit.

Although she hadn't had any experience as an editor, her meticulous nature, and vocation as an educator, proved to be valuable. Mari edited chapters for me when I had no clue that what I was writing was expository. We knew something was missing, but we didn't know what it was until I met Jane Chagaris-Albanese at a women's church retreat in New Jersey.

Jane, who'd been writing her own book, referred me to Barry Sheinkopf, a published author, editor, and writing professor, who directs Bookshapers.com. Under his tutelage, this once expository book, as well as my previous one, *Still Standing: The Story of My Wars*, turned into a life of passion and raw elements that have brought forth tears from men and women alike.

One of them was Darwin Laidley, a Vietnam veteran I became friends with while living in LA. Darwin was going to school for ministry, and one day shared a prophecy with me. Without knowing I was a writer, he felt led to pray for my hands, saying that God was going to use them to reach people. He'd said I would go places I never dreamed of, meet people I'd never imagined meeting. . . .

Afterward, I told him that I was a writer and let him read a rough draft of "Inner City Princess" (a chapter from my first book). My brawny friend cried. I thank Darwin for relaying God's message; I believed it then and I believe it now.

I thank Yavaun Swanson, a lovely lady I met at a Sherman Oaks salon one afternoon, who showed me how quickly one can be great friends. Every month we'd meet for lunch at a different place, trading personal stories, laughing, and crying, until the day I left. I miss her still.

Last but certainly never least, I want to give an extra-special thank you to my buddy Burns, who, just as in the Gulf, has stood by me: always united and never divided. I want to thank my buddy's friend Patricia Casey for believing my story must be told, and for sharing two of the chapters from my first book with Dr. Angelou.

It's humbling to see where life has taken this kid from down the block, for that is, in essence, how I see myself—an average girl from Union City, New Jersey, who refused to be knocked down.

With that in mind, my heartfelt desire is that the children, women, and men who've been, are, or will be, in similar predicaments will seek God's purpose for their lives and find hope for themselves, bringing restoration to relationships with family and friends.

Our criminal justice system doesn't always work; there was no reason for me to have to stay longer in a violent marriage in order to obtain enough concrete evidence to make a case. I don't expect anyone to have to do that either, nor do I suggest it, for matters do escalate.

Just as domestic violence laws need to be amended to ensure the safety of the victim, so should a perpetrator be charged with aggravated assault on a police officer, whether DV or not, if he or she knows that the person is a cop. If law enforcement officers are done with a shift and see a crime being committed, they take *action*, which means they're always acting in an official capacity. It's essential that this change in the law is implemented.

Regarding the cases briefed, I chose some agencies I did

U/C for, but they are by no means, the only work I performed or the only departments I worked with. That would take volumes, and this book had to end at some point.

Know that Law Enforcement is not always exciting, but I didn't think you'd want to read about the mundane: tedious report writing; waiting in full gear in a car or a van for endless hours on jobs that don't happen; targets who leave you flat; search warrants that produce little or no evidence; mobile surveillance or primary back-up scenarios with cops who appear mute, making the time appear longer. . . .

However, surveillance may contain moments when: instant rapport is built after a cop shares personal experiences; you kiss a partner to avoid being made; U/C work can bring: speaking in accented Spanish to dealers who try to rip you off, change prices, or sell bogus drugs; sources/informants working both sides of the fence. . . .

The situations are as different as you can imagine, keeping U/Cs on their toes to adapt without warning, while maintaining a believable rap, a likable personality, and ensuring evidence is obtained. In my opinion, the not knowing what to expect is what makes it a cool and unique thing to do: No doubt, if I could do it all over again, I would.

And now, this book ends, but not my life. God has an abundance of great plans for my future, and I anticipate experiencing all of them. Whatever they are, there will probably be enough material for a third book, and a fourth, and. . . .

So I say see you later, and thank you for letting me share some of my life stories with you.

"He lifted me out of the slimy pit, out of the mud and mire; He set my feet on a rock and gave me a firm place to stand."

—Psalm 40:2

TF 194

DRUG ENFORCEMENT ADMINISTRATION
UNITED STATES DEPARTMENT OF JUSTICE

THIS IS TO CERTIFY THAT **JULIA TORRES**, WHOSE SIGNATURE AND PHOTOGRAPH APPEAR BELOW, IS DULY APPOINTED AS **TASK FORCE OFFICER** IN THE DRUG ENFORCEMENT ADMINISTRATION, UNITED STATES DEPARTMENT OF JUSTICE, AND AS SUCH IS CHARGED WITH THE DUTY OF ENFORCING THE CONTROLLED SUBSTANCES ACT, AND OTHER DUTIES IMPOSED BY LAW.

Office of the Administrator
Drug Enforcement Administration

BY ORDER OF:
The Attorney General
of the United States

8/2003

SIGNATURE

I

Methods of Instruction

"POLICE FILMS ARE A GROSS EXAGGERATION of the intricacy of law enforcement, not to mention undercover work." Using his hands to make his points, our instructor paced back and forth. "Actors don't run out of ammo, and if they do, their weapon doesn't lock to the rear, they just keep shootin'. I'd like to have that gun."

The academy cadets and I loved listening to a professor who taught with a sense of humor. At nine o'clock in the morning, Vito Palumbo made it seem as if lunchtime was in the next five minutes.

"They don't follow chain-of-evidence but check out what they do. They toss evidence around in the squad room like it's a ball. I'd like to see my boss walk in to find a bag in his face. We'll all be under investigation—without pay, too. We don't dodge bullets from high-powered rifles on a regular basis, or leap over tall buildings consecutively. Hell, I can't even jump one."

Laughter followed.

"And guys, the most important thing. . . ." Students leaned in closer, hanging on the last words the short Italian with an unsuspecting police presence would speak. "When it comes to conducting search warrants, don't follow their lead, or you'll get killed."

Peers sat up straight—the word *kill* has the tendency to do that, bring respect to it, thus changing the environment. That morning was no different as the reality of death hung in the air, but Palumbo moved on.

"Honestly, I never shot out of my car while in hot pursuit in the middle of the city. . .too many people, somebody's gonna get killed, the city's gonna get sued, and probably me, too. That's Hollywood."

A student raised his hand. "Sir, how often do you chase a suspect?"

"As an undercover?"

"Yes."

"I never have. That's not my job."

"What is?" someone called out.

"The U/C walks the walk, talks the talk, and gathers information and evidence to make a solid case. Then he or she writes articulate reports. Surveillance teams can chase 'em."

"I have a surveillance question," I said.

"Okay, shoot."

"How close are the teams, and how much can they hear?"

"It depends how close they can get without being made, but just 'cause they're there doesn't mean they can hear shots fired."

Chairs screeched and remarks were made.

"Why not?" asked a man seated in the rear.

"Murphy's Law."

Expletives were uttered.

"Okay, guys, look—it's great to have back-up, don't get me wrong, but the U/C must always work thinking that he or she is alone. Use your personality, but remember you're acting. Don't lose yourself in the role. Be a good bullshitter, but know how to get out without getting killed."

"Do you always carry?" asked a young man.

"No."

The student mumbled under his breath.

"I know how you feel, but I can't always explain having one."

The instructor made his way to the center of the class, standing still as if for effect, before glancing at everyone. "Guys, listen, what you learn here is book knowledge. It's what you need to know to get certified, but by no means is this the street. Let me ask you this. Would you take your gun to buy a dime bag from a street dealer, or to discuss bank transactions with a money launderer, or to place a bet with a bookie—or better yet, if you're gonna be introduced to a wise guy?"

Some classmates nodded or shook their heads. Others shrugged.

Having made his point, his arms went up. "Exactly. See how you don't know? It all depends on the circumstances. In my opinion, it should be up to the undercover to make that decision, if experienced, or the supervisor if not."

The invaluable lesson had been absorbed: I'd be alone, armed or not. If I couldn't talk myself out of a situation, then undercover work was no longer for me.

Graduation came that December, and I beamed with pride at my police certification. Having returned from the Gulf War that July, I'd been ecstatic when things had begun moving along to my benefit. Now there was nowhere to go but up, yet I knew it wouldn't be at Sussex.

It was lame. At that time, deep-cover investigations meant wearing a hair net in a cookie factory where it was presumed there was narcotics activity. Luckily, employees smoking a joint outdoors during their lunch break did not fall into that category, and that job was short-lived.

As the months dragged by, I'd take compensatory time to break up the monotony. That May was no different when I flew to Miami Beach to stay with my older sister Marlene and got in touch with Roman.

We'd met in March 1990 at a nightclub near the beach. Whenever I was in the area, we'd get together. Although we shared a mutual attraction, there hadn't been any intimacy. The bad habits I'd developed from my 1985 prom rape of having sex in the dark, with a buzz or not, entertaining dead end relationships or sabotaging good ones, had made me hesitant.

I had hurt George, the guy whom I had shared a deep love with back then; I had not been able to fathom how those malicious, intrusive thoughts could have entered my mind when we finally made love about two years after beginning our relationship. No words could've described their vulgarity at such pure and intimate moments. All I'd wanted to do was plead them out of existence, but being of a surreptitious nature,

I'd been unable.

It had been such a traumatic event that I'd volunteered for Operation Desert Shield in September 1990, hoping to die. Only one person had known about my trauma—my then best friend Marissa, who'd been seventeen—and though her response had been comforting, I knew my mother's and brother's would not have been. I'd remained silent, and also said nothing to my sister, whose support I was uncertain of.

However, on May 13, 1992, the final night of that trip, after spending a fun-filled evening dancing at a beach club, I decided to spend the night with Roman. I wanted to see if the demons still hovered, but how precise could I have been at spotting them? Neither of us had been drunk, but I'd had a buzz. The lesson for my action would come forth, though. Before I fell asleep, I knew I had conceived.

About a week later in Jersey, I made an appointment to see an OB-GYN, who confirmed my pregnancy. Carrying the child of a man who was, in essence, a stranger brought the realization that my negative behavior had to cease, but I was happy—he'd be someone to love wholly. There was no doubt in my mind that I'd give birth to a boy.

I boarded a flight to relay the news to Roman the following month. I had no ulterior motives, no desire to marry him, nor any money to demand. Simply, he had the right to know.

Roman's response was contradictory—supportive at first, then doubtful. Not appreciating his lack of character, I advised him not to contact me and returned home.

Work resumed, but I said nothing, opting instead for the first trimester to pass. Things took on a different turn in mid-June, when my sergeant sent me to a two-week DEA drug-training course in South Jersey.

I arrived early on the first day of class and was assigned to be the greeter. A twenty-something-year-old, olive-complexioned Filipino with high cheekbones entered. Notebook under an arm, Dunkin Donuts coffee in one hand, he extended the other one to me. "Hi, I'm Rick DeLeon. Nice to meet you." His smile was warm, noble.

"Julia Torres—but I'm the greeter, not you," I teased.

"Okay. Should we try this again?"

I laughed at his wittiness. "No, that's okay. Have a seat. Class will begin when everybody's here."

"You sure about that?"

"Don't shoot the messenger," I said, raising my hands.

His loud laughter resonated confidence as he strolled off.

When everyone had sat, I went to the available seat in the first row. There was Rick, seated to my left.

Moments later, I accidentally dropped my pen. *He's gonna pick it up.*

"Here you go," he said.

"Thank you."

"You're welcome."

He's gonna start a conversation.

"What department are you?"

"Sussex County Prosecutor's, Narcotics. You?"

"Hudson County Prosecutor's, Narcotics."

"Cool!" I said. "That's where I wanna work."

He drank some coffee before saying, "Put your resume in."

"I did."

"Really? And Hudson didn't call you?" He seemed puzzled.

"No. I took the first agency that did."

"I'm surprised. You're Spanish and female. Send it again."

"Yeah, I was too, for those same reasons. I'll try again after I get some experience."

"In Sussex?" he laughed, causing others to turn in our direction.

I shrugged. "At least I got the academy done."

"You're right. It's easier to get hired after that paper's in your hands. Saves departments time and money. That's smart. You live in Sussex?" he asked, finishing his coffee.

"You crazy?" I answered rhetorically, slapping his arm. "I live in Hudson."

He chuckled. "Easy, there. Remind me not to say that again. So where do you live?"

"Union City."

"Oh—I live in Jersey City, Greenville."

"We're neighbors."

"You wanna carpool?"

"Yeah, that'd be great," I said before the training instructor entered the room, filling it with his musky fragrance.

Commuting two hours each way gave Rick and me much time to talk. My analysis of him began one afternoon on our drive back home as the radio was playing softly.

"You know, I like Filipinos."

"Really? Filipinos? Why is that?" Rick asked, taking a puff of his cigarette.

"I've had good experiences with them."

"Good how?" His small brown eyes expressed curiosity.

"Well, one of my best friends in high school was Filipino,

and so was my pediatrician," I said, lowering the window, allowing the summer breeze to make cartwheels with my hair.

Bursting into laughter, he asked, "Your pediatrician?" He took another drag before flicking the ashes outside.

"Yeah. What's so funny? I saw him 'til I was twenty-three."

"Twenty-three? Are you crazy?"

"No. I was really comfortable with him."

"You don't say," he said in mockery.

I ignored his remark. "You know what ended it?"

"No. Tell me." He brought the cigarette to his lips.

"He said I had to see a real doctor."

"What?" His cigarette almost fell out when he snickered. "He *is* a real doctor."

"That's what I said, but he said I had to see a general practitioner, not him, and I said, 'But, Doctor, I love you.'"

He roared. "You're crazy. You told the doctor you loved him?"

I shrugged. "Yeah, why not? He said he loved me, too."

Rick giggled and flicked his cigarette out the window. "So that's the reason you like Filipinos?"

"And because of my friend, too. Plus I really admire their work ethic and that they're family oriented."

My comfort level led me to share the news of my pregnancy. I was glad I did; having a man's optimistic opinion was comforting.

One afternoon, my career began to unfold for the better as we waited for the instructor. Surrounded by a smorgasbord of cologne, tenor whispers, and baritone laughter, I heard my name and turned.

"Hi. I'm Jon Tillwater."

Jon, a burly blond six-footer with blue eyes, could've been a spectacular sports anchorman. His bass voice was clear and articulate. "I'm a detective with the Lakewood Police Department, Special Operations Unit," he said. "We're conducting a narcotics operation this summer in a high drug-trafficking area known as the Jungle. We're looking for undercover cops, and I think you'd be great. Would you be interested in coming on loan?"

It was what I had been waiting for. "I'd love to!"

"Great. Let me have your sergeant's number, so we can speak with him."

The classroom instructor entered, and I quickly wrote my info on a piece of paper and handed it to Jon.

On one of our return trips, I brought up the subject of rape to test Rick. "You know, I have a friend that was date-raped in college, and she had a hard time getting over it."

"Getting *over* it?" he asked, brows furrowed.

"Yeah. Why are you looking at me like that?"

"I don't know if those are the words *I'd* choose."

Good man. "What do you mean?"

"College date rapes are more common than people think, and just like rapes in general, they're highly unreported."

"Why?"

"Most reported rapes are made by adults who understand it for what it is. Don't get me wrong—some adults don't report them either, but they're not in the majority. Kids don't know what to do. Things like denial, shame, personal blame, accusations from others, you know, some of what we call rape trauma syndrome, prevent them from going to the police."

"How do you know that?" I asked.

"I read a lot, and I paid attention in the academy."

He's scoring big points. "But why deny it?"

"It's easier to ignore the trauma than to address it."

"Makes sense." I nodded. "But why feel ashamed if she did nothing wrong?"

"Assuming it's a she, maybe she drank a little too much, made out with him a little, and the guy didn't take no for an answer when she wanted him to stop."

I shook my head. "No, that wasn't it for my friend."

"Well, maybe your friend felt people would accuse her," he suggested.

"But why would someone do that?"

"It happens more often than people realize. Even the mother sometimes blames the daughter."

"How *could* she? It's her own daughter."

"She might be an old-school parent, maybe ignorant, maybe doesn't wanna deal with it. . .without even knowing, she's actually making it worse."

"So why not ask for advice?"

"Some parents find the whole ordeal shameful and don't want to acknowledge it. Some even tell the kids to keep quiet if they know the perp."

I was indignant. "But it's not about *them*! They'd rather have their own flesh and blood live in torment than tell the police?"

"Sometimes—but remember, if they're not acknowledging the rape, they're blind to their pain. The perp may, at times, live in the same home."

"That's horrible. There's no healing."

"No, that's why it's often repressed. Then people wonder why a rape victim snaps and kills someone years later. They should look at the root instead of asking how it could've been done."

"So how do they heal?"

"They start talking about it."

"To who?"

"A professional, a friend, someone who won't judge them."

"But what if they don't?"

"They have to start *somewhere*, Julia."

"That's a lot of heavy stuff to talk about." I turned to stare out the window.

"Yeah, but it should get done."

I had been content with his answers but didn't think it was the right time to disclose my rape. Instead, I said, "Working in that field must be tough. I don't know if I could do that."

"I'm sure you could."

I shook my head and grinned. "I don't think so. I'd have a hard time with the interrogation. I'd wanna hurt them."

"Some cops feel that way, but it makes them want to get a confession rather than hurt them. In the end, it's about putting them behind bars, so they don't do it again."

"You're right, but I don't know if I could do it, especially with kids." I twirled the piny air freshener he had over his rear-view mirror.

"Yeah, that's tough, too. But it's all the same premise."

I decided to keep in touch with Rick after our course ended. On that final drive home, I asked, "Wanna stay in touch?"

"Sure." He double-parked in front of my apartment.

"Okay, great. Thanks for all the rides, the coffees, doughnuts, and, most of all, the talks."

"You're welcome. Thank you, too." He smiled.

"It was nice talking to someone intelligent and open-minded," I added.

He nodded. "Same here. I know what you mean. Be safe."

"You, safer. Remember, I'm in Sussex." I leaned back to grab my purse and notebook.

He laughed. "That's right."

It wasn't the last time we saw each other.

A week later, my sergeant called out, "Julia?"

Having finished eating a turkey sandwich at my desk, I headed to his office. The wooden floors in the old, undisclosed two-story house we used as our base for narcotics operations creaked.

"Yes, Sergeant?"

He placed his telephone in its cradle. "That was Lakewood Special Ops. Come in. They want you to do some undercover work for them. You can go, but I told them they can only have you for seven days: four days the first week, three the next." He paused.

"When do I begin?"

"July 27, when you're back from A.T. Give them a call." He handed me a message slip. "The detective's name is Jon Tillwater. He'll tell you where to report. They're paying for your lodging and meals. Good luck, Julia."

"Thank you." I could've shouted with glee. There was a week left before I went with my reserve unit to our two-week annual training in Fort Dix, New Jersey, and then I'd get some excitement.

Back at my desk, I dialed Jon's number, and we agreed on a time and place to meet for my assignment.

I went home that night and called Rick. "Let's celebrate!"

"You're going, huh?" He was as excited as me.

"I told you. Come on—hurry up, and come get me."

"Okay, okay. Give me fifteen."

I rushed out of my apartment. When I saw his black Saab pull around the corner, I flagged him down and threw myself in it.

"Hey, catch your breath," he said, smiling.

"I'm *sooo* happy."

"Yeah, I see that. Ice cream okay?"

"Sure. We can eat it by 80th Street Park."

"Sounds good." Before you knew it, we were both sitting in his car, eating chocolate and vanilla ice cream in cups.

"Listen, J.," he began, concern in his eyes clear. "I'm really happy for you, but are you gonna be all right?"

"You mean the baby?" I asked, savoring the chocolate scoop.

"Yeah, I mean, this is gonna be your first time."

"I know, but we'll be fine." I rubbed my small belly, glancing at the swings, where toddlers were shouting with glee.

There was a vital factor to consider—the captain's five-year pregnancy warning in the Gulf—but it hadn't crossed my mind.

"Do they know?" he asked.

"No, only the military. I'm restricted from being near the gas chamber. You know that's what I teach, it wouldn't be good. It may seem irresponsible, but I don't wanna say anything until I'm showing. It's not like I'll be doing daredevil stuff. I'm just gonna be buying off street dealers."

"I know, but I worry about you. What about the baby's dad?"

"After he said he'd be supportive, he began to hesitate when a friend questioned it, so I told him not to call me. Now he calls Rose—you know, my old college friend—to check up on me."

"Because he cares." The Mr. Softee ice cream truck pulled over near Rick; its whimsical tune brought a group of teenagers.

I shook my head. "No, because he feels guilty. I like him, but if he's gonna believe his friend over me, then I don't want him. I won't try to change his mind. He's a grown man. . .and by the way, I don't even like his last name."

"What is it?"

"Pupo."

He laughed.

"It sounds like poop," I said.

He roared, almost spilling ice cream on his jeans. "You didn't tell him that, did you?"

"Not the poop part, but I did tell him I didn't like it. Why wouldn't I? And I also made it clear that I didn't want or need anything from him, nor did I have an ulterior motive. I said I was only telling him 'cause he was the dad and he had a right to know."

"You're right, but be careful, okay? If you need anything, page me." He finished his cup and tossed both in a garbage can.

Indeed my friendship with Rick had evolved, and I wouldn't know how great a man he'd be until a few weeks later, when a devastating event altered a few lives.

2

Returning to Me

ONE HOT JULY MORNING ten weeks into my pregnancy, I was listening to supplemental instruction on nuclear, biological, and chemical warfare with my peers during A.T. Every word the sergeant spoke began to fade until it became unintelligible.

Staff Sergeant Penney, who was standing to my left, looked at me. "Torres, are you all right?"

"Yes," I replied meekly.

"You sure? Your color doesn't look right."

"Yes, I...I just need to sit down." My eyes fluttered, and, feeling woozy, I grabbed the chain link fence beside me.

"Excuse me, Sergeant," he said to the instructor. "Call an ambulance. Sergeant Torres is about to pass out."

Class stopped. Within minutes, screaming sirens arrived, and I was whisked to the base hospital. From there, snippets of scenes flashed before me—a slight prick in the forearm, body shivering, medical staff remarks—until I was out.

A few hours later, I awoke tired but clear-headed in a private hospital room, sun shining through the window.

Immediately I placed my hand on my queasy tummy. Something was different.

On the wooden nightstand to my right, a note read *Julia, I came to see you, but you were asleep. I'll call you later. Your pager's in the drawer. It was ringing. I turned it off so it wouldn't wake you. Hope you feel better—Kathy.*

Kathy Coury-Maixner, an officer and a friend, belonged to another platoon in the same company as I did. During the Gulf, she had sent me encouraging letters and assisted Mom with my sexual harassment complaints.

I checked my pager—Rick's number was followed by Mom's. Although I'd told him about my pregnancy, she had learned of it in a comical way. Wondering why I hadn't been feeling well, she had accompanied me to the pharmacy. The Cuban pharmacist had placed a pill container of Materna in a small bag.

"What's that prescription for?" asked Mom.

Uh, oh. I had raised my eyebrows and widened my eyes at him, hoping he'd glance my way.

He'd stapled the paper bag, answering without looking up, "It's a vitamin for pregnant women."

There was a pause.

When he handed me the prescription, he saw my facial expression and realized he had spilled the beans. "Oh, but it's not just for that. I take them, too," he'd blurted.

I had almost laughed at his absurd cover-up attempt.

Afterward, I had shared the news with Mom, who had not been upset, figuring I was a grown woman living alone and accustomed to making my own decisions. It had been a pleasant surprise when she suggested that I work nights while she worked days in order to care for the baby ourselves.

As I chuckled out loud at the thought of a man taking pregnancy vitamins, a doctor and nurse entered my room.

"Miss Torres?"

"Yes, Doctor?"

Stethoscope around his neck, small rectangular wire-rimmed glasses over expressionless eyes, he asked, "How do you feel?"

"Better."

"Do you know what's going on?"

"No."

"You're going through the beginning phase of a miscarriage."

I gasped, covered my mouth, and closed my eyes.

"It'll be all right," said the nurse, who'd been silent.

I brought my head down, my shoulders slumped, and I took a slow deep breath.

"Your body will expel the fetus when it's ready."

I looked up. "...Expel?"

"When there's a defective fetus in the womb, the body will automatically reject it. Do you understand?"

"Yes...I'm going to lose my baby," I said, the rise and fall of my voice a whisper.

"I'm sorry, Miss Torres. You'll be under observation. Irene will be your nurse. If you need anything, pull the cord behind you. She will tend to you until the end of her shift.

Another nurse will take over from there," he advised, and left.

Irene approached my bed, drawing the crisp white sheets over me. "Miss Torres, you're not alone. Approximately twenty-five percent of pregnancies become miscarriages in the first trimester. Most of which are male fetuses."

"I understand, but it doesn't make it easier," I said.

Her big brown eyes softened. "No, it doesn't, sweetie. I had a miscarriage once, too. I know how you're feeling."

"Thank you."

"Please let me know if you need anything."

Once the door closed, I turned on my side and cried.

My baby. . .my son. I touched my stomach again. *Why is this happening? Was it the Gulf?*

Needing a friend, I returned Rick's page. "Hey, it's me."

"Where are you, J.?"

"At the hospital in Fort Dix."

"I knew something was up when you didn't return my call. What happened?"

"I'm being observed. I'll be having a miscarriage soon."

". . .I'm sorry. How do you feel?"

"Not good," I said, looking around the room.

"You need anything?"

"No."

"I'll head that way after work."

"Thank you."

"No need to. Your mom know?"

"No, I called you first."

"Okay. I'll bring her with me and tell her on the way."

When they arrived, Mom, having had her own miscarriage before my sister's birth, was empathetic and did most of the talking. They left around eight o'clock, but two hours after their departure, I began having excruciating abdominal pain.

Rising from the bed with the urge to urinate, I wheeled the shepherd-hook IV to the bathroom. As I opened the stall door, the torturous pangs increased.

I bit my lip, held my scream. Dizziness took over. Sweat dripped down my forehead. I sat on the toilet and looked down; the water had turned a bright crimson. Globs of red and pink spewed from inside me.

The reality was worse than the pain. Feeling faint, I slowly moved my hand to pull the emergency cord on the wall. It was hard to grasp, until at last the light string made contact with my skin.

A nurse pushed open the stall door. "Miss Torres?"

"Y-Yes."

"*Medic, stat!*" she shouted.

Medical personnel ran in, strapping me on a gurney. I felt as light as a feather.

The sirens of an ambulance wailed; I was in it, falling in and out of consciousness.

When I opened my eyes, a man in green scrubs was standing over me. In that cold operating room, he mumbled about anesthesia. Moments later, I was out again.

In what I assumed was the early afternoon of the next day, I awoke in a well-lit, open room surrounded by unknown voices, light music, and rubber soles moving to and fro. Several blankets were draped over me.

A nurse pulled a curtain wide open. "Miss Torres?"

"Yes?" My mouth was dry.

"How do you feel?"

"Tired and thirsty. What happened?"

"The doctor will be in shortly."

Within five minutes, a thin doctor entered, fixing his tie. "Miss Torres, you're out of recovery. That's good. You began hemorrhaging heavily late last night. Fort Dix was not equipped to handle it, so you were rushed here. We had to perform an emergency D&C."

"Where am I?"

"Rancocas Hospital in Willingboro. You arrived at eleven p.m. An ambulance will take you back to the Fort Dix hospital once you're cleared."

"Will it be today?"

"Yes. A nurse will bring you discharge papers."

I felt alone, empty; the sadness hurt.

But God gave me a reprieve. When I reached Fort Dix, I was able to spend time with Rick. He had walked into my room for his usual two-hour visit; I almost cried.

"Hey, J. You okay?" He greeted me with a kiss on the forehead.

"I'm better now," I said softly.

"Your nurse said you were pretty banged up." He fluffed the pillow behind my head.

"I was. Thank you so much for being here."

"That's what friends are for."

"I don't know how I can ever repay you."

"No repayment here. We're friends. If I was jammed up, you'd do everything in your power to help me, right?"

"No doubt."

He winked. "That's right, kid. I know you would."

"I'll be discharged in the morning. I'm on light duty until

we're outta here Friday."

"Good, you could use the rest. Pick you up at the barracks tomorrow? What, six o'clock?"

"Eighteen hundred for you," I teased.

"That's good. You got your color back and your sense of humor."

Rick was punctual.

"You wanna go watch the planes take off and land at McGuire?" I asked him the next night.

"Sure, sounds good."

He parked his car on the grass outside the chain-link barbed-wire fence.

"Let's sit on the hood," I suggested.

I sat with my legs crisscrossed, hands folded, and began looking far off, speaking with melancholy. "You know, I always felt that, if I had a son, I'd raise him to be the kind of man women love—personable, smart, funny, athletic, faithful, and generous, but not a pushover."

"The baby was a he?" asked Rick.

"Yes, but a doctor didn't tell me. I just felt it."

I wasn't wrong either. About a month later, Mom ran into Arsenio, my grandma's boyfriend before she died. He told her about a dream in which he saw her rocking an infant boy. When he asked my grandmother who the baby was, she'd replied, smile beaming, "My grandson. Look how beautiful he is."

That was my son Roman. I wondered where miscarried babies went; it was God's way of telling me he was with Abuela in heaven. I'd meet him one day.

"Are you gonna tell the dad?"

"When I'm home."

"You gonna see him next time you're in Florida?"

"No...Rick, I wanna tell you something very personal."

"I think we've been down that road. Shoot."

Better to be direct, I thought. "I was raped."

"Ah. That explains a lot. All those questions you asked on our rides from DEA."

"I'm sorry if you think I set you up."

"No, I don't think that. You were testing me."

"Yes, but why?"

"To see if you could trust me," he answered.

He understood me, and I told him everything.

"Sounds like he wanted to gain your trust."

"What do you mean?"

"If he was a perfect gentleman at the prom, you wouldn't suspect any deviant behavior from him when he suggested going down the shore later."

His words were clear despite the vroom of planes. "I never thought of that. Makes sense." I paused before adding, "You know, all that effort in trying to do the right thing and keep my virginity worked out for nothing. This jerk-off took it like it didn't mean a thing. If I'd given it up to my high school sweetheart, it never would've happened. Things wouldn't have ended, 'cause we would've been having sex."

"For the most part that's probably true, but don't do that to yourself. You don't know how it would've played out. You might've broken up before the prom and ended up going with this alleged friend anyway."

I sighed, considering his words. "I guess you're right. Rick, do you think it's normal to wanna have a buzz before sex or have the lights off?"

"Yes, based on your situation. In the dark, the memory isn't clear, and the alcohol helps to keep you from remembering."

I nodded. "That's right. So can you help me?"

"With what?" He was baffled.

"I'm very comfortable with you. You're the first guy I've told. I want you to help me overcome it."

"How?"

"I want us to have sex with the lights on, and off, but not because I have to, but because I want to, and I don't wanna drink. I want to have a normal sexual relationship."

"Why don't you speak to a therapist?"

"Because it's easier for me to handle the physical than the psychological."

"I see."

"Do you?" I asked rhetorically. "Rick, I gotta tell you, I was watching how you talked to people in class, what you did. To see if I could tell you without being judged."

"That makes sense. So I guess I passed, huh?"

"You sure did." I smiled, adding, "But remember, you being Filipino helped, too."

He laughed. "J., you're a smart cookie and a tough one, too. If I was a woman, I'd be like you."

"Thank you. That's a great compliment. So will you do it? . . . It's not about you teaching me how to have sex."

When he said nothing, I filled in the gap. "It's about you helping me overcome this heavy burden."

His eyes spoke before his mouth moved almost in a whisper. "I know. I understand." He paused, then added, "This is serious. It's a big responsibility. I don't wanna hurt you by doing more harm than good."

"I was hoping you'd think that way. So what do you say?"

"Okay. I'll do it, but please let me know if it's not working out how you want."

I exhaled. "Thank you. I will."

With Rick, I began to feel hope. My ability to trust had not been completely shattered. He taught me about gratifying relationships, and I began to be set free. The unnatural, ugly portions of my life were at last being removed one layer at a time. What he did for me had a positive impact, and I am indebted to him for his unconditional help.

Our feelings for one another grew more than platonic as the months passed; however, we realized our friendship was more valuable. Today we remain friends who share mutual respect for one another.

In hindsight, although I understand the need to ignore the trauma, the right thing to do was to pray and immediately seek counseling from a professional. Had I done that, perhaps the angst I had experienced would not have been as traumatic.

3

The Jungle

EXHILARATION FILLED THE CAR as I drove down the shore on the New Jersey Turnpike in my white undercover Cutlass Supreme. With my older brother Frank's free-style cassette blasting, the cool summer wind was pouring through open windows, too. I passed endless stands of trees and mile markers.

Three unmarked vehicles were waiting on an unpaved road. Jon waved; the other four men turned as I approached, gravel crinkling under tires.

"Hi, Julie, glad to have you," said Jon when the door thudded behind me.

We greeted each other with a kiss. "Glad to be here."

He began introductions. Jon turned to the tall, older gentleman standing beside him. "This is Tom Sheehan, our supervisor, whom I'll be running with. We'll always be here, but there'll be a different group with us every day."

The fifty-five-year-old extended his hand, smiling warmly. "Nice to meet you."

"You, too." I liked him and the confidence he exuded.

"Okay, here are some of the guys you'll be working with today," said Jon. Two men climbed out of their nondescript gray car; further away, another guy wearing sunglasses slid off the trunk of his vehicle.

"Hi, guys." I raised a hand in greeting.

"Hi." The two thirty-somethings were polar opposites. Mick was fit, good-looking, and clean-cut. Harry was heavy-set, cute, and sported a beard.

"Mick and Harry will be riding together. Pete over there will be solo," Jon continued.

"Hello," said the handsome young Greek, heading toward me, removing his hands from his pockets and placing his sunglasses on his head.

Jon didn't miss a beat. "Usually, we ride two to a vehicle. That can change, but you'll always have at least three cars on surveillance. We all have radios. Here's yours. We've checked her in, right?" Jon looked at Tom.

"Yeah, she's good. I have the key."

"Okay, Julie, here's how it'll work." Jon nodded. "From now on, with today being an exception, you'll meet that day's team once you're wired. Someone else will be with me when I wire you in the hotel room. We'll make sure it's secure and in proper working order before we leave to a pre-arranged location. It's important the team gets a good look at you before we head out."

"I understand," I said, glancing at them.

"You'll have danger signals in case something goes wrong, but we'll be there like white on rice, don't you worry about that."

"Okay."

Jon continued, following protocol, "After each buy, we'll re-group, field-test the drugs, and show you a lineup. When you make a positive ID, you initial the back of the photograph, and we'll continue with another buy, unless it's too late."

"Will you have every target's picture?" I asked.

"Good question. Tom, you wanna answer that?"

"Sure. Julie, we know all the street dealers, and we have photographs of all of them. Surveillance teams will be in the field while we're waiting here with you." He pointed to the three detectives, who were listening. "They'll call out a suspect's location. We'll already know who he is, but you won't. We'll tell you how to get there and follow you in loosely. Once you make a buy, one of them will prepare a photo array with the target you bought from, and others with similar likeness from the hundreds of pictures we have."

Jon entered the conversation. "You should know that some of them use different street terms. When we know who's selling, we'll also call out that dealer's terminology. They normally sell ten or twenty-dollar bags of marijuana or cocaine."

"Can I just ask them what they have?"

"Sure, if that's what makes you comfortable."

"Okay. Am I driving or walking?"

He and Tom exchanged looks. "Usually driving, but you may have to walk up to some dealers and into some places. Is that okay with you?" Jon asked.

"Yes. Does anybody around here carry?"

"Another good question. . .not usually, but that doesn't mean you should let your guard down." Jon raised an index finger, as if recalling an unmade point. "No buy is ever the same, Julie. If you make a bogus purchase, don't worry about it. They still get locked up for selling with intent."

"When do they get locked up?"

"Girl, you've got some great questions. You sure you haven't done this before? . . . They'll get locked up when the investigation's over, which may be at the end of August or September. We don't know, but it will not be while you still have buys to make."

"Okay."

Jon turned to Tom, who took over from there. "Julie, it is very important that you relay the danger signal loud and clear." The lines on his forehead, and his thick white hair, showed he had seen plenty.

"I will." I looked down at what I was wearing: loose jeans, a sleeveless button-down shirt, and sneakers with no socks. "Are my clothes all right?"

"Yes, what you have on is fine," answered Tom.

"Okay. When do we start?"

Jon responded quickly. "Now. Follow Tom and me to the hotel. The guys will check out the area. Put your stuff in the room, and we'll head out once you're wired. When we're done for the night, we'll go back to the hotel, take the wire with us, and you can relax for a bit. We'll pick you up for dinner at seven."

In the bright hotel room, Tom pulled the curtains closed. After securing my personal items, I unbuttoned my baggy light-blue shirt, and Jon wired me. The rectangular box felt a bit awkward in the small of my back. "What if it slips?"

"That's why we have to secure it really well. The box may get hot after awhile. I'll put extra tape so it doesn't burn your skin. I'll be bringing the mike that's connected to the wire up and around to the front of your breastbone so we can hear you clearer. Your skin might be a little red when we remove the tape. It might hurt a little."

"No problem. Just take it off fast."

"You got it."

"Is she good?" Tom asked from across the room.

"I think so," he answered. "Julie, let me hear you talk while you're walking around."

I went into the bathroom, closed the door, opened it, flushed the toilet, and let the shower and sink water run while saying, "Testing, one, two, three, testing. Copy?"

"10-4."

I said, "Okay. I'm ready."

I followed them in my U/C vehicle to the pre-set location, where we made small talk until about ten minutes later when the team reported, "Okay, the target's standing. . .blow and weed. . . . Bring in the U/C."

"10-4," Jon affirmed. He turned to me, looking for signs of fear. "Ready?"

"Yes."

"Good luck," Tom encouraged.

"Thank you."

Entering my car, I hoped the first buy would go without incident. There was nothing noteworthy in starting something new on a bad note.

Near the area, I called out, "I'm turning off." After securing the radio beneath my seat, I cruised in slowly. With the music low, I glanced around and spotted the target.

"Yo!" he shouted from down the block of housing projects, waving me over.

I stopped in front a young black eighteen-year-old with short dreads, wearing a black tank top and baggy denim shorts. "What up?" he asked.

"Whatcha' got?" I countered.

"Blow."

"Gimme two."

From the right front pocket of his jeans, he withdrew a handful of clear plastic Baggies containing white powder and handed me two.

In exchange, I gave him a twenty-dollar bill.

He left, and so did I.

Further away from the area, once my radio was pieced together, I communicated with the rest of the team and drove to meet them.

"Good first job. Smooth," Jon said as he handed me a Scott Reagent Field Test Kit. After putting some powder in the packet, I crushed the ampules inside and waited. Seconds later, the pink-and-blue results confirmed the presence of cocaine.

Tom placed the Baggies in an evidence bag, which I signed, and Jon showed me a photo line-up. I identified the target and initialed the back of his picture.

"Okay, Julie, this is the way we'll be working. You good?"

"Yes."

"Okay. Wanna head back out?"

"Yeah. I liked it. It was nice and easy."

"Yes, it was, but don't think they're all like that."

"I won't."

By evening's end, I had made seven purchases of marijuana and cocaine from different street dealers.

CRUISING AROUND ONE AFTERNOON a few days later, a good-looking, olive-complexioned Puerto-Rican guy standing on a street corner next to an African-American caught my eye.

I stepped on the brakes. The Hispanic waved to me. *Oh, too bad he's a dealer.* I pulled alongside. "Hi."

"Hello." He approached the window of my car. "How you doin'?" He smiled coyly.

"Good."

"Where you from?" he asked, leaning in.

"From around," I shrugged.

"Can I get your number?"

"No."

"I can cook Puerto-Rican food."

I laughed. "Good for you."

"I'll cook for you. Anything you want."

The African-American approached my car. "Is he bothering you?"

"Hey, man, I ain't bothering her. Mind your business."

"No, he's okay." I put my car in Park. It looked like I might be buying from both twenty-something-year-olds.

"What you need, *mami*?"

"Whatcha' got?"

"I got weed."

The Puerto-Rican interrupted, "Hey, I got blow. She don't

want your shit. She wants mine. Right?"

I laughed. "I dunno. I don't want you guys to fight."

The black guy came to my window. "How many you want?"

"Two."

He handed me two Baggies containing a green leafy substance; I gave him twenty dollars, and he strolled away.

"How 'bout me?" the Hispanic one asked with a pouty expression, brown eyes softening.

"How 'bout you?"

"Two okay? I got something better."

"Besides Puerto-Rican food?" I teased. "All right, I don't wanna hurt your feelings."

He smiled, handing me two Baggies containing white powder, and I gave him a twenty-dollar bill.

"Will you be around again?" he asked.

"I dunno."

"Maybe I can get your number next time."

"Maybe not," I chuckled, and drove away.

I met up with the guys.

"Hey, Julie, we're gonna have to send your boy a Puerto-Rican cookbook in jail," said Jon. His remark brought laughter.

"What a shame. A good-looking guy like that selling drugs on the street." I shook my head.

We called it a night.

Things moved along in the same manner until the second to last day, when I met a guy who made me doubt my appearance.

A light-skinned Puerto-Rican guy was walking down the

block wearing jeans, sneakers, and a buttoned-down sleeveless denim shirt. We made eye contact, and I pulled over. "Whatcha' got?" I asked, lowering the music.

He stopped and looked at me. "I ain't got anything. What are you looking for?"

"Some blow."

Squinting, he said, "You look like a narco."

"Go fuck yourself."

He raised his eyebrows.

"You gonna tell me where I can get some or what?"

He leaned into my window and searched my eyes. "All right, but you gotta take me. I don't know the house number."

I stared at him. "You're not gonna try anything, right?"

"No. I just don't know how to get you there."

"All right. Get in."

After making a few turns, he said, "Stop here. I'll get out. It's that house in the middle of the block."

"Which one?"

"See those guys on the front porch?" He pointed to an old house on the left. "You can get something there."

"From who?"

"Ask for D., Daryl."

Once he left, I parked on the corner and walked to the house. Several long steps creaked as I hopped onto them.

Two men sat on milk crates, drinking from bottles covered with brown paper bags; another two stood on the porch, smoking cigarettes. We exchanged glances. "What up?" asked one.

"Not much. D. inside?" I answered, opening the flimsy front door, pretending I'd been there many times before.

"Yeah, in the back."

The door rattled when it closed; inside, I made a speedy assessment. Talking loudly to my immediate right, six men of varying ages were sitting on mismatched chairs and tables. Some were smoking cigarettes, others drinking canned beer. Another two were watching television on an old cloth sofa to my far left; one was drinking rum out of a bottle as the other flicked his cigarette ashes into an empty beer can.

If Daryl was the dealer, he wouldn't have been in that room doing nothing; he'd be serious about making money, I figured.

"Where's D.?" I asked, raising my voice.

The smoker on the couch glanced my way. "Yo, D.!"

Seconds later, the heaviest, oldest, and most talkative man in the group called out. "Hey, *mami*!" He leaned forward in his chair, extending a large, calloused hand. "Come here." He grabbed my hand and started pulling me to him. "Sit on my lap, honey," he chortled. "I wanna see how much you weigh."

Raucous laughter ensued. All eyes were on the charlatan.

His strong grip drew me closer. My sneakers squeaked as I tried to resist. He'll feel my wire, I thought.

When I felt his knee close to me, I knew it'd all be over if he succeeded. I punched his chest hard. "Get your fuckin' hands off me."

He raised his eyebrows, dropped his hand and mocked, "Ooh. . .a hot La-*ti*-na."

"*Yo*, man. Let her be. Come over here, *mami*." A tall, thin black man had come out from a side door.

Hiding my relief, I strode his way, straightening my shirt. "What's up with the old man trying to feel me up?"

"Ah, he's just an old-timer who can't get any." He shook

his head. "What do you need?"

"Blow."

"How many?"

"Two."

He unzipped the smaller pocket of the fanny bag strapped around his waist and removed two Baggies of white powder.

After handing him a twenty-dollar bill, I left.

The guys and I met, completing the usual post-day work. "You all right?" asked Tom.

"Yeah, but I was worried about the wire."

"You handled it well, Julie," said Jon.

My lesson to adapt in the blink of an eye had been learned.

By the end of my seven-day assignment, I'd made forty-nine buys of marijuana and cocaine.

When all the purchases made by the six undercovers were tallied, the number of arrests totaled ninety-six. A dinner was held in our honor, and we could bring a guest.

At home, I called Rick. "Hey, it's me."

"What's up, J.?"

"You'll never guess where we're going," I teased.

"We? Ooh...where?"

I clued him in.

"J., that's *great*. I'm proud of you, kid. Thanks for inviting me."

"Who else? But do me a favor."

"Anything."

"Don't wear any of your old-man ties. I'll buy you one."

Rick chuckled, asking, "You don't like 'em, huh?"

"Never did."

Two weeks later, Rick was by my side, wearing the nice

tie I'd bought him for that special occasion. In my white skirt suit, short-sleeved pink top, and white leather bolero hat, I rose to receive my Exceptional Duty award.

Things were moving along in my private and professional life.

4

Squad B

HUDSON COUNTY WAS THE PLACE narcos hungered to go to, myself included. Three of the towns were responsible for the criminal element that kept undercovers on their feet: Union City, West New York, and Jersey City.

It was innate; people of all ages were street savvy, suspicious of others, and defensive, trying to keep you from getting over on them. I was one of them, and having grown up in Union City enabled me a first-hand understanding of residents' psyches.

After the Jungle's assignment terminated, I resubmitted my resume to the Hudson County Prosecutor's Office, optimistic that someone would reach out to me this time around.

One mid-morning Saturday in October, I tore open an envelope from Hudson and raised my arms in victory. An interview had been scheduled for me that following Thursday at eleven o'clock.

I called Rick to share the thrilling news. "Rick, Rick, it's gonna happen!"

"You got the letter, huh?" He was laughing.

"Yes. I'm so excited!"

"I can tell. You're out of breath."

"You better believe it. If you have plans for tonight, cancel them. We're celebrating!"

"But you haven't gotten the job yet," he teased.

"I will."

"I know you will, kid. So where are we going?"

"I don't care. You pick the place. Eight o'clock good?"

"Yeah, that's fine. I'll honk the horn."

"Are you kidding? You won't have to. I'll be standing outside at attention, in a sexy dress and high heels."

"Be careful someone else doesn't pick you up."

THE DAY OF MY INTERVIEW, I marched up the steps of the dismal-looking administration building on Newark Avenue in Jersey City in a new double-breasted pin-striped skirt suit, heels clicking past the heavy glass doors.

When the lobby elevator doors swished open, I followed others in, entering with the confidence that I'd leave as a new hire. A receptionist seated at a desk behind Plexiglass buzzed me in, directing me to sit outside the deputy chief's office.

Moments later, I heard my name from inside and entered to find a handsome thirty-four-year-old white guy wearing glasses. He rose, buttoning his double-breasted navy suit.

The light from the window behind him revealed hues of light brown in his short, cropped hair. "Come on in, Ms. Torres. I'm Deputy Chief William Jenning." He extended a strong, manicured hand.

"Nice to meet you, sir."

"Likewise. This is First Assistant Prosecutor James Hall." An older gentleman in a brown suit, cowboy boots on his feet, stood up from the leather chair he'd been sitting on.

"Please have a seat," said Jenning.

After discussing the information on my resume, he asked, "Ms. Torres, what is your background?"

"I'm Cuban."

"So is my wife. Were you born there?"

"Yes."

"So was she, but she's got family from the Canary Islands."

"Me, too. That's not uncommon in Cubans."

"Do you have other ancestry?"

"My dad has Native Cuban Indian on his end."

"That explains your healthy hair."

"Thank you."

Hall asked, "Ms. Torres, are you married?"

I turned to him. "No."

"What is the tan line on your wedding finger?"

"I wear a band on the beach sometimes, so men don't hit on me."

He chuckled, exchanging looks with Jenning. "Really? I never heard that before."

"It gets old when you're trying to read a book and all you want is some peace and quiet."

"I suppose." He shrugged.

"Ms. Torres," Jenning said, "you do realize that Hudson

County doesn't pay well?"

"Yes, sir, I know that. I'm not here for the money. I'm here for the crime."

"And where would you like to work?"

"Narcotics."

He nodded. "You can certainly be utilized there. I'm sure you can, but I have to ask if you're able to read, write, and speak the Spanish language?"

"Yes, I am."

He clasped his hands. "James, do you have anything further to ask?"

He shook his head.

Jenning rose; Hall followed. "Well, Ms. Torres, thank you for your interest in the Hudson County Prosecutor's Office. You'll be hearing from us shortly."

We shook hands, and I left his office confident I'd been hired.

Two weeks later, a job offer arrived in the mail, one I quickly accepted, wasting no time in submitting my resignation to Sussex. However, there was someone important I wanted to share the news with—Mimi, my mentor. I'd begun my first law enforcement job as an agent for the Middlesex County Prosecutor's Office in January of 1990, after graduating from Rutgers University the previous May. She'd worked undercover in the Narcotics Task Force at a time when it was rare for Hispanics, let alone women. Her visits to my office for Grand Jury testimony were laden with suspense stories of high-risk exploits in street operations, exactly the excitement I had been craving—they served as my motivating factor to work undercover.

At home, I plopped myself on the futon, kicking the shoes off my feet. The dial tone couldn't ring fast enough. "Girl, guess who hired me?"

"Well, I know it wasn't us," she joked.

"You got that right. Although we would've made a helluva team."

"That's right, cuz. Well, *nena*, I know your goal's Hudson."

"Yup!" I couldn't contain the euphoria.

"That's great, *mamita*. Major leagues, honey. *Bendito*, I'm so proud of you."

"Thank you. That means a lot to me. You know you're the original bad ass."

She laughed, "Yeah girl, if you say it, then I am."

"So tell me, how long did it take you to buy your first key?"

"About a year."

"Okay. I'm gonna beat your record." We laughed at our friendly competition.

TWO WEEKS LATER, I entered the Narcotics Task Force, was given my gold shield, Glock 17, and my new assignment: Squad B, the four-to-midnight shift; Rick worked with Squad A, from nine to four. The unit was made up of a fun group of guys whose personalities complemented one another. We cracked jokes on each other to defuse the tension of having a stressful job. Everything and everyone was fair game except children, who had to be respected.

Bobby Garcia, an experienced undercover, was Cuban, awesome, and my new partner. He taught me the most important lesson of undercover work one night as we sat in our squad room.

"Julie?" he called out to me from his corner of the room, pronouncing the "J" as an "H".

I looked up from the case files I'd been working on while I sipped some coffee. "Yeah?"

Leaning back in his old chair, eyes studying me like a good detective, he asked, "What's the most important part of the job?"

Full of invincibility, I didn't hesitate to answer what I considered a simple question, "Buying a lot of drugs."

He shook his head. "No, that's not it."

"No? Then what?"

"To go home."

"To go home? ... Hm."

"Hulie, there will always be drugs, but there won't always be another Hulie. The most important part of the job is not who has the biggest seizure. The most important part of the job is to go home. Remember that." He nodded for effect.

Bobby didn't try to change the undercover style I had already developed, nor did he try to teach me how to be an undercover. However, he did share insight.

That November in West New York, I bought my first kilo of cocaine with Bobby. In that particular case, we role-played a husband and wife. After he made several purchases, he introduced me to Jairo, the target, and negotiations to purchase a kilo of coke were made.

At ten o'clock the night of our deal, with surveillance teams in the area, we were crossing the street, holding hands.

"You good?" he asked.

"Yeah, you?"

"Yeah, yeah. I'm good." He smiled. "Let's do it," he added, patting me on the butt.

"*Oye, cojelo suave*," I said in friendly reprimand.

At the target's four-story residence, we stood in the small vestibule and rang his bell. Bobby faced the glass-door entrance while I stood sideways, keeping an eye on the door behind us.

The door buzzed. Wooden steps creaked as we ascended to the second floor where Jairo stood in the hallway. "Over here."

"Hey, what's up?"

"How you doing, man? Come on in."

"Good. You remember my wife?"

"Yes, of course. How are you, ma'am?"

"Fine, thank you." The scent of garlic and onions was wafting from pots on the stove to my far right. To my left, a television was on low, and two rumpled throw pillows adorned the living room couch, evidence of where Jairo had been sitting. Closed windows with tan blinds, and striped curtains cascading to the floor, covered what would be a clear panoramic street view in warm weather. "You wanna see it?" asked Jairo, getting straight to the point.

"Yeah."

"Okay." He reached into the back of the top shelf of the entertainment center and withdrew a rectangular package covered in brown paper, wrapped in gray tape, and marked with black letters.

"Here you go." He handed Bobby the package, along with a razor blade from the top of a lacquered coffee table displaying ceramic figurines.

Turning to me, Bobby placed it on my hands, carefully cutting a tiny sliver, inspecting the contents. "Looks good, hasn't been touched."

"I told you it was good shit. Look at the color."

"Yeah, I see. Nice, pure white." Bobby turned to me. "What do you think?"

"I think it looks good. How much?"

"Twenty-eight thousand dollars," Jairo said.

"That's high," I complained.

The target rolled his eyes. "Partner, we agreed. Twenty-eight."

"I know, but the wife didn't know."

"So what are we gonna do?" Jairo asked, hands expressing impatience.

Bobby looked at me. "I'm sorry, honey. I thought it was a good deal."

"If you already agreed, what can we do?" I shrugged.

Jairo sighed.

"All right, Jairo. The wife's okay with it. You know how it is."

"Yeah, I do. What time will you be back with the money?" Bobby asked, "What do you think?"

"An hour, maybe two?" I suggested.

"Okay, two hours then," replied Jairo.

We left, returned to our vehicle, and after we were out of the neighborhood, I radioed our return to base.

Once there, the lieutenant handed me the money from the evidence vault, and I made Xerox copies, putting the cash into a briefcase. Within the hour, a team briefing was held, assigning specific roles. Then we all headed out.

The most dangerous time in a drug deal is when the drugs and money are together; anything can happen at that point. Since it was a key, the stakes were higher.

On the drive there, Bobby, whose job was to page me once he saw the package again, turned to me from the driver's seat. "You nervous?"

My job was the flash roll. "A little."

"Me, too. It's okay. It keeps you alert."

Once the surveillance teams were in place, I said, "Good luck. I'll be right there when you call me."

"Thank you, Hulie."

I took the briefcase, entering the BMW that another cop had parked in a lot. Bobby drove off.

Waiting for a partner's signal can be stressful. Calls may not be relayed on time, transmissions can be unclear, or, worse, a radio can suddenly not work. I always preferred to be on the other end, acting in the undercover capacity.

After what seemed an interminable delay but was merely minutes, I received Bobby's cue and left the lot to enter his area. When I saw multiple marked units, flashing lights, and uniformed and plain-clothed cops as I double-parked across the street, I knew it was over.

The target had trusted our roles and had shown Bobby the drugs with the certainty that I would bring the money. I stayed in the area until the target was placed into a patrol car, handcuffed; Bobby, brandishing another set of cuffs, had been placed in another.

Once the area was secured, I returned to base, logged the cash into the evidence vault, and headed to our de-briefing, all with the understanding that we were going home.

The following night I called Mimi. "I did it."

She knew what I meant. "Bitch." It was a compliment.

Sometime later, Bobby was transferred to the homicide unit, where he worked until he retired. It was sad to watch him go; we had become fond of one another, but it was a good move for him.

During the time I was waiting for a new partner, the same man who had chased me in my sleep when I came back from the Gulf resurfaced.

It had been after midnight when I awoke for no reason to see him standing by the slightly parted blinds of my bedroom window, in black garb, weapon in his right-gloved hand, watching me.

He's here. Very slowly, I reached for the Glock beneath my pillow, slid off the rattan bed, and crawled low to the light switch on the opposite side of the room.

I stood and turned on the light, but when I aimed my weapon in the man's direction, no one was there. *What the hell's going on?*

He hadn't been a blur to me, but rather crystal clear. I wondered if Post-Traumatic Stress Disorder had been the culprit. My head spun until morning broke.

At the office, I approached Andy Martinez, a Vietnam Veteran and a cop from Bayonne Police who was on-loan with us. He was sitting alone at his gray metal desk reading the newspaper.

"Hey, Andy, can I talk to you about something?"

"Sure, Julie. What's up?" He removed his glasses.

After describing my unsettling experience, he asked with

fatherly concern, "Have you told anyone else?"

"No."

"Okay, good."

I grinned. "They'll think I'm crazy, huh?"

"Yeah, but they don't know what it's like. Sweetheart, that's PTSD."

"But I haven't had any nightmares in a long time, and I've never hallucinated. Andy, I could've sworn he was real."

"It can happen like that. Julie, listen to me." He took my hands in his. "You're not crazy, okay. A lot of other guys here, maybe...but not you," he chuckled.

I smiled at him, thankful that an esteemed professional knew my sanity was intact.

"Here's what you do. Don't sleep with your gun loaded. This way if it ever happens again, which I don't think it will, the sound will wake you up when you rack it."

"Okay."

"Don't think too much about it. You're fine, honey," he said, tousling my hair.

Andy was right; it never happened again.

Then my new partner arrived—Jerry Burgos, a twenty-something-year-old Puerto Rican patrol cop from the Hoboken Police Department. He fit right in.

On occasion, we'd meet some of the guys at a local cops' bar after work where I'd have a drink and Jerry, who didn't drink, would order a soda. Sometimes Jerry and I went out after work to grab a bite and unwind before going home. It was about spending time together, building rapport.

We had clicked immediately, not having to speak to know what was on each other's mind, responding to situations exactly as we expected the other would. Having come from the road, he hadn't had any undercover experience, but Jerry was a quick learner. I was happy to teach him what I'd learned from Bobby as well as what I had developed on my own, but I taught by example.

One night a few weeks later, our lieutenant approached our desks. "It's dead here. You guys wanna hit the street?"

We drove to the area of 8th Street and New York Avenue in Union City, as surveillance teams watched. I saw a guy from Edison, my old grammar school, at a bus stop. Our eyes locked, but I didn't greet him.

About half a block further, I saw Pedro, someone else I knew from Edison. He waved, calling out, "Hey, Julia!"

We hadn't seen each other since I was thirteen years old.

Jerry and I pulled up alongside him as I rolled down the window.

"Wow, it's been a long time." He smiled, leaning into the car to exchange a hello kiss. "How you doing?"

"Yeah, it has. I'm good, can't complain. You?"

"Visiting family. What's Frankie up to these days?"

"Working, nothing special."

"Yeah, same here. What are you guys looking for?" he asked, glancing at Jerry.

I knew he meant drugs. "Nothing," I replied. "We're just hanging out."

"My cousin's up the block. You can ask him if he has anything," he offered.

"Nah, I feel weird buying from your cousin," I countered.

"Don't worry about it. Tell him I sent you."

"It's okay."

"Well, at least stop by and say hi."

Jerry and I drove up the block and spoke with Pedro's cousin but didn't discuss drugs. When we drove off, I turned on the radio, relaying, "Nothing here."

"Wanna try West New York?" The lieutenant suggested.

"10-4."

Wanting to explain my inaction to Jerry, I lowered the music and began, "You know, I grew up here."

He nodded as we proceeded up New York Avenue, passing scattered passersby on foot or bicycle, closed businesses, an open late-night *bodega* here and there.

"I went to grammar school with Pedro, not his cousin—I never saw him before. Pedro was a couple years older than me, that's why he knew my brother. I remember him 'cause he was one the best-looking guys in Edison, but he moved at some point in high school. I know the guy at the bus stop, too, José. We graduated Edison and Emerson together. There's a lot of people here, but somehow everybody seems to know everybody. I could've bought from Pedro's cousin, but for what? For a nickel-and-dime bag, I would've blown my cover. News like that travels fast. It'd be all over the street in a heartbeat. Sometimes, you gotta walk away."

"I understand, and I agree." Indeed, Jerry was learning fast.

On Hudson Avenue and 54th Street in West New York, a tall, thin Mexican was leaning against a corner building. As Jerry drove slowly, I made eye contact with him.

"Let's turn around. I think he's got some."

We pulled up in front of him, and he sidled to my window. "*Hola.*"

The conversation resumed in Spanish. "What's up?" I asked.

"You looking for something?"

"Yes. You got powder?"

He hesitated. "Who's he?" He pointed to Jerry.

"My boyfriend."

"He looks like a cop."

"Nah, he's just big."

He shrugged. "Okay. How much do you want?"

"Six."

He removed six Baggies of white powder from his right front shirt pocket and handed them to me in exchange for sixty dollars.

"You always here?" I asked.

"Um, I'm normally here at this time on Fridays, but. . . well, take my pager number. If you're thinking of coming by, beep me, and put two nines after your number. I'll call you back. You tell me what you want so I can have it ready."

"Okay."

I turned to Jerry. "Honey, you got a paper and pen?"

"Let me see." He reached into the center console and handed me both.

As I wrote down the guy's number, we exchanged names.

Once done, surveillance teams followed us to base while my partner and I talked about his appearance. "See what I mean? You're too clean-cut. Plus you're big." Jerry's cropped hair, muscular physique, and serious demeanor smelled like cop.

"What should I do?" he asked, hazel eyes eager.

"Get scruffier—five o'clock shadow, a goatee, hair and

clothes not so neat, you know, whatever works for you. It's not your fault—you came from patrol—but people on the street pick up those cop mannerisms. Just be looser. You can do it. Somebody told me that once, too."

That was Jerry, the partner I grew to care about in a short period of time. Today he is a sergeant in another department, and, like Bobby, we remain in touch. Without a doubt, I would've taken a bullet for either one of them.

I am indebted to Hudson for the experience and relationships I encountered, as well as the additional training schools that ensured one remained privy to developments in the underworld.

That March of 1994 was no different, when I was sent to a DEA Undercover Training course in Paterson, New Jersey. There would be one exception, however: It would catapult my immediate future, but first, I had to speak to my brother about unfinished business.

5

Incarceration

ONE COOL SEPTEMBER AFTERNOON in 1993, I went to speak with my brother about an overseas conversation that we'd only glossed over.

The phone rang as I sat in a mobile trailer full of soldiers relaying redeployment news. "Hello?"

"Marlene, it's me."

"Hel-*lo*, Julieta!" She was in her usual good spirits.

"I'll be home soon."

"Great! When?"

"Before the Fourth."

She had cheered. "O-kay, congratulations! Just in time for fireworks. Did you call Mom yet?" Her tone brought suspicion.

"No. What's up?"

"Well, I don't know if I should be the one to tell you."

"Tell me what?" My sister had never been good at keeping secrets.

"Well. . . ."

"Marlene, just say it."

"Frank was arrested."

"For *what?*" I hadn't seen that coming.

"Drugs."

There was no way she could be right. "Who told you?"

"Mom. She called me, crying."

"When?"

"Oh, I don't know. A few months ago."

"A few *months* ago? And *now* you tell me?"

"She said not to tell you, so you wouldn't get upset."

I flailed my hands. "I wouldn't get upset. I'd get *pissed.*"

"Well, she said you had enough things to worry about with all those stupid men over there."

"What kind of drugs? What department? Where is he now?"

"Oh, I don't know. That's cop stuff. Call her."

I hung up with my sister and dialed Mom's number.

"Ma, it's me."

She sighed, "Oh, how good to hear your voice."

"How are you?"

"Good. And you?" She sounded strained.

"Ma, what's up?"

"What are you talking about?"

"With Frank."

She let out a breath. "Oh. . . ." She began to sob.

"Ma, stop crying. What happened?"

"They arrested him!"

"For what?"

"Selling cocaine."

"How much?"

"Oh, Aurorita, I don't know. I just know it's cocaine. Can you believe it? I didn't teach him any of that."

"Ma, it's not your fault."

Her voice spiked. "Dirty money! All for dirty money. It's better to make a little money and be at peace than to make a lot of money selling drugs. Where did I go wrong?"

"You didn't. He's a grown man. He makes his own decisions."

"I never taught any of you to break the law. On the contrary, I taught you to respect it."

"Ma, this has nothing to do with you. Listen to me. He's accountable for his actions, not you. Stop it. I just called to see how you were doing after I heard, and also to let you know I'll be home soon."

"Oh, thank God! I can't wait. Maybe when you're home, you can talk to him. Aurorita . . . ."

"What, Ma?"

She sighed. "Your brother needs money, and I don't have money to give him."

"I gave you power of attorney. Take the money I made here. Just make sure I have some when I get home, so I can travel."

"Okay. Thank you, Aurorita. When will you be here?"

"I don't know the exact date yet."

"I'll be there. Thank God! We've been praying for you, and a man on the radio wished you well."

"What man?"

"A radio host was mentioning soldiers who were in the Gulf, and one of my co-workers gave him your name."

"Oh, that was nice."

"Yes, and another thing, a woman from work said she dreamt about you coming back home. She said nothing was going to happen to you. You don't know how that helped me."

"I'm sure it did. Gotta go. Someone wants to use the phone."

"Okay."

"Ma?"

"Yes?"

"Stop worrying. There's nothing you can do."

The irony of life, I thought, after hanging up. I volunteer to go to war, and my brother gets arrested for selling drugs. *Why'd he do it?*

I parked in his driveway and stepped out, not looking forward to our conversation. I rang my brother's doorbell.

Standing in front of the single-family house where he lived with his wife and two-year-old son, Adrian, I wondered if a house payment had had anything to do with it.

He opened the door, vacuum cleaner cord in his hand. "Hey, what's up?" He greeted me with a hello kiss.

The light gray living-room carpet looked immaculate. Frank, ever the neat freak, often told his wife to leave for a few hours while he cleaned the house and vacuumed. Now that they had a son, he was no different. He enjoyed his time alone listening to music as he put things in order.

I sat down on the comfortable white leather sofa, kicking off my shoes, purse beside me.

He lowered the music and sat across from me in a plush

white leather side chair.

"Can we talk?" I asked.

"What's up?"

"You tell me."

"Julia, I don't know what to tell you. I made a mistake."

"No shit. That's obvious. What were you thinking?"

"I don't know. I guess I just wanted to get out of debt. You know...the house, the cars, the kid, the wife...."

"And you didn't see any other way out?"

"Not one that could get me out quickly."

"So you're saying this was a one-shot deal?"

"Yeah. I was delivering a key. Just this one time."

"Come on, Frank, you know better than that. You would've done it again if the situation had presented itself."

"Well, I'm not gonna lie. You're probably right. So I guess it's a good thing this happened, huh?"

"Yup. Next time it would've been for higher stakes. Didn't you think you'd get caught?"

"Honestly? No. I had a good thing going—a couple of steady professional clients, and that was it."

"So what happened?"

"I was set up."

"Cut the bullshit. They all say that. You got greedy, and you got caught. That's what happened. That's what always happens. It's the nature of the beast."

"...You're right. I should've kept it how I had it, and I would've been fine."

"No. You shouldn't have been dealing, *period*. You didn't learn that from any of us."

He nodded, appearing ashamed.

"You know Mom blames herself."

He shook his head.

"Yeah, that's what I said. Not her fault. But you didn't think about her or how hard she's worked. You didn't think about me either. I got a drug dealer for a brother, and I'm a cop. What the fuck? What about Vic, Adrian, and the baby that's coming? What are they gonna do?"

"That's what I wanted to talk to you about. I took a plea . . . . Do you think you can live here while I'm gone, until the bank takes the house?"

"When you going in?"

"October third. I got a flat two."

"When are they taking the house?"

"Maybe a few months after I go in."

"And then what? Where are they gonna go?"

"Her mom's house. I just need you to stay here so they're not alone and, you know, make sure they're taken care of."

"Okay. I'll tell my landlord I gotta move."

"Thanks. I'm sorry. It's never gonna happen again."

"It better not. I'll put the cuffs on you myself. Listen Frank, I'm gonna visit you one time only, when you first go in. Having a brother in jail is not something I want broadcasted, and I don't want it to look like I'm in agreement with you. I'm not gonna send you things either. Jail's a place for rehabilitation, not recreation. I'll send you books to read for Christmas and your birthday, but that's it."

"I understand."

That October, true to my word, I moved into Frank's house to care for his family, and visited him once during his first month's incarceration. Mom went to see him religiously those two years. She deposited money into his account, brought hot steak sandwiches from Dos Amigos, a Cuban restaurant in West New York, New Jersey, and provided luxuries that I did not agree with: a television, a boom-box with compact discs, a silk robe, sunglasses, even a Rolex replica. It was hard for me to rationalize how she bought things he asked for when he had broken the law. How could he acknowledge the wrong and make amends if he was surrounded with items of comfort? I wondered.

I thought of my service in the Gulf and how I hadn't asked for anything. Care packages had come from different people, her included, but never because I requested something. My mentality was that I had volunteered and I'd take responsibility for my actions. No one needed to make my stay better.

Mom's mindset was that I had chosen to be in the Gulf and had been prepared. She said he wasn't like me; I could get through the eye of a needle, whatever that implied.

Frank, she added, did not want to be in jail and was unprepared, which meant he needed her help. It wasn't logical to me; if someone broke the law, I believed (and still do), the price had to be paid.

I wondered if my independent spirit reminded her of my dad so much that I was somehow paying for the animosity she held for him, especially when I knew without a doubt that she wouldn't have supported me with my rape had I disclosed it. It brought me to question how a parent could support a grown-up son in jail on a drug charge and not a daughter who was raped at eighteen. But, as barbaric and wrong as her actions were, I chose not to dwell on them. It'd only serve to anger me. Instead, I chose to be supportive of Vic, her pregnancy, and Adrian.

On Frank's release date two years later, I drove Mom, Adrian, and my brother's baby daughter Nicole to bring him home. His marriage did not survive, and his divorce distanced our families. Mom and I became collateral damage. The price that my brother paid was more than his prison term.

Today, we continue to rebuild our relationship with his kids, hoping for the day that God brings us all to be as united as we once were.

6

Deep Cover

SEATED IN ROWS OF LONG CLASSROOM TABLES in March 1994, colleagues engaged in lively conversation while waiting for the first speaker of our undercover training class to arrive.

Throaty voices and chortles permeated the testosterone-filled room. The confined, rectangular space had led some of the men to open the windows, and others to step out and have a drink at the water fountain in the hallway.

As I glanced at the empty white-board, sipping my light-and-sweet coffee, a muscular, dark-haired cop sitting in front of me turned. "Hi, I'm Jack West." His voice was soft, pleasant.

"Julia Torres."

"What department you from?"

"Hudson County Prosecutor's, Narcotics. You?"

"Passaic County Prosecutor's, Narcotics. . .how long you been there?" He tilted his head to the side, small brown eyes curious.

"Not too long, a little over a year."

"But you're in Hudson."

I smiled, understanding his implication. Months in Hudson equated to years elsewhere in terms of the number and depth of investigations.

"My office is conducting two-week prostitution stings. Would you be interested in coming on-loan?"

That'd be an additional experience I could add to my resume, I thought. "Sure."

"Okay, let me have your number, and I'll tell my captain to give you a call. His name's Vinny Moschetta."

No sooner had he placed my number in his pocket than the Southern lilt of the instructor's voice brought everyone's interest to the platform he had mounted.

Cowboy hat on his head, bolo tie on a collared shirt, boots under flared pants, the Texan began speaking in a southern drawl. "Can I get everyone's attention?" He scanned the room, blue eyes behind glasses above a thick mustache. "Let's talk body language."

It'd be a practical lesson in applying simple observation to daily operations. In addition, it'd be highly beneficial in your personal life, where day-to-day nuances were often overlooked.

Back on the street after those two weeks, having forgotten the conversation with Jack, I was pleasantly surprised in mid-April. As I was sliding my key in the lock after returning from the gym, duffel bag in hand, I heard the telephone ring. *Oh* crap.

A smooth male voice greeted me. "Hello, may I speak with Julia?"

"This is she," I said, tossing my bag and keys on the futon.

"Hi, Julia. I'm Vinny Moschetta. Jack said good things about you."

After a brief conversation and scheduling an unofficial interview, I wrote down the directions, slipped them into my fanny bag, and prepared for work.

ON THE DAY OF OUR MEETING, I got lost on the way, arriving about an hour late. I entered a paved area where a slew of unmarked cars were parked. An intercom hung next to the entrance of the nondescript brick building, previously a morgue. I pressed the button. "Yes?"

"I'm here to see Captain Moschetta."

At the sound of the buzzer, I opened the heavy door and walked up two flights of stairs. A well-lit corridor contained offices where cops were moving about—coffee mugs in hands, handcuffs at waists, guns on hips.

I strolled down the hallway looking for the captain's office and found it: *Vinny Moschetta, Captain, Narcotics Task Force.*

My sneakers squeaked when I stopped short. "Captain?"

An attractive, dark-haired Italian in his late thirties looked up from the yellow legal pad he'd been writing on. He put his pen down and rose, standing about five-ten.

"You must be Julia." He approached me—striped shirt, sleeves rolled up, jeans, black shoes—and extended his hand, smiling.

"I am. Nice to meet you," I said as I shook it.

"Come on in. Have a seat."

"Thank you." A metal filing cabinet stood to the left of the desk, behind it a window with closed blinds.

We began bullshitting, and I sensed him analyzing me. "Did you see Jack?" he asked.

"No."

He called out to someone crossing in the hall and asked them to summon Jack.

In moments, he stood in the doorway, which appeared to have narrowed. "Yes, Captain? You wanted to see me?"

The captain nodded, pointing towards me. "Julia's here."

"Hi." He turned to me.

"Hey, Jack." I waved.

"Can you close the door and sit down for a minute?"

Jack lowered himself onto one of the chairs by the wall.

"I'd like the two of you to perform a pencil test," said Moschetta with ease, alternating his glance between us.

I had no idea what he was referring to but said nothing.

"Okay," Jack said.

The captain addressed me. "You're in a bar, and you come across Jack, a well-known coke dealer, who is alone and sitting on a stool." Leaning back in his chair, hands clasped across his waist, he added, "Seduce him."

It's a cold buy, I thought. *Easy enough.* . . . "Okay," I replied. Without hesitating, I lifted my chair and moved it closer to Jack, getting into character, creating a make-believe environment in my mind. My approach had to be smooth enough to be believable yet professional enough to legally ensure that he would offer me what he normally did: cocaine.

"Hi," I began, looking in Jack's direction.

He glanced at me, nodded, and continued to look forward. My imagination developed over jukebox music. "What are you drinking?"

He raised his imaginary glass. "Beer."

"That's what I'm gonna have. You want another one?"

He shrugged.

I ordered two Coors Lights from the invisible bartender.

"Here you go." I handed it to him amid a spritz of running water.

Surrounded by cackling laughter, murmured dialogue, and television news, I glanced around, pretending to look for someone in the smoke-filled room.

He stared ahead impassively.

"You meeting someone?" I asked, amid the clack of a pool game.

"No, I'm alone."

I nodded, after taking a sip of the cold beer. "Yeah, I might be, too. What's your name?"

"Jack. Yours?"

"Julia. My friends were supposed to be here." I grinned.

"Maybe they're late."

I shook my head. "No, I was late. They should've been here by now." I shrugged, scanning the room again, catching a glimpse of a guy with a crew cut whose dart scored the center of a bull's eye.

"You were going out?" he asked.

"Yeah. We were gonna have a couple of drinks, then go clubbing." I raised my drink and took a swig. "It's Friday, we wanted to party. You know."

"You were gonna party?" Inflection in his tone expressed

sudden interest.

"Yeah, but now I can't."

"Why not?"

"They were bringing something." I had another drink.

"What were they bringing?"

"...You know."

"Coke?"

"Shh." I tilted my head towards the bartender.

Jack turned to the captain. "It's over."

"Thank you, Jack. Shut the door on your way out."

"You got it, Captain." He looked my way before leaving. "See you, Julia."

"I'm impressed," Moschetta said to me. "You know why I asked you to do that?"

"To test me?" I asked.

He sat up straight. "Yes. I wanted to see how you'd handle yourself in a situation where you're alone and know nothing."

I nodded.

"Do you have any family or friends in the Paterson area?"

"No."

"Any cops you know?" He searched my eyes.

"No."

"Good. Let me explain what we've got going. The office is setting up a social club in downtown Paterson for the purpose of eliminating the illegal gambling activity in the area. We'd like to get a cop in as the owner, someone unknown to the area, who can hire someone as an interim club manager in order to move around freely."

There was a tap on the door. It opened slowly.

The captain looked over.

"Hey, Cap, can I—" A lean, muscular guy stopped short. "Oh, I'm sorry, Captain. I didn't know you had a meeting."

"It's okay, Bobby."

Vinny continued after the thud of the door, "There are businesses in the area handing out pay-outs on keno, horseracing, and joker poker machines. There is also illegal horse betting. We're looking for a cop who can form a rapport with the other club owners to infiltrate their establishments, play machines, get pay-outs, and bet on horses."

I interjected on his slight pause. "Captain, I'm not looking for a job."

"Will you hear me out?"

I shrugged. "Okay."

"There will be video surveillance but no backup, except for random drive-bys. Residents will think there are cops hanging around, and it'll raise suspicion about the newest person, the undercover, in this case. Follow me so far?"

"Yes."

"Good." He cleared his throat. "The head target, who rents machines for a cut of the proceeds, has a shop up the block from ours. When payments are made to him, a wire has to be worn, at which time there'd be surveillance. Afterward, reports have to be written in the office. In order for that to happen, the investigating officers will go to a pre-arranged location to pick up the undercover, who'd lay low in the back seat, and enter the office through a back door after the officers ensure no one is present. Once done, they'll take the undercover back to the original spot. No one can know what's being done—not family, friends, boyfriends. You know cops talk, right?"

"Yes." If he's giving me this much information, he's already hired me, I thought, reading into his determined blue eyes.

"Then you know something like this will be found out right away, and it can pose a threat to the undercover?"

"Yes, I know that, Captain."

"Great. That's the reason why there are only seven people aware of this investigation: the prosecutor, the chief, two investigating officers, their supervisor, the tech guy, and me. If you were to accept this job, you'd have to advise Hudson that you're resigning from law enforcement."

I sat up straight in my chair. "Captain, it all sounds pretty cool, but I came here 'cause Jack said you were doing two-week prostitution stings, and I haven't done that yet."

He shook his head. "No, I wouldn't ask someone to come on-loan for that. I have investigators here."

"So why would he say that?"

"I don't know. I can't answer for him." A few seconds passed before he asked, "What can I do to change your mind?"

"I don't know. I like where I am. I'm not looking to leave."

"All right, entertain me. What would you want ideally?"

I sighed, "Well, I'd have to say a lot more money, a nice car, a cell phone, a gun, freedom of hours. I go to school part-time during the day and won't be available until December. In January, I'll be doing my teaching internship, so I can't work 'til after four. On Saturdays, I teach from 9:00 to 5:00, and on Sundays I go to church."

"None of that's a problem."

I leaned forward. "I could come and go as I please?"

"Yes, you'd be able to do that."

"I'd be on my own? No one breathing down my back?"

"You'd be your own boss. Consider your requests done. You'll hear from the chief for an interview because that's protocol, but it won't have any effect on you being hired. I want you to work for me."

I had made no decision, but I wanted to see where this would take me. "Fine, Captain. I'll wait to hear from the chief."

"Terrific." He rose, and we shook hands. "He'll call you soon. I'll walk you to the door."

Back in my car, my head was spinning, wondering what I had just stepped into. I went back to base and said nothing. Work went on as usual, but within a few days, I received a phone call to schedule an interview with the chief and the prosecutor.

At the end of April, Chief John Nativo, a white-haired Italian with thick glasses, was sitting on a leather wingback chair across from me. "Miss Torres, Vinny said to give you a weapon."

He paused, glancing up at an old framed newspaper clipping of a case he'd worked on. "Ahem," he continued in his nasally voice, "since the state police requires paperwork to register a weapon, and we don't want anyone to know who you are, Vinny says I can give you one of mine. What would you like?"

"A Glock 17, Chief."

"Okay. I have one of those."

My head was spinning faster as I headed to Prosecutor Ronald Fava's office.

"Good to meet you, Julia." The prosecutor came across the plush carpet, extending his hand. "Vinny speaks highly of you."

I shook his hand. "Nice to meet you, Prosecutor. Thank you."

He pointed to two nail-trim leather chairs in front of his desk. "Please make yourself comfortable."

Walking to the front of the room, he stopped at the coffeepot and called out, "Do you drink coffee, Julia?"

"Yes, Prosecutor."

"How do you take it?"

"Light and sweet, sir." I was flabbergasted that he would take the time to make me a cup. It didn't happen in law enforcement.

He moved casually towards me—single-breasted navy suit jacket unbuttoned, pressed shirt and slacks, buffed shoes, and the ever-present red, white, and blue-striped tie. He handed me the mug.

Once behind his desk, the prosecutor, his straight brown hair combed to the side, took being direct to another level. "Julia, Vinny has asked me to hire you, and I'm going to do just that."

I said nothing.

"Now tell me, how much do you want to make?"

"Fifty thousand."

He widened his eyes. "That's a lot, Julia."

"I'm worth it."

"I am sure you are, but my investigators don't make that much money. If they hear about it, there will be problems."

"I won't be telling anyone," I assured him.

"I understand, but these things have a way of leaking, and it will create animosity." He grinned. He removed a heavy book from one of the shelves behind him. Shifting through pages, he paused to fix his tie, and turned the book. "Please take a look at the two pay scales I can offer you, and let me know which one you'd prefer."

Both were more than I was making; I chose the higher of the two.

"Perfect. Julia, congratulations and welcome to the Passaic County Prosecutor's Office."

As simple as that, I had been hired.

"As you've been made aware, this investigation is only known to seven people." He folded his hands on his desk. "Vinny will give you his home number, as well as the chief's, in the event you are arrested."

"Okay."

"Vinny has placed a lot of trust in you. I trust his judgment."

"Thank you. I won't let either of you down, sir."

"Great." He clapped his hands and rose. "I will swear you in at Vinny's office as soon as the time is appropriate once you come on board in December. Let me walk you to the door."

I rode down the elevator in awe. It had all been so quick that I hadn't had time to think. I drove to Hudson, radio off, needing silence, knowing I had to prepare a two-week resignation in November.

The squad knew that I was going to school during the day; my teaching internship would follow that January. Leaving law enforcement for a teaching career would make sense.

At that time, I was working on a case where I'd made various cocaine purchases from two Hispanic guys. It was good, I thought, that I'd work until my last day and Jerry—scruffy, goatee, Chinatown Rolex on his wrist—would be there backing me up. In that same six-month time frame, I knew I could bring Jerry in as an undercover on my other open cases.

Resigning created a quandary; although I wasn't lying to him, I was omitting the truth. It didn't make me feel good. We trusted each other. He was a stellar partner, one I would've gladly worked with for a long time, but I had given my word.

That November at base, I headed to the small, ordinary office in the corner and rolled a blank sheet of paper into a typewriter: *Please allow this memorandum to serve as notice of my resignation effective December 02, 1994.*

My career in Hudson County would end; my mind spun its reel. My first week, I'd been thrust into the wire room on a big West New York narcotics and gambling investigation that later turned the town upside down. I'd leapt from one end of the room to the other, noting the time and footage of the call at each electronic buzz.

The action was what I had dreamed—being arrested with targets, executing search warrants, finding drug vials in awkward places, extraditions, buy-bust operations, collaborating with New York agencies. For me, conducting surveillance meant I'd talk with a partner for an undetermined time without raising suspicion, sit shotgun ready to follow perps on foot, or find a way to overhear targets negotiating.

Although Bobby's motto was ever-present, every case increased my boldness and creativity, whether I was entering a bar cold, striking up conversations with suspects, getting my hair cut while arranging a purchase with the hairdresser, or meeting a dealer outside a supermarket in aerobics attire. It was easy to find a commonality with people who in reality were no different from me. They were simply making poor choices.

Yes, I'd acquired a slew of experiences of which I was grateful. I'd miss the guys and the mayhem, but it was time to go.

Julia Torres

7

Casting the Unwitting

TWO NOVEMBER WEEKENDS BEFORE I BEGAN the deep cover investigation known as the Wake Up Café, I interviewed a variety of men and women for the manager's position. Although each person appeared shadier than the next, I wasn't convinced about hiring anyone until I met Jimmy Nocella.

While I was savoring a cappuccino, staring out the storefront window, a thin white guy about five feet five inches caught my attention. As people trotted to and fro, bundled in coats, he strode with ease from across the street in a sweatshirt. He stopped in front of my door, put his face to the glass, and peered in, causing his small nose to be squished.

A sudden bitter wind seeped in when I opened the door. "Can I help you with something?"

A scar ran along the left side of his face from the top of his right ear to his jaw. "Uh, yeah, I'm not from around here.

I'm looking for Julia. You her?" He shuffled his feet from side to side, hands inside his pockets.

"Yes. Jimmy?" I asked.

"Yeah, that's me."

"Come on in." I held the door for him. "Aren't you cold?"

"Nah, I'm always hot." He shrugged, removing his hands—rough, calloused, scars on some knuckles—from his pockets. "I don't own coats."

"Never?"

"Not since I was sixteen."

"Get outta here." I headed towards a table in the corner, leaving my cappuccino on the counter, and motioned him to a seat.

"After you." He pulled out a chair. "Pop always said, 'Jimmy, you gotta let the woman sit first. It's what a man's supposed to do.'"

I chuckled. "I like Pop."

"It's the whole truth," he said, once seated across from me.

"The coats, or Pop?"

"Everythin'."

"You from New York?"

"Nah, Passaic. Well...I was born in Brooklyn, raised in Bensonhurst, and moved here with Pop when I was sixteen after my mom threw away all the coats, underwears, everythin'. She was a crazy Irish, drinkin' all the time. When she got crazy, she'd throw it all out. One day, Pop said, 'That's it,' and we left."

"What happened to her?"

"She died from drinkin' all those gins and scotches and vodkas right outta the bottles. She was a raving beauty and died a hag."

"That's very sad."

He shrugged. "Pop said she was a no-good mom."

"What do you say?"

"She was an angel when she didn't drink." He paused, sounding melancholic, looking far off. "But wudya gonna do? She didn't want no help. There's only so much a man could take."

"Where is he?"

"Florida, with his sister Gina. Got too cold for him here, his knees you know, but he didn't wanna go. He worried about me. I said, 'Pop fugetaboutit—go.' And he did."

"When was that?"

"When I turned twenty-five."

"And you are?"

"Twenty-eight on Valentine's Day. Ma wanted to name me Rudy, but Pop said it wasn't a man's name like Rocco."

"How'd you get 'Jimmy'?"

"Ma said Rocco was too *Eye*-talian. She wanted Jack. Pop said no, too Irish. They agreed on Jimmy—not James, not Jim."

I laughed. "Sounds like quite a character, your pop."

"Yeah, I love him to death."

"That's good. . .you want a cappuccino?"

"Yeah. I'll make it myself."

"All right. Make me one, too."

"No problem." He spoke on the way to the counter. "Been makin' 'em since I was eight. The fellas on the block threw me quarters when I did." He looked around the machine.

"Coffee's in the fridge."

"Lavazza! Bee-*you*-tee-ful," he exclaimed, and then turned to me, grinning broadly with a gap-toothed mouth, dimples on either side. "That's Pop's favorite. Danesi's the other."

"Mine, too."

"No shit?"

"No shit." I smiled.

After putting my unfinished counter cup in the sink and frothing both cappuccinos, he walked over to me with them in hand, napkins beneath, and set them on the table. "Well, wudya think?"

"Nice color."

"It's all in how much stick you put in the milk." He slapped his mouth. "Oh, man, I'm sorry. That don't sound right. Feel free to smack me. Pop would."

"It's okay. Don't worry about it. Sit down."

"Nice classy lady like yourself don't need to be hearin' stuff like that. Really, forgive me, please." He sat, placed his hands in a prayer position and brought them up to his face. "*Marone*."

"Forget it."

"Pop always said there was two things I did a lot, fightin' and talkin'."

"Is that how you got the scar?"

He fanned his sweatshirt. "It's hot in here." Muttering under his breath, he looked away embarrassed.

"You're just blushing. It's okay."

"Thank you. I blame it on the Irish—it's the white skin, you know. I hate it. Pop was olive, like you. Sure wish I had that color all year round."

I laughed. "Yeah, I like it too. It's a forever tan."

"Yeah, it is. Anyways, being that I'm being honest with you. You sure you're no shrink?" he chuckled. "I got this—" he pointed to the long scar— "at a bar fight when we moved to Jersey. I had a hard time gettin' used to the school and the people—it ain't no Bensonhurst, you know what I mean, and a good-lookin' Puerto Rican girl named Jasmine—I'll never forget that name—showed me around the school, you know, like took me under her wings. She was a doll."

He paused, glancing onto the street, where a woman was entering a double-parked car with a toddler wearing earmuffs and a scarf.

"Anyways, we was good friends, and her boyfriend didn't like it 'cause he kept hearing rumors." He stopped to have his first sip of the cappuccino. "You know people talk?"

"I try not to let other people's opinions bother me."

"You're a good woman for that, 'cause it bothered me bad. At a bar one night, I was drinkin' a beer, and her crazy Puerto Rican boyfriend snuck up behind me and cut me with a knife. He hadda be weak, or he had a cheap knife, 'cause it didn't go deep, and I felt my jaw over here." He touched the lower part of the scar. "It was wet, so I looked at my fingers and freaked out when I saw blood. I cracked my beer bottle and cut him with it a couple times."

"And nobody screamed or called the cops?"

"Yeah. The lady that was sittin' by me, she screamed and fainted, and her husband went to the pay phone to call for help."

"So how'd it end?"

"I dunno. I heard the sirens down the block, ran out with the bottle, threw it in somebody's backyard and ran home. Pop said not to worry. He was in Vietnam, so he stopped the bleeding and gave me painkillers. By the time the cops got there, I was sleepin'. Pop said I hadda go with 'em. I did two years 'cause they never found the bottle, but some friends of his said it was me."

"What about the other guy?"

"He did twice that when he came outta the hospital, 'cause his knife was next to him."

"That's some story." I lifted my glass to drink some more. "Let's talk about work. You reliable?"

"Yup. Pop always said, 'A man is as good as the money he brings to the table.' Even if I married a rich lady, he said the man hadda provide. No bums in my family—maybe crazy people, but no bums, not on the Italian side anyways."

I chuckled. "You drive?"

"Yeah, I got an old Lincoln."

"As long as it gets you here, I don't care how old it is. This is a cash business. If I catch you stealing, you gotta go."

"I wouldn't do that to you, I swear." He made a cross with his fingers over his heart, kissed the tips and raised his hand up to heaven. "May God strike me dead right now. 'A man's gotta have honor,' Pop always said."

"Pop was full of advice. What's his name?"

"Sabino, but he goes by Sonny. You Italian?"

"Somewhere along the line. So tell me, when can you start?"

"Right now. Gotta get somethin' steady. I ain't broke or nuthin' like that, you know." He reached into his front denim pocket and removed a wad of bills wrapped with a rubber band. "See?"

"You don't have to do that."

"I don't want you to think I'm a bum or livin' off the streets, or worse, women. I got different bills here." He shuffled them to show tens, twenties, fifties, and a few hundreds.

"I don't think that at all. I like you, Jimmy. I appreciate you being direct. This is what I'll do. I'll be in and out of here the next couple of weeks, so I'll need you to run the shop, make cappuccinos, take care of the people, you know?"

He moved his cappuccino to the side. "I could do that."

"If a problem comes up, don't call the cops—page me with a nine-one-one."

"No cops, don't worry. Grew up around social clubs. I know the deal."

"Good, then we're on the same page. I'll pay you in advance, four hundred and fifty dollars a week for six days, no Sundays. You open up at ten a.m. I'll get here whenever. If I stay late and nothing's going on, I'll let you know if you can go, but if I'm busy out there, you stay. Okay?"

"You got it, Julia. I won't let you down."

I handed him an extra set of keys. "You begin tomorrow. I'm locking up now—just give me your address before you leave. I have your number." I rose and extended my hand.

"You got a deal. Hold on, let me get this." He rose, took the glasses, washed and dried them, and put them where they belonged. We walked out together, and I was content that I had found someone sketchy, personable, and reliable.

8

Playing the Role

IN THE PLAIN TWO-ROOM ORGANIZED CRIME OFFICE, the senior investigators, Robert Mulick and Leon Tauris, their supervisor, and the tech guy briefed me on the Wake Up Café case. Targets, addresses, and expected key words were discussed. Photographs of main players and the locations of their establishments were provided, emergency contact numbers for the chief and captain secured, cameras in my club revealed, and video recording review dates determined.

Once the data was committed to memory, I drove out in a confiscated Nissan Maxima registered under my fictitious name and address: Julia Tirado of Jersey City. Before entering the front door of my business that first rainy night in December, I canvassed the immediate half-mile stretch of downtown Paterson, where Lou Costello's monument stood and every other business was similar to mine. A few passersby were hurrying to their destinations, covered with hooded raincoats; others ran with newspapers overhead.

A number of patrons were talking around tables and chairs in the front room, cigarettes in hand, ashes in trays. Jimmy stood behind the long serving counter by the cash register, giving a young girl change.

"Hey, Jimmy, everything clean?" I asked, shaking my umbrella before buttoning it.

"Yeah—come on, I'll show you," he said, leading me to the middle room, where I greeted two men playing pool as another straddled one of the scattered chairs while watching the television positioned on metal brackets.

I slid the tall, movable shelf that covered a hidden area in the right-hand corner. Focused players were placing bets on keno machines, the money regularly noted in reports and submitted into evidence. "I got everythin' in your office laid out nice," said Jimmy as he picked up an empty can from the floor and tossed it into a small trashcan on the way out.

"Okay, show me." A desk with an executive chair and a filing cabinet next to a small sofa were the only items of furniture in the small, square space. A clock, and thin gold-framed prints, hung on ivory walls.

"Thanks, Jimmy. I'll take it from here. You're doing a great job."

"You got it, boss." He winked.

I looked around the office, ensuring nothing was out of place before beginning what would become my routine: socializing with customers over cappuccinos while players gambled away their wages and disability checks. By the end of our investigation, I'd develop different levels of dialog with all sorts of colorful characters, and I'd consume about seven coffee beverages a day.

Some area residents and business owners came in that week to introduce themselves. The usual players were happy to meet the owner Jimmy had spoken of. Although there had been a welcome reception, I proceeded with caution, not wanting to appear suspicious by talking too much or asking questions.

Things moved along with ease the first two weeks, less one exception: I hadn't received the promised Glock 17. One evening soon after, I decided to speak with the captain.

I dialed his extension from the Organized Crime office. "Captain, I'm here doing reports. Is anyone up there? I'd like to talk to you about something."

"No one's here. You can come on up."

Once I arrived, he asked, "How's the social club?"

"Good. Been meeting some people, walking around sometimes, playing it loose 'til people get more comfortable."

"So what would you like to talk about?" he asked, interlocking his fingers on his desk.

"When am I getting my Glock?"

"That won't be necessary. You don't need one."

Leaning forward in my chair, I said, "That's not your fuckin' call. It's mine."

He shook his head. "You won't need it."

"How do you know?"

"I know the area." Calmly, he asked, "How would you explain the presence of a gun if you were pulled over by the police?"

"That's easy. I'd say I have a cash business in downtown

Paterson and work late hours."

"They'd arrest you. It's not in your name," he challenged.

"You're assuming they'd see it, or that I'd give 'em consent to search my car."

The captain remained unstirred. "It's more trouble than what it's worth, Julia. Same reason for not having a badge."

"I'm not talkin' about the shield, I'm talkin' about the gun."

He shrugged. "You won't need it."

I flailed my hands. "It's what we *agreed* to. That's not fuckin' right. How am I supposed to protect myself? There's all kinds of shady people there."

"You'll find a way."

"What if I don't?"

"You will."

The issue was moot. I stomped out of his office.

On my drive home that night, I thought about this unusual predicament. Things had just begun, and they were already on the wrong foot, but I could not simply leave. Being hired elsewhere would take time, and going back to Hudson was not an option, since the prosecutor didn't rehire those who resigned.

By the time I arrived home, I'd concluded that the absence of a gun would have to be disregarded or tunnel vision could cloud my judgment, preventing me from seeing danger signals. I opted to convert my already guarded state into hyper-vigilance, as I had done in the military.

At the social club, funny tales and boisterous pool games resumed while gin rummy hands were dealt. Music played in the front room; the television blared in the back. Players often filled the machine room with smoke, leaving behind ashtrays and empty soda cans.

In piles of snow, puddles of rain, or high humidity, a cast of characters came and went. However, a few regulars—Half-a-Cup Eddie, Gianni the Captain, Doc Dennis, Gustav the Russian, Cool Hand Carl, and Gio the Actor, each as engaging as the next—would keep me company until I locked up for the night.

While the radio beats echoed during a Friday night card game, Gio squinted as he took a drag of his cigarette. Picking up a card, he blew the smoke out slowly. "Julie, you have a boyfriend?"

It was the first time anyone had asked me anything personal. "Yeah."

The other two men, a thick-mustached Armenian named Hamik, and Hugo, an Argentine-Italian, who often slouched, looked up from their hands.

"What's he do?" Gio continued.

"He sells insurance." It was the first thing that came to me.

"Really? Insurance?"

"Yeah, why?"

He tilted his head, peered at me, and placed a card on the pile. "I don't picture you with an insurance guy."

"Why not?"

He shook his head, short ponytail moving about. "Not manly enough."

"Well, he *is* manly enough, believe me," I laughed.

The other men had been silent, enjoying their smokes. I emptied out one of the ashtrays.

"*Grazie,*" said Hugo.

"*Prego,*" I said.

"Gin," said Gio.

Hamik left as quietly as he had entered.

"Julie, you see that? See how it's bitten?" Gio pointed to Hamik's extinguished cigarette.

"Yeah?"

"Look at the teeth marks. Nobody bites their cigarette when they smoke."

Hugo and I leaned in closer.

"See mine? This is normal. Look at Hugo's."

I did. "Hm."

Gio's eyebrows went up in confirmation.

"So what are you tryin' to say?"

"He could be very frustrated, have pent-up aggression. Whatever it is, it ain't good. You be careful with him. A guy like that can snap at any moment."

"That's right," agreed Hugo.

"I've been watching that character," added Gio.

"Why?"

"Honey, I'm an actor. We're trained to look at everything. It's how we act—we feed off a person's actions."

"You must be a good one. Don't tell me what you think of me. Besides the boyfriend thing, I might not wanna know."

He laughed, and so did Hugo. "Julie, you're a sweet, beautiful girl."

"Yeah, she's just *testa dura*," joked Hugo.

"Nah, she's a sweetheart," Gio winked.

One of the gamblers came out from playing keno and asked me to head over to check his winnings, so he could be paid. The other two had lost; they were all leaving together. Recording payouts became as normal as using right or left English at the pool table. Watching television meant endless debates over O.J. Simpson's guilt or innocence.

THE FIRST SET OF SEARCH WARRANTS, based on the places where I'd received payouts, were executed a couple of days before Christmas. The captain called before it went down. "Julia?"

"Yeah?"

"Get lost for a bit. We're hitting your place and others. Get back in time to overhear."

"Okay."

I told Jimmy I needed to go to the market before it closed.

When I returned with shopping bags, cops were swarming the street. Standing in the midst of the crowd of bystanders, I overheard comments, but none suggested an undercover was the reason for the raids.

"Julie?" Gustav, who had, one night, said I walked like a soldier, called out.

"Yeah? What's up, Gus?" I asked, nudging with my chin in my club's direction.

He ambled slowly towards me, hands in denim pockets. "Don't go in. They're asking Jimmy questions."

"Why?"

"I think it's routine."

"That's what everybody's sayin', but I feel bad leavin' him there. It's my place, you know."

"Don't worry, he'll be all right. Go home."

"Okay." I slipped away, noticing the crowd had dwindled.

The next day was business as usual, but everyone eyed new patrons with suspicion. Jimmy had played it cool with the police, denying any gambling.

For me, returning home after the social club meant I never took the same route twice. I noted the day's events and kept them sealed in a large manila envelope at a friend's house, asking that my notes be taken to the press in the event of my incarceration or death.

Paranoia had set in when I wasn't provided a weapon. I considered my deep-cover status and thought it could be explained differently, since cops, my old and current agency included, didn't know I was an undercover, let alone one of them. I figured that, if I were to become hurt on a job that turned out bad, I'd be labeled as a cop who had become an informant and my paycheck would be explained as payment. I even imagined the headlines-*Corrupt Undercover Cop Goes Rogue*.

Imagination or not, after my distrust of fellow soldiers overseas, I didn't want to chance it. I took the safer route and protected myself, trusting no one, including colleagues.

The social club life resumed. While Jimmy tended the patrons, I frequented neighborhood shops, befriending the business owners who'd invite me to play their machines. In the back room, I placed bets on live horse races, watching them on large screens, joining the men who cursed and cheered boisterously. Someone would often show up with focaccia, soda, and beer, which became consolation prizes for those who lost more than expected.

One spring day, Fabrizio Calabrese, a heavy-set club owner with thinning hair who'd started a rumor that I was an FBI agent, appeared at my shop's entrance. Until then, he hadn't entered; our conversations had been carried on from afar.

"Hey, Julie." He waved and put his hand in his pocket.

"Come on in, Fiz," I said, smiling.

"Nah, that's okay." He glanced away sheepishly, squinting through his thick-prescription glasses, pretending to notice the kids walking up the block. "I don't have a lot of time."

"Time for what? We're not getting married."

Fiz laughed. "You're funny, Julie."

"Yeah, and I'm FBI, too. So come on in. You don't have anything to worry about." I motioned.

"Oh, that." He stepped inside, coming up to the counter where I stood drinking my fifth cappuccino, and extended a hand towards me. "I'm sorry, Julie."

"It's okay," I said, shaking it. "You have some imagination."

He shrugged. "I'm an old timer. Heard you were at Tony's club the other night. When you comin' to mine?"

"You haven't invited me. I'm a lady. I don't go without one."

"Well, you got it. Come over whenever you want."

"Thank you. I'll take you up on that offer one of these days if you make me a cappuccino—no cheap coffee."

"No, nothing cheap in my place, nothing but the best for you. You come in anytime, okay? I'm heading back now," he said, shuffling out.

With Gio pointing out the kind of men I didn't date, Gustav comparing my walk to a soldier's, and Fiz guessing I was an FBI agent, it was no surprise when twelve-year-old Lamar, a black adolescent who lived above my shop, claimed I had characteristics that were unusual for a social club owner.

One early evening in late May 1995, some folks were sitting near the Lou Costello fountain while groups of men hung around outside storefronts, smoking and talking.

Lamar rushed in through the open door while Jimmy and I were conversing over a cappuccino. "Something's wrong with my dad!" the kid said, out of breath, a frantic look on his face. "He needs *help!*"

My antenna rose when I heard *help*. "What is it?" I asked.

"He's having a seizure, and his eyes are moving crazy."

"Call an ambulance," I said to Jimmy, and ran out, following Lamar up the stairs.

In the small, hot, dark apartment, his dad, Winston, lay on the linoleum floor, body thrashing, eyes fluttering. I began moving things away from him that could hurt him. "Get me some pillows," I said to the kid.

"Winston, can you hear me?" I said, placing the couch pillows at a safe distance on either side of his head.

His eyes were glassy and unfocused, and there were beads of sweat on his face. I turned to Lamar. "What's he on?"

"Nothing. He's epileptic," he said nervously.

"This is more than a seizure. You gotta *tell* me so, I can tell the medic."

"Uh, uh—"

"Lamar, he's *tripping*. He's not gonna get in trouble."

Resigned, he answered, "He was smoking a pipe."

"How much? When?"

He shrugged.

At that moment, emergency medical service technicians

came through the open door, making a quick assessment of the situation. One relayed a message through his radio as the other prepared the gurney. The two men struggled to lift Winston, a six-foot, two-hundred-pound, muscular man, onto it.

"What's he on?" grunted the smaller, thinner man of the two.

"He's having a bad crack-cocaine trip," I offered.

"Who are you?" the younger, muscular technician asked as his partner checked Winston's vitals.

"I own the business downstairs. Lamar asked for help." I pointed to him.

"Is he his son?"

"Yes."

"Okay, kid. Come with us."

They left hurriedly, and I returned to my club realizing that I might have reacted too professionally. I hoped Lamar hadn't noticed, but he had.

The next day he entered my club to thank me, but I wasn't there. When I came in a few hours later, Jimmy said, "Julia, Lamar was lookin' for you."

"Oh, how's his dad?" I asked, putting my handbag on the counter's interior shelf.

"He's good. It was a trip...but he said you already knew."

"Knew what?"

"That he was trippin' bad."

"Yeah, it was obvious," I said, grabbing a soda from the fridge.

"That's what I said. But he said you knew exactly what you was doin'."

I shrugged, "*Doin'?*"

"Yeah, you know, movin' things, askin' for pillows, knowing what he was trippin' on. Said you knew a lot for a club owner."

"Club owners supposed to be stupid?"

"Guess he thinks so," Jimmy chuckled.

"Yeah, well he's twelve. I'm twenty-eight."

"Yeah, that's what I said."

Street smarts—one of the perks of growing up in the inner city—could save your life or someone else's. At twelve, Lamar had them.

PERIODICALLY, I'D WALK UP THE BLOCK to see Giuseppe Civita, the machine owner, to pay him his percentage and discuss business operations. Before entering, as agreed, Mulick and Tauris would meet me at a designated spot to sneak me into the office, where I'd be wired. Afterward, they'd take me back and I'd hop into my car, heading to Civita's place, where they would conduct loose surveillance. Once done, they'd drive me to the office for my report writing, and I'd hand them the wire.

At the six-month mark, it seemed the case was going to run longer than expected. "You never know," remarked Mulick. "This might turn into another FBI, Joe Pistone case. His was supposed to be short-term, too." I hoped that wouldn't be true.

Finally, in July 1995, after obtaining a substantial amount of information, and adding more defendants and target locations from other areas of Paterson, the second and final set of search warrants was handed out. Some cops conducted raids and executed multiple arrests; others seized evidence and loaded confiscated machines into trucks. When the police raided my place, I was present, but Jimmy was not. A crowd on the street had formed outside my club.

Once the police entered, the front door was locked and the blinds were closed. Mulick and Tauris led me to the rear office, where one placed his badge around my neck. "Julia, this will let the people know you're a cop. It's better that they think that, so they won't come after you. If they think you're a rat, they may." We left the club, pausing at the door so the crowd could see our badges. "Pretty bitch," someone shouted, as others clapped. That case was considered the biggest investigation the Passaic County Prosecutor's Office had had in twenty-two years.

I never saw Jimmy again.

Indictments were handed out, businesses closed, and the streets were cleaned. In the end, I was glad to have been selected for that job. Most of all, I was happy to return to my normal life.

I was assigned to the Task Force, Street Narcotics Team, run by Robert "Rob" Prause, a no-nonsense former marine. The five-nine German-Italian was a cop's cop, firm but fair, with the team and the suspects. I liked him and trusted his instincts.

Our squad conducted surveillance and short-term investigations that led to arrests and search warrants, causing the days and nights to move fast. Soon enough, months had gone by, and the year drew to a close, bringing with it a higher level of law enforcement. Perhaps it was my reward for triumphing from a personal malevolent deed that previous Spring.

9

Deliverance

ON A BEAUTIFUL SUNNY APRIL AFTERNOON in 1995, my family was celebrating my niece Nickie's christening party in a private room at a Secaucus restaurant. The mood was festive as music played, relatives danced, and loud laughter resounded.

I sat on a corner chair, rocking a wide-eyed Nickie in my arms while absorbing her sweet baby scent. Suddenly, her mom entered the party room and headed towards me with determination.

"What's up, Vic?" I asked, curious.

Eyes hot with fury, mouth tight, she practically snarled, "Judas is in the lobby."

Not too long before, I had confided my rape to her. Vic hadn't betrayed my trust by relaying the news to anyone. She'd understood why I hadn't shared it with my family, but to say the least, she felt I'd been given a raw deal in every way. "That's a fucked-up thing to do. I can't believe he got away with that! And you couldn't even tell your family," she'd said adamantly.

And there she stood before me, ready to wage war.

I nodded, rose, and headed out the entrance door, ready to confront him. My subconscious, however, must've known I'd need an emotional crutch: Nickie remained with me.

My heels echoed on the shiny tile floor, leaving the comfort of familiar sounds and voices behind me. I stopped by a gold railing with steps that stood between the lobby of the adjoining hotel and me.

From across the room, I saw him conversing with someone. In a black suit, he stood with his back to me, but he must've sensed daggers pointed at his head.

He turned, and his mouth dropped. He stood there motionless.

I remained staring, no expression in my dark eyes. From that distance, I flatly asked, "How you doing?"

"Good," he answered nervously.

"You going to the reunion?" Soon we'd be having our ten-year high school reunion.

"I don't know." His words were weighted in fear.

I nodded, said nothing, and turned away. My lovely niece had remained silent, perhaps sensing the dire environment.

In the party room, where balloons, streamers, and refreshments abounded, everyone remained joyful but me. Having been unable to confront him, I felt disappointed with myself, victimized again. I thought of the unspoken words I had prepared for many years.

My mind remained in a fog until the party ended about an hour later. In silence, I strolled to the parking deck with Mom, not mindful of the birds that hovered on nearby trees. The ground was as gray as my mood when I started the ignition and began driving away.

Then I saw him standing outside the rear entrance of the hotel, smoking a cigarette, with his back to me again. It was my second chance.

Pulling the Nissan to the side, I placed it in Park. "Ma, I'll be right back," I said without expecting a response.

I headed toward him. He'd just finished stomping his cigarette when he looked up, and there I was.

He flinched.

Hit hard. Not mincing my words, I asked, "You remember what you did to me?"

He gaped, startled, afraid to respond.

The tension could have been cut with a chainsaw, and I enjoyed it, waiting for his response in a fighting stance. *Bastard.* I did not care to pardon the awkwardness he showed; it'd work in my favor.

His facial expression changed from startled to snagged. "I took advantage of you," he replied.

Cynic! He had taken the spineless route. It could have been easier, I thought. All I'd wanted was a sincere apology, an explanation.

I scoffed, "What nice choice words for rape."

He flinched again. But I saw embarrassment on his face, not remorse. He'd had the opportunity for atonement, but he had chosen to defend himself. I knew his demons would follow him.

I asked, "You know what I do now?"

He shook his head.

Seven years of shame, denial, lost relationships...and that

poor excuse of a man could not even speak. I wanted to hurt him bad, to knock his teeth out, to make him suffer. God protected me that day from a prison sentence. If I'd had a weapon at my side, I don't know what I would've done.

"I'm a cop."

Another flinch.

"You know what I regret? The five-year statute of limitations has passed. I cannot charge you with the crime." At that time, the law in New Jersey stated that, if the victim of a sexual assault was an adult, the crime had to be reported within five years.

He was proving to be quite the mute, but cowards don't usually have much to say when confronted.

"You going to the reunion?"

His uncertainty was laughable, pitiful. "I don't know."

"Don't. I'll pick up that microphone and let everybody there know what you did to me."

Of course he said nothing.

I wasn't done. "You have kids?" I asked.

He said, "I have a son."

"I hope your son doesn't pay for what you did." Abruptly, I turned and left. No other words were necessary.

Entering the vehicle in triumph, I became aware of the birds. Perhaps they'd sensed a moment of vindication.

I drove off without looking back. Mom must've perceived the tension because she asked, "What were you talking about?"

Although my initial perception that she wouldn't support me still dwelled inside me, at twenty-eight, I was confident that it had not been my fault. I was also strong enough not to give a damn if her opinion hadn't changed.

Turning to her at a traffic light, I asked one question. "Ma, if something bad happened to one of your kids, would you want to know? Think carefully before you answer."

"Yes, I would want to know."

She didn't think about it. I waited a few seconds before asking again, more slowly. "Really *think* about it. You answered too quickly."

"Yes, of course I'd want to know. What is this about, Aurorita?"

Mom's use of my middle name signaled her displeasure. Her quick reply convinced me that she was only thinking about herself, wanting to be aware of information she hadn't been privy to, rather than to know something that she could help me with. But since I had confronted Judas, I thought it was time she knew.

I parked on Boulevard East, the panoramic view of Manhattan soothing me, providing encouragement. Two young girls strolled by with a small dog while a couple sat on a bench, arms wrapped around each other.

I turned off the engine and started telling her everything.

Her body language and facial expression were not promising. The scowl on her lips expressed disdain, but it didn't stop me. I had waited long enough to talk; the weight had been mine alone far too long. Words overflowed. With each came a release, strengthening me, until there was nothing left to say.

She began, "You should have known better. What did you expect? What would make you think that, if you drank and passed out, it wouldn't have happened with any man?"

She hadn't even considered the possibility that I had been drugged.

"You and your independent spirit! Liberated, just like your grandmother," she went on. "You never listen! You always do what you want to do. How could you expect to drink to that point and not pay the consequences?"

Mother or not, I had had it. "Enough. That's why I didn't tell you ten years ago. I knew you'd say that. What a shame. You're still living in the '40s. Your mind has not evolved."

She said nothing—not even an apology—and worse, no remorse or shame for those bitter words.

"You're lucky you're my mother—otherwise I'd beat the crap out of you right now." I added, "He was my *friend*. I didn't tell him to *rape me*. No one does that. And all men don't rape women when they pass out. What you said is not what you say to *any* victim. That's why rape is so unreported. The stigma is horrendous. No one should have to face being raped and then judged by their own family!"

She was silent. How could she not say anything? I thought. "I'm glad that God gave me the discernment to know how you'd respond back then, but it's unfortunate that I couldn't tell you so you could've helped me. That's what you were supposed to do. And still now, ten years later, look—you blame me."

I wasn't done. "Whose side are you on? I'm your daughter. Remember I said I hated you when I was nineteen? I meant it then. I don't know what your ridiculous thinking would've done to me at eighteen. Who knows what would've become of me?"

No matter what I said or how I said it, my harshness

hadn't stirred her one bit. "Ten years, Ma. It's been ten years, and you don't even know how it affected my life. And you're my mother." I scoffed and shook my head in disgust.

I started the ignition, knowing she would not say a word. We drove in silence until we parted ways.

A short time later I told Frank, whose initial response was just as predictable. "You should've told me, so I could've fucked him up."

Although I would have appreciated it at that time, his answer hadn't been what I'd needed.

He should have left it at that, but he didn't. "You shouldn't have put yourself in that position anyway. Everybody knows that all girls have sex on prom night because they don't wanna go to college as virgins."

"What?"

"Yeah, come on, you know that. They go down the shore to get laid."

"No. Where do you get those ideas? Am I the only one in this family that's normal?"

He shrugged. "Well, anyway, that's not rape. You got drunk and passed out. He didn't beat you. If the woman isn't beaten, it's not rape."

"I don't wanna hear it. That's despicable, ignorant." I left knowing his support would also not be forthcoming.

To this day, some people maintain the same antiquated view that, if a person passes out, then it's not rape. Along with that, a misconception remains that, if rape is non-violent, or if the victim knows the attacker, then it is not rape. The truth is quite the opposite: Many sexual assaults are non-violent, and most perpetrators are known by the victim.

I wondered what views my sister held and whether she'd agree with me that rape is a crime, not of sex, but of power and opportunity. Marlene was the last family member who did not know, but I wasn't willing to risk telling her because I valued her opinion.

However in 2001, while visiting Mom and Marlene in Florida, my sister confessed. "Mom told me what that creep did to you."

"What creep?" I stopped short on the way to Mom's bedroom.

"That jerk you went to the prom with."

So my mother had betrayed me again, I thought. Rape was not something to share as mere gossip. "What do you think?" I asked.

Hurt in her eyes, tears beginning to pool, she said, "I think it's the worst thing that can happen to a woman."

"Thank you, Marlene." At that moment, I loved her more.

After the initial confessions to Mom and Frank in 1995, I went to see a hypnotist to learn who'd clothed me. She regressed me to that night and from there, the answer became clear--it had been Mandy.

Had she realized when it was too late, and had it led her to dress me and sleep at my side? Regardless, I don't blame her, as I'm sure it affected her, as it did Marissa, who still won't be alone in her house. Crime is never independent.

On the drive home, I stopped at the Sunrise Inn and walked up the exact steps toward the same room from that day. Looking through the glass, curtains parted, I stared. If walls could speak, I thought. How many people had stayed in that room after me, friends having fun, couples making love, none aware of what had happened before them. I said goodbye to that stronghold. No words could describe the freedom I experienced. The liberating sensation would coincide perfectly with my next assignment where I'd soar higher than ever.

10

Mr. and Mrs. Russo

On February 1, 1996, Rob approached my desk amid our squad room's leftover lasagna, radio transmissions, and one-way telephone conversations. "Torres, Cap wants to see us in his office."

We headed past the steel-barred holding cell where two detectives were securing the last prisoner for transport to the county jail. At times, music from our boom boxes would trump the murmurs or curses coming from the cage.

"What'd you do, Torres?" Rob teased, climbing the steps two at a time.

"It wasn't me. It was *you*. I'm just backing you up."

Shaking his head, he said, "That's *you*...got an answer for everything."

"Would I be me otherwise?"

We strode down the narrow, well-lit corridor where

framed photographs of drug seizures hung now and again, java remained on constant brew, and investigators working long-term investigations collaborated with one another.

"Come on in and sit down," Moschetta said, looking up at us from behind his desk, signaling to the two chairs in front of him. "Will you close the door, Bobby?"

"Sure, Cap."

The captain clasped his hands. "I received a phone call from DEA Newark Field Division this morning about HIDTA, you know, High Intensity Drug Trafficking Area? Either of you familiar with it?"

"No."

"It's a task force comprised of federal, state, and local law enforcement. It was implemented to combat drugs in the five counties with the most narcotics activities—Hudson, Essex, Bergen, Union, and us. They asked for two bodies, and I thought the two of you were the best qualified."

He paused.

"When do we go?" I asked, eager to learn new investigative methods from other agencies.

"Next week. You two will be the first to represent us. I know you won't let me down or embarrass this office."

The following Monday, we reported to HIDTA. While waiting in a small break room for further instructions, the rumble of a beverage vending machine turned our voices into whispers.

An older, heavy-boned white gentleman in pressed cuffed khakis, a navy polo shirt, and polished black loafers peered into the room. "Hi." His gentle smile and inquisitive eyes were a stark contradiction to his strong voice and command presence.

We straightened up in our seats.

"Where are you two from?"

"Passaic."

He looked at me. "Please come with me."

I waved good-bye to Rob.

"Had a nice ride in this morning?" he asked as I walked beside him down a long carpeted hallway with new office furniture.

"Yes, I did."

"Good. Traffic can be a challenge sometimes." He made a right turn at the end of the corridor. "Here we are in my humble office. Have a seat."

The bonded leather chair was comfortable, its nail-trim arms untarnished. He'd been a marine; I smiled at the framed USMC flag displaying its colors above a bookcase.

Seated behind his desk, he introduced himself. "I'm Renzo Novotni, Customs Group IV Supervisor. What's your name?"

"Julia Torres."

"Torres? Where are you from?"

"I'm Cuban."

"Ooh, a high-class Spanish," he joked.

I chuckled, shaking my head. "No, not at all."

"Are you fluent?"

"Yes, I am."

"How do you feel about traveling?"

"I love it."

"Do you have a valid passport?"

"Yes."

"When was the last time you used it?"

"Last summer, on a cruise."

"How'd you like it?"

"I loved it so much I gained eight pounds."

He had a loud, contagious laugh. "I know what you mean. You like to eat, like me, huh?"

"Probably more. Those midnight desserts did me in."

"Ah, yes. They are yummy. That's how I got this." He rubbed his belly. "But you don't have to worry about that."

I laughed.

"How much time do you need to get your stuff together if I tell you that you have a plane to catch?"

"Enough to get my passport if I need it. I'll buy clothes when I get there."

He nodded. "Ah, independently wealthy."

"Not yet." I smiled.

"I like that. There isn't anyone you have to check with?"

"No, I answer to no one."

"Good. You're gonna work for me. You'll be getting a cross-designation as a Task Force Officer. The first will be from DEA because you're assigned to HIDTA, and the other from Customs because you'll be in my group. There are a couple of things I want you to know before you begin. If there's a blizzard and there are no pressing matters, there's no need to work that day. If there's a family emergency and you can't notify me, don't worry. Take care of it. Family comes first. Call when you can."

"Alright." I knew we'd get along.

"Do you have any questions for me?"

"Is this a big group?"

"No. With you, there's six—one will retire soon, another soon after, and one is here part-time. That leaves Paul and Matthew to do most of the work. You'll be working with them."

"Are you a Vietnam veteran?"

He nodded. "Yes, I am."

"I'm honored to work for you."

"Honored? Why, thank you."

"You're welcome. Marines are my favorite branch of service."

"Why is that?"

"I think they're the most squared away."

"We think so too," he teased.

"Yes, you do. Not to mention you wear the best uniform." I pointed to the photograph on his desk where he sat in dress blues, next to a woman.

"Ah, yes, the uniform. That's my beloved wife. Did you serve?"

"Yes, but I was army."

"Oh."

"You normally say, 'I'm sorry to hear that.'"

He laughed loudly. "Yes, that sounds about right. You sure do know us well. So why not marines?"

"They didn't have split-option for women. I didn't want to lose time from college."

"Good reason. What college?"

"Rutgers."

"The public ivy-league."

I chuckled.

A FEW HOURS LATER, I MET PAUL WOLF from Customs and Matthew Vail from DEA, both agents whom I'd work with on wiretaps, proffers, and warrants. As with prior agencies, craftiness on surveillance was key, whether I asked to use a suspect's bathroom to get a search warrant layout or entered a deli to ask a target for car help to effect his arrest.

On occasion, I'd see Rob in his group. One night, he called me over. "Torres, you know that Franco wire-tap?"

"Yeah."

"You wanna be my wife and back me up?"

"Sure. When?"

"Don't know yet. We're gonna have a sit-down soon. I'd like you to be there as back-up. You can relax the situation at the same time."

"Alright. Do I tell Renzo?"

"Nah, my G/S will talk to him."

Renzo ambled towards my desk the next afternoon. "Julia, Tommy and Bobby are ready to discuss that job."

The four of us sat in Renzo's office, and Tommy began the meeting. "Bobby's been doing an excellent job on the Franco case for almost a year. There's an important meeting coming up where Bobby and the targets will be discussing doing business with the meth-amphetamine source in California. He thought of adding a different spin to the case by bringing you in as his wife, so that he could have a primary back-up. We've spoken to the ASAC, and he's on board."

"Okay. What do you want me to do?" I asked.

He turned to Rob. "Bobby, you take it from here."

"Torres, here's the deal. I told Franco I have a Cuban wife whose dad lives in Miami. You know Billy Garces, the Cuban group supervisor?"

"Yeah."

"He said he'll play the role of your dad if we need him. I told Franco that he runs an operation in Miami where they sell stolen merchandise from trucks. You got me so far?"

"Yeah. Your story works with Miami Cubans."

"Good. We've already given them a whole shitload of Heineken for free when they had the San Gennaro Feast. He thinks I'm running the show for your dad."

"Why?"

"'Cause I told him your dad wants me to take over the business. He's old, he's tired, and he doesn't want the headache. Since I'm your husband, he trusts me."

"Makes sense."

He nodded. "We're supposed to have a sit-down soon."

"Who?"

"Me, Mark, Joey, and another Italian I don't know. It's gonna be at a restaurant in Long Island. I asked about the food, and they said it was good, so I said I'd be taking my wife to dinner."

"Alright. What do I do?"

"Just follow my lead. And if they say it's okay to meet them, be yourself and use your personality to ease the tension."

"Okay."

"Bring the Russo driver's license with the undercover apartment address."

Recently, I had gone to the state police in Trenton to have a fictitious license made under Julia Russo. It coincided with the passport I had for a possible trip to New Delhi on an FBI Nigerian heroin wiretap. "Okay, when's the meet?"

"Don't know yet. I'll give you a heads-up as soon as I do."

"Any other questions, Julia?" asked Renzo.

"No," I said. "I'll prepare a marriage license in case it's needed."

LATER THAT WEEK, BOBBY CAME UP TO MY DESK. "Torres, we're on. We're leaving in an hour."

"What colors you wearing?"

He snorted, "Aw, Torres, I don't know."

"Come on, man. We gotta match. We're married."

"Uh, okay. You're right. I'll wear dark green slacks and a shirt with different colors on it—uh, green, brown, ivory. You get the idea, Torres? I'm not a fashion plate."

"No, you're definitely not," I teased.

"Okay, killer. You be ready."

"I'm leaving right now." I grabbed my purse. "See?"

An hour later, surveillance teams followed our black Ford Probe GT, making good time until we hit traffic on the Cross Bronx. Crawling our way with three teams behind us, I wiggled in my seat. "How much longer?" I asked Rob.

"I don't know. Doesn't look good." He glanced at me. "What's the—" he began laughing. "You gotta pee?"

"Yeah. What's so funny?"

"You dancing?"

"If that's what you wanna call it."

"Torres, what am I gonna do with you?"

"Nothing. Just get me a bathroom."

"Hold it."

"If I'm doing this, it's 'cause I reached my limit."

"Limit of what?" he said, cracking up. "Your craziness?"

"Stop laughing. You're gonna make me laugh, and it'll be worse."

"But you look real funny, Torres." He burst into laughter.

"Yeah, yeah, ha-ha. Pull over."

"On the Cross Bronx?"

"Where else, Oshkosh? Tell the guys I gotta take a personal." I got napkins out of my purse as he called it out on the radio and pulled over on the shoulder. The other cars lined up behind us.

I couldn't get out quick enough. "Just tell 'em to look the other way," I called out to Rob as I jacked up my skirt to pull down my pantyhose and crouch.

I wasn't the only one with a full bladder; a couple of the guys went into the woods. Once finished, I shouted, "I'm good."

We continued to the Italian restaurant, arriving on an upscale street lined with old trees. Once parked, we entered holding hands. "Hi, two please," Rob told the pretty, dark-haired Italian hostess.

"Where would you like to be seated?" she asked.

"In the back."

"Follow me." She grabbed two menus and led the way.

Rob sat across from me, facing the front of the restaurant. Wall-to-wall mirrors provided a complete vantage point. Two agents were sitting in the bar section; others outside waited for the targets—Mark Franco, the main player; Joey Tessareri, his right arm; and the third, a John Doe.

During the succulent surf-and-turf dinner with a scrumptious side of broccoli rabe and a dry white Bordeaux, Rob was laughing at something silly I had said when purposeful footsteps caught my attention. From the corner of my eye, well-polished black cowboy boots under black jeans and a black leather blazer tapered the muscular frame of a man in his early thirties.

"That's Mark," Rob whispered.

"Wow! He looks good," I said, noticing his intense eyes and strong jawline as he headed past us to a back room.

"Torres, things catch your eye easy," said Rob before pointing out Mark's right-hand man. "Joey's here, last table by the bar."

Through the mirror, the other dark-haired Italian who stood about six feet, wearing a sweater and jeans, was just as good-looking and muscular. Mark had joined Joey, and I hoped the beer bottle he had in his hand would relax him. Although it was warm inside, he hadn't removed his jacket. The fourth, the unknown guy I'd seen briefly through the mirrors, had come and gone.

"I'm gonna go hang out with them," Rob said, taking a Heineken with him.

While I was savoring the lobster's tender, buttery taste, an idea occurred to me. I called the hostess over. "Will you send my husband and the boys a bottle of wine on me?" I pointed to them.

"What would you like?"

At that time in the Northeast, Santa Margherita was a popular pinot grigio with the Italians, but wanting her to make the suggestion, I asked, "What do you recommend?"

"Santa Margherita. It's seventy-five dollars."

"That's fine."

"You must love your husband."

"He's a great guy. He deserves more than that."

"It's nice to hear women speak well of their husbands. I'll send it right over."

Twenty minutes later, Rob was at the edge of our table,

grinning, hazel eyes glimmering. "Torres, I don't know what you did, but the guys wanna meet you."

I smiled. The government money spent had been worth every cent. "I wanted to score you some points."

"You did. Thanks." He held his hand out for me.

Mark, who'd sat down but was still wearing his jacket, rose when I approached the table with Rob. Joey had been standing. "Mark, Joey, this is my wife, Julia."

"Nice to meet you," they said warmly, extending their hands, giving me a peck on the cheek. Rob removed a stool for me across from Mark.

The night was going well until Rob caressed the back of my neck, throwing me off. I turned to him. "What are you doing?"

His eyes widened slightly. From the corner of my eye, I noticed the targets staring at me and caught myself. Whispering loud enough for them to hear but low enough to appear intimate, I said, "You know that turns me on in public."

Rob let out a chuckle. The guys hung their heads in embarrassment.

Charisma and wit resumed as deep voices vied for attention, bringing with them popular movies for discussion. We began reciting famous lines in films we loved; *Scarface* soon appeared.

"I got an even better one," I said excitedly. The targets' body language had changed: shoulders relaxed, eyes expressing interest. Mark removed his jacket, hanging it over his stool.

"Ready?"

The targets nodded, seeming eager.

Rob egged me on. "Go ahead!"

I raised my hands to my waist, pretending to be holding a MAC-10 machine gun. "Ju wanna play ruf? Say he-llo to my leettle fren," and ended with bullet sounds.

The men let out guffaws while applauding. That was the ice breaker.

At the end of the night, Mark walked us outside, where we exchanged kisses and handshakes. He remained watching while Rob and I strolled to our car with hands entwined, until Rob opened the door for me.

Surveillance following, I turned to my partner. "Man, you almost got me when you touched the back of my neck, but when I saw that look in your eye saying, *Torres, I'm your husband*, I said the first thing that came to me."

"Yeah, that was good. I thought we were fucked. You cleaned it up perfect."

"Yeah, but what was up with that?"

Sheepishly, he answered, "You know I love short hair."

"That's right. It's your kryptonite." I laughed.

"It is. And it looked so good the way you had it. I couldn't help myself."

"Well, you definitely kept me on my toes."

"Did you see their faces?"

"Yeah, they didn't know where to put themselves."

"You were great, Torres! They're totally in now. It was tense at first, but you were able to make them laugh, and you got Mark to take off his coat."

"Thanks. What happened to the third guy?"

"Oh, Rocco's the owner. He was busy and couldn't stay."

Surveillance teams broke off when we entered the building to brief our G/S, who was content that Rob's position had been solidified. The comment Rob had made about things catching my eye easily would prove accurate a few weeks later in early December.

Julia Torres

II

Fate

WHAT IS LOVE—THAT UNEXPLAINABLE, incomparable, extraordinary sensation that, at its peak, edifies the spirit and promotes insight, setting the mind adrift into a mystical state? I had experienced the essence of its core for the first time with George from 1985 to 1987, but having had the residual effects of rape hovering over me, I'd ended it.

After him, I'd become an emotional cripple until 1992, when Rick, a good friend, helped me overcome the psychological issues behind the physical trauma. As a result, love ceased to be an ambiguity for me.

Domingo Cruz, or Dom, as I called him, was seven years older than me, a former marine, a cop, and through him, I learned how much I could love again. To love with such exaggeration embodied the surrender of my life for his if given a choice; to me, it meant there was nothing we could not overcome.

Our relationship began in 1994, two years after we met through a mutual colleague. It had been full of joy, but it wasn't meant to endure.

When his dad, the very epitome of fatherhood, the man he most admired, respected, and cherished, became terminally ill, he chose to separate himself from me without saying a word. I yearned to care for him, but he wouldn't accept it. I could not understand it, and although it grieved me, I respected his privacy.

Time passed until, one cold November afternoon, I found the courage to call him. In my attic apartment, where I'd been living for a few months, I lifted the heavy handset.

"Hello?" His voice was strained.

I closed my eyes, took a breath, and said, "It's me."

His breath was labored. I heard its depth. "Hi, Julie."

Leaning against the refrigerator, glancing out the window at the untainted snow covering the rooftop, I sighed. "How's your dad?"

"Not good, Julie. Not good." The man I had considered my soul-mate could not fathom happiness as his father lay dying.

"Dom," I paused, needing yet not wanting to know his response, "do you still love me?"

Time stopped.

He took a deep breath. "No."

I gasped. The rug under my feet had been yanked. I fell, weightless into a dark unknown, and there I floated.

He sensed my turmoil, but he'd known his answer would make me retreat. "It's okay, Julie. Let me call you back." He did not. Those words had hurt him as much as they had me, for he confessed many years later that he hadn't meant them.

I sobbed as never before; it came from the pit of my stomach, the recesses of my soul. I hadn't thought I'd love another man that way again, for it had been paradise when we were together, a wretched howl when we were not.

From then on, dating equaled comparisons—fair to no one. I focused on my career, putting love on a back burner again, becoming further goal directed, consumed by self-imposed deadlines: marriage by thirty, children by thirty-five. The mere desire had been shallow, and I hadn't placed any value on the essence of marriage.

In November 1996, while completing a DEA 6, Report of Investigation, at my desk, I overheard a foreign language interpreter and Matthew talking about an all-inclusive trip for friends and families to Cancun. Knowing travel to Mexico could be completed at that time with a driver's license, and that Frank would want to go, I interjected, "Can me and my brother go?"

SIMPLE MOMENTS CHANGE THE COURSE OF EVENTS. That ordinary conversation would be the catalyst for my immediate future as early December rolled around and we boarded a resort van at the airport. Warm weather, picture-postcard scenes, and island music surrounded us on the ride to our destination. Billboards advertising real estate and travel had been a common sight, but a specific one with daily flights to Cuba caught my attention.

It had been a trip I'd thought of taking on and again, but there had always been an impediment. Cuba had seemed a paradox. The beauty and richness of *La Perla de Las Antillas* was available for foreigners to enjoy but forbidden to Cubans living on the island.

It was one of those prodding moments. Pointing at the advertisement, I nudged Frank. "You wanna go?"

"Yeah."

"How do you go to Cuba from here?" I leaned forward between other tourists to ask the driver.

He glanced at me in the rear-view mirror. "I'll have an agent call you."

At our destination, palm frond fans oscillated on ceilings in the vast, open reception hall while toucans cackled in grand cages. A slight breeze carried scents of coconut oil and salt water past the pool, where music was blasting.

We hurried to our rooms and changed into swimwear. Frank was looking for his suntan oil when the phone rang.

"Miss Julia Torres, please?" asked a low male voice.

"This is she."

"I am the travel agent, to see you about your Cuba trip?"

"Oh, that was fast. We'll be there in a minute."

Downstairs, Fernando introduced himself and said, "Have a seat.... How long do you want to travel for?"

"Just one day," I said.

He shook his head. "You'll have to go for at least three."

Frank and I exchanged glances. He shrugged.

"Okay," I said.

"Do you have a passport?"

"I do, but he doesn't."

The agent scratched his head. "He can't go without it."

"I guess we're not going," said Frank.

"No, *you're* not going, but I am."

"Where do you want to stay?" asked Fernando.

"I don't know. I've never been there."

He removed a binder from a drawer. "Take a look in here. There are several hotels."

Mom often mentioned Hotel Capri while I was growing up, and there it was. I took it as a sign that it was where I should stay.

Itinerary established, Frank and I headed to the pool and jumped right in, maneuvering our way towards the bar, where we met a young couple from New York over margaritas. The four of us kayaked, snorkeled, rode banana boats, and danced in resort clubs until it was time for my trip to Cuba.

At five a.m. that morning, for unknown reasons, I woke Frank. "Something phenomenal's gonna happen. If I don't return, call Renzo. His number's here," I pointed at the nightstand.

"O-kay," he mumbled.

Aboard the aircraft, I made small talk with the lady seated to my left until we landed at the Jose Marti International Airport. The enigma of Cuba began to manifest itself when I provided my travel documents to a brown-complexioned immigration agent.

"This travel permit is incorrect. Your American passport says you were born in Cuba, but you gave me a tourist visa."

"Yes, I'm an American tourist."

"No, you're Cuban. We don't recognize American citizenship for Cubans. A Cuban is always a Cuban," he admonished.

"Okay. Let me have my papers," I said.

"No. I have to keep them until I know what to do."

"What do you mean?"

"When someone arrives here with the wrong documentation, one of two things happen: Either the person sleeps in the airport until the next flight, which in your case is tomorrow, or the person goes to jail until the next flight."

Without any basis, I asserted, "God is big, and I am going to stay."

He dismissed me with a wave. "Sit over there and wait."

Once the remaining travelers left the airport, a government agent, holstered gun on his hip, marched up to me. The six-foot mulato who stood in a defensive posture spoke as if he knew me. "Hello, Miss Torres. What are you doing in Cuba?"

"Visiting my homeland."

"Why?"

"I wanted to."

"For what reason?" He eyed me with incredulity.

"I never have."

He shrugged and left.

Ten minutes passed before a man in plain clothes appeared, ID pinned to his shirt pocket reading *Ruben Antonio Rodriguez-Martinez, Seguridad del Estado*. "What brings you here, Miss Torres?"

"I'm just visiting."

"Who?" His voice carried an undertone of intimidation.

"No one. I'm visiting where I was born."

He frowned. "Why not family?"

"I don't have any here."

"You're here alone?"

"Yes. Is that a problem?"

"Where's your luggage?" The suspicion in his hazel eyes was clear.

I pointed to my beach bag. "Right here."

"What were your plans?"

"I was going to the beach."

He raised his eyebrows.

I raised my vest. "See?"

He turned around and was gone.

Soon enough, an older, black Cuban in a military uniform sat down on the chair to my right. "Miss Torres?"

"Yes, that's me. But you already know that."

He ignored my remark. "Do you have any family living here?"

"I already answered that."

"Where is your family?" He combed his thick mustache with his fingers.

"In the United States."

"What do you do for a living?"

"What don't I do?" I answered. "I'm a teacher, photographer, and I sell houses." It was all true: I worked as an adjunct professor on Saturdays, had studied photography, and had obtained my real estate license. I wasn't foolish enough to mention the military or law enforcement and risk being considered a spy or thrown in jail.

"Why are you here?"

I let out an exaggerated sigh. "I'm tired of answering the same questions. My answers haven't changed, because they're true."

"Hmpf." He rose, clicking the heels of his boots. Two more men followed: one in uniform, the other in plain clothes.

I rolled my eyes.

"Miss Torres, we're just curious why you don't have any luggage," said the younger of the two, a Chinese-Cuban.

"I'm only here three days. I don't need much."

"And you have no family here?"

"I answered that twice." I raised two fingers.

He pointed to the uniformed man. "He'll stay with you until a decision has been made about you."

I shrugged and turned to the last man. "What's your name?"

"Jorge Luis."

"Jorge, I'm starving. Is there any food around here?"

"Upstairs. Come on, I'll take you."

Once there, he pointed to an area with various tables. On one, there were several Canadian tourists. "That's for tourists."

A pretty black waitress came over. "We have chicken, *moro*, fries, and mango juice."

"Okay, I'll have that." I pointed to Jorge, who had sat further away, and added, "Bring him whatever he wants."

By the time we returned downstairs, the agent who had taken my documents five hours prior had also. "Miss Torres? Come here quick. They're letting you stay."

"I told you!"

I waved good-bye to Jorge and ran outside. Immediately, I was struck with the smell of diesel fuel, and by the thought that I was in my homeland and had no one to share that moment with.

I hopped into a taxi, conversing with the driver as waves crashed against the *malecon*, splattering over the ledge; *bicitaxis* transported passengers through busy streets; natives of all colors and sizes lolled about.

At the pre-1959 Capri Hotel, I checked in and rode the small elevator to my room. The furniture was from the 1950s: two twin beds, cloth chairs, old fixtures.

Once refreshed, I spoke with the lobby concierge who suggested the scenic walk to an ice cream parlor at a park called Coppelia, and that evening's nine o'clock aquatic dance at the rooftop pool, followed by ballads at the piano bar.

Antique cars rumbled along the street in an island appearing to have been suspended in time. Rooftops of dilapidated buildings displayed old-fashioned styles on clotheslines. Men and women, in jeans or shorts, strolled aimlessly, laughing and telling stories, flip-flops or sneakers on their feet.

Near Coppelia, I noticed a young, ill-placed mulatto in dreadlocks walking across the street: alas, another simple moment that changes life. From the distance, he asked, "Hey, lady, where are you going?"

"Coppelia's." *He seems harmless.* "You wanna come?"

"Sure." He crossed the street. "Hi, I'm Misael."

As we walked, he told me things I didn't know. "Four rolls of toilet paper cost a dollar, and people make between five to fifteen dollars a month."

"And a dollar for toilet paper! Why doesn't anyone complain?"

"We'll be thrown in jail. Besides, there's nothing to fight with. The government seized our weapons a long time ago."

On our return, he asked, "You like to dance?"

"Yes."

"There's a club across from Hotel Capri, Club 21. It's good after midnight. You wanna meet the DJ now and ask him about it?"

"Sure. I'm near there."

At midnight, I met Misael at the corner of the club. As we approached the door, a very good-looking man standing to my left, in jeans and a white shirt with the sleeves rolled up, caught my eye. Before you knew it, he stood before us, blocking our entrance.

I glanced up, but honey-colored eyes simply stared at me. I waited for his inviting mouth to move, but he didn't speak. Then I heard it: *You're gonna marry this man.*

I broke the silence. "What, I gotta pay you?"

"Yes. It's a dollar fifty each."

I handed him a five.

"I'll go get you change." He turned and entered the club.

Wow, what a body. He had a perfect athletic build: small waist, broad v-shaped back, and big legs.

After he returned, I entered with Misael, wondering how I could meet him. I surmised that, if I spoke with the DJ long enough, Misael would leave. That's what happened.

By the DJ booth, I asked Vladimir, "Is the bouncer married?"

He was intrigued. "I don't know."

Hmm, he must live with someone.

"Do you like him?"

"Yes. I'm going to marry him."

"Hotel California" began to play. The bouncer approached me. "Are you going to dance?"

"No," I said. It wasn't a song I danced to.

"My name is Narciso. Here's my business card." It read *Narciso Nadal, Cocina Internacional y Criolla.*

"You cook?"

"Yes, I'm a chef. I went to culinary arts school. This club is a restaurant during the day, and I'm a chef here."

"What are you doing here as a bouncer?"

"There was a fight here last weekend, and since I'm the biggest guy, the owner asked me to work this weekend in case it happens again. . . . Turn the card around. I wrote something. I'll be back. I have to go watch the door."

On the reverse of the card, he'd interpreted a phrase from Spanish to English—*Es mejor fracasar intentando un truinfo, que dejar de triunfar por temor a un fracaso.* In English, it read "It's better to fail trying to succeed than fail to succeed for fear of failure."

I don't believe in coincidences. That voice had been crystal clear: *You're gonna marry this man.* I hadn't doubted those words. There had to be a reason for the both of us, who were only there that weekend, to have met.

He had two of the three ideals I wanted in a husband at that time, as fickle as they were: a nice last name and cooking abilities. The former two had been confirmed with his card, but would the last? I wondered.

On his next approach, I asked, "Are your genetics natural, luck, or steroids?"

"Natural. My dad was called 'Tarzan' when he was young. He's a tall Spaniard, six-three, taller than me. I'm only six-one. My mom had a tremendous physique when she was young—she's *mulata*." That had been the icing on the cake.

We went for a walk around the *malecon* once the club closed a few hours later. People lolled about; some leaned on windows, talking to their neighbors, while others rode bicycles through the streets, friends on handlebars shouting or laughing.

Narciso asked, "What are your plans for tomorrow?"

"I'm gonna go on a tour of Old Havana."

"Let me be your tour guide. I have the day off. If you want, we can also go to the beach, Mar Azul."

With plans set, we strolled to the Capri, and there parted ways.

The next morning, while brushing my teeth in my orange bikini, I heard a knock on my door. Thinking it was Narciso, I opened it, toothbrush in hand.

Two men stood before me—one in civvies, the other in military uniform. *I'm being followed.*

I signaled for them to wait. Moments later, after dressing, I asked, "What do you want?"

The uniformed guy spoke. "We want to confirm the details of your return flight. May we come in?"

"I have no intention of staying," I said, allowing them limited entry, and provided them the info.

"We're not all bad here," said the one in civvies as the other made notes on a pad.

"I didn't say that. . . . I saw you yesterday on the street."

"You must be mistaken," he said as both exchanged glances.

"No. I'm a photographer. Faces are pictures to me."

They left without saying anything further.

The phone rang. "I'm in the lobby." Narciso's voice was stressed.

Seated on a chair, jaw clenched, he greeted me curtly moments later. Outside, he explained, "The male employees in the lobby were asking me to leave because Cubans are not allowed inside hotels."

Hm, just like Coppelia was only for tourists. Misael had to ask an employee to bring the ice cream.

He hailed a cab to the beach.

Sitting on the hot sand, staring into the limitless sea, an idea came to me. "How does someone leave Cuba?"

"There are three ways. You can win the Cuban or American lottery. Someone sends an invitation letter to a person over fifty-five years old, and an interview determines your approval. Or you marry a Canadian, European or Mexican."

"I'm gonna get you out of here," I said.

He said nothing.

After we left the beach and toured Old Havana, he asked, "Do you want to see the cannons fire at the Fort tonight?"

"Sure."

However, that evening, we spent the night together, bypassing the fort. My contention had been to experience what I deemed a meant-to-be moment.

The next morning, after agreeing to stay in touch but before leaving for the airport, I mentioned having two sisters in Havana. "Where in Havana?" he asked.

"I don't know, I only have a partial address. Can I tell you when I'm home?"

"Sure, I'll find them for you."

The weekend's adventure replayed in my head on the flight to Cancun. Falling in love was not something I did easily, but it was evident that Rob was right—things did catch my eye easy.

I'd only witnessed that excitement through actors in films,

living vicariously in their place, seated engrossed for two hours. Our encounter was not something that often occurred in the real world, leading me to surmise that destiny had called.

And I suspected that, even if the marriage did not work out, at least I'd have gotten someone out of that measly existence that had once been the jewel of the Caribbean. What did I really know? Nothing at all. I was merely going with the moment.

12

Paris

Julia, it's Renzo. The answering machine kept playing as I turned on the heat in the one-bedroom North Bergen condo I'd bought the year before. *I hope you had a fabulous time in Cancun.* Thankful for the resort's laundry facility, I unzipped my suitcase, putting things in order. *Please come in at nine a.m. Monday morning. I got a job for you. Have a nice day.*

Knowing it had to be something good if Renzo was calling me at home, I jumped in the shower, thinking how well things were moving along. In PJs and a plush red robe, I left the bathroom refreshed and made a light dinner of white rice and chicken breast in white wine. It was the perfect end to a great vacation, I thought, turning off the light at bedtime.

AT WORK THE NEXT DAY, I draped my jacket over my chair and hurried to Renzo's office. "Okay, what is it?" The excitement in my voice was clear.

He was drinking his early-morning coffee. He gulped and put it down to say, "You're gonna love this one. Have a seat."

I did.

"I received a call from Paris DEA on Thursday—"

"I'm going to *Paris?*"

He laughed loudly. "*Oui, oui, Mademoiselle,* I guess I don't have to ask you if you're interested in going."

"No way—that's a no-brainer."

He resumed, "They're working on a heroin case involving international travel between France and New Jersey, and they need to get Newark Customs on board. Ebi, a Nigerian woman who is part of the operation, is waiting for an American mule to telephone her to pick up a brick of heroin and smuggle it into the United States. DEA asked if I had anyone who could make it happen, and of course I said yes."

I laughed. "When do I go?"

"In two days. Special Agents Gino Liberti from Customs, and Mike Menter from DEA, will be traveling with you. Gino doesn't speak French, but Mike does. He worked in Paris for a few years, so you two won't feel totally left out."

"Phew. Thanks, Renzo. This is the moment I wish I'd stayed in French class in high school."

"Why didn't you?"

"I was a junior, and there were a whole bunch of freshmen in it. Two weeks was enough."

"Ooh, of course," he said, wiggling his fingers, "no junior wants to hang out in a class full of freshmen."

"Oh, well. So what do I do?"

"On this end, fill out your travel paperwork. The front

office will make sure your air and lodging are set. Get a bag ready for five days, and don't forget your passport. Matthew will drop you guys off in Newark. An agent will be waiting at the airport in Paris. He'll fill you in from there."

I clapped my hands. "All *right*. I can't pack soon enough."

"Yeah, I figured it'd be right up your alley."

"You got that right. How's the weather?" I pointed with my chin to the window.

"Cold like here."

"Okay. Anything else?"

"Congratulations."

"Thank you for thinking of me, Renzo."

Two afternoons later, we landed at Charles De Gaulle and met Agent Lee Ianozzi, who warned us to get used to people smoking everywhere in Paris. Intercoms were blaring in French when we headed out of the sliding glass doors with our bags and climbed into Lee's vehicle.

Small cars tooted horns on busy streets as we drove by boutiques, restaurants, and cafes. Passersby, loaves of bread under their arms, winter hats on heads, hurried by.

The Champs-Élysées was lively: a couple, having come out of an exclusive shop, bags in hand, ran from a wide sidewalk across the street to catch a cab at a stand; an older, salt-and-pepper-haired man left a bistro, fedora on his head, newspaper curled in one hand, and a coffee cup in the other.

We turned at Rue La Boetie, where we stopped in front of the revolving doors of Hotel Rochester. American, British, and French flags hung beside two whinnying horse statues, hooves resting on a golden globe.

Inside the six-story building we found a reception lobby where lighting from wall sconces cast a soft glow on marble floors. After agreeing to meet the team there at nine o'clock, we checked into our rooms to cope with some of the jet-lag. In my room, I quickly unpacked and fell asleep.

Later that night, we met Lee in the lobby. He had company with him: DEA Special Agent Benjamin Kearney, and Pierre BoBois and Rene Bisset, from the French police. We all went to a festive restaurant where waiters were moving to and fro in slacks, crisp white shirts, vests and bow ties. The scents of a French cuisine, my favorite, drifted across the room: soufflé, *filet mignon, moules marinière.*

"What are you having?" asked Mike when we were all seated.

"I have no idea. It's in French."

"Would you like me to suggest something?" he asked.

"Yes, please."

He turned to Gino. "Would you?"

He nodded.

He recommended *boeuf Bourguignon* and *boudin blanc*, respectively, with complementary wines. It was one of the rare times that I savored a mushroom garnish—that subtle blend of red wine, cognac, vegetables, and herbs.

I heard a high-pitched yelp. I looked around and was surprised to see a poodle seated on a chair behind a dinner plate of dog biscuits, and just as poised as the older woman across from it. I asked Lee. "Do they allow all dogs in restaurants?"

He set down his wine glass. "No, only small breeds."

"Oh. Let me ask you another question. . . . Is it normal to eat this late?"

Pierre interjected in accented English, "It's customary to dine around nine p.m., sometimes later."

"How does everyone stay so thin?"

"Rene can tell you that," he joked.

He looked up after finishing his brandied roast goose, its flavor of seasonings and brandy sauce wafting over the table. "He's referring to my smoking habit. I believe *that* is how we Frenchmen stay thin," said Rene.

The waiter arrived. "*Le dessert quelqu'un?*" A platter of *crème brulee, croquembouche,* French apple tart, and *crepes* with vanilla ice cream were rolled to our table.

By evening's end, inquiring minds satisfied over interesting talk, Pierre and Rene bade us *adieu*. We rode with the agents to our hotel and agreed to be ready for the next day's ten a.m. briefing.

That morning, after going through embassy security, we followed Lee into a private office where coffee was percolating. "Help yourselves," said Benjamin.

Seated around a table, Lee began the briefing. "In the next hour, me, Mike, and Julia will head to the train station in an attempt for Julia to contact Ebi, the Nigerian female target who is expecting a phone call from an American mule to smuggle the heroin into the U.S. During that conversation, our goal is to establish a time and place where Julia and Ebi can meet. We hope that Ebi will bring the heroin to the meeting and show it to Julia. Immediately following, Julia provides the hit signal, and Ebi gets arrested. "Julia, any questions about your phone call to Ebi?"

"What language does she speak?"

"Ebu and French."

I grinned. "No English?"

"It's broken."

Mike assured me, "You'll be fine."

Lee continued, "You can call her to introduce yourself."

"What name do I use?" I asked.

"Lisa Bravo," said Benjamin. "That's the name that'll be entered in INTERPOL after we complete the investigation."

"Okay. What do you need me to say?" I drank some coffee.

"Tell her you're the one picking up the merchandise, but you want to see it first. Have her come out to meet you."

"Where?"

"Élysées Café."

"Will she know where it is?"

"Yes, everyone does."

I leaned forward. "Can we drive by it so I can see it?"

"Yes. When we get a room for you at the hotel nearby, we'll show it to you."

"What's the room for?"

"To have her bring you the heroin."

"Can I see the room, too? I'd like to get a feel for it. Make it look like someone's been there, just in case. You know...."

"Yes. No problem. I understand."

"When's this going down?"

"Well, hopefully you'll get in touch with her soon to arrange a time for tomorrow."

"Okay."

"Anything else? Anyone?..."

"I think we covered it all," said Benjamin.

Lee turned to me. "Ready?"

"Yes."

"All right, everyone," he said. "Remember, safety first. Let's head out."

The train station bustled: some people rushed by, newspapers or bagels in hand; others had dogs on leashes as business owners sold magazines, loaves of French bread, and the ever-present cigarettes.

"Okay, Julia, you know what you're gonna say?" asked Lee, standing by the pay phone next to me and Mike.

"Yes."

"Okay. Go ahead and dial her number."

The overseas tone rang hollow while thoughts of Tom Cruise in *Mission Impossible* came to mind. It was ironic that, in that same depot, I was acting in an undercover capacity, getting paid paltry thousands compared to Cruise, who pretended to play my role and earned millions.

"*Bonjour?*" a sweet soprano voice answered.

Giving Lee the thumbs up sign, I said, "*Bonjour. Ebi, s'il vous plait?*"

"*Oui, c'est Ebi.*"

"*Je m'appelle Lisa. Je Americane.*"

"*Ah, bon. Ca va?*"

"*Très bien. Et vous?*" Destinations blasted over the intercom when one train stopped and another sped away, blowing hot windy air, twirling my hair.

"*Bon. Parlez-vous francais?*"

"*Comme si, comme ca. Et vous? Parlez-vous anglais?*"

"*Un peu.*"

Our lack of fluency in either's language clearly wouldn't keep us from communicating. She asked, "You have girdle?"

"A girdle? *Non. Pourquoi?*" I glanced at Mike, shrugging. He moved his hands, signaling to let it roll.

"*Securite de mouvement. If non girdle, vous* swallow."

"Swallow?"

"*Oui.*"

Shaking my head, I said, "*Non.* I don't wanna do that. Girdle's better, but *je ne sais pas,* uh. *Vous* show *moi comme?*"

"*Oui.* I put in girdle. *Vous see moi.*"

"*Bon.* What will you be wearing?"

"*Que? Je ne comprends pas.*"

"Uh...." Searching the air for words, I saw a man drop a coffee cup. "*Merde!*" he barked when some splattered on his suit. "Uh, clothes, fashion, *moda*...."

"Ah, *oui!*" she exclaimed. "*Oui, moda, mes habits. Naturellement. Un brun pantaloon et une bleu chemisier. Et vous?*"

"*Noir* sweater *et* Levis." I didn't know how to say "jeans," but she'd know what I meant. Mike had bought Levis for some of the men, saying they had been solicited. Because of their high cost, they were synonymous with wealth.

"*Bon. Quand?*"

"*Deux* tomorrow? Élysées Café?"

"*Oui. Bon.*"

"*Magnifique. Au revoir,*" I said, ending our call. Phew!

"That was great, Julia," Lee said, smiling. "You introduced yourself in French and tried to speak as much as you could in her language. You certainly picked it up quickly."

I sighed. "Thank you. I tried to recall what I knew from high school, but hearing the Frenchmen last night really helped."

Mike chimed in, "I told you she was sharp."

"How do you feel?" Lee asked.

"Good—I think it worked despite the language issues."

"All right. Let's go back to the embassy to debrief and plan for tomorrow's meet." The three of us headed up the stairs, past people moving in all directions. Once out in the brisk air, we left in Lee's car, passing the glorious *Arc de Triomphe* on the western end of the Champs-Élysées.

Before our debriefing, we drove by the hotel and the café.

Using the key that Lee provided, I headed upstairs to room 406, lay on the bed, and rolled around, making it appear slept in. I threw one of my shirts on it, considering it gone. In the bathroom, I opened the toiletry packets, dumped some out, and put a bar of soap in the tub.

At the café, the glass windows would provide unobstructed views for surveillance. The bathroom was small and private enough to converse in and keep watch over.

Once done, we continued to the embassy, where we entered a conference room and met Benjamin and Gino.

"All right. Let's talk about how we're gonna get this done," Lee began. "Julia, when the target arrives, do something obvious so surveillance knows who she is."

"I'll stand up to greet her, and wave her over."

"Sounds good."

"Where will you see the heroin?"

"In the bathroom."

"Okay. Make sure you arrange for her to meet you at the hotel, and once you see the drugs, leave the café and give us a hit signal. What will it be? Again, make it obvious."

"Okay. I'll take off my hat."

"You'll put it on before opening the door?" asked Benjamin.

"Yes."

He noted it on the ops report he was writing.

"How soon after will you give the hit signal?"

"When I pass the café. In case anyone's looking, I'll scratch my head; I don't want anyone getting suspicious that I took off my hat in the cold."

"Okay."

"Where do you want me to go once I'm gone?" I asked.

"A car will pull up to the curb, and me and Mike will be sitting in the front. Gino will be in the back. He'll open the back right passenger door for you. Get in right away."

"What's the hurry?"

"Undercover work is not recognized in France."

"You're kidding."

"I wish I was, but no one does it. . . . You won't be carrying either."

"That's fine," I said.

"Julia, you would be considered an *agent provocateur*," interjected Mike.

"What's that?" I asked.

"A person associated with suspicious people who provokes trouble."

"So what does that mean for me?"

"If the French police get to you before we do, you'll be arrested. Pierre and Rene will give you five minutes to leave, but if it takes longer, they have to do their job. Don't worry, if you end up in jail, we'll get you out, but it may take a bit of time."

"Okay. No problem."

"Anybody have any questions?"

"Are we taking the drugs with us?" asked Gino.

"Probably not. France won't let the package leave."

"What'll happen to Ebi?" I asked.

"When she knocks on your hotel room door to exchange the drugs for the money, agents will be waiting inside. She'll be arrested then."

Mike asked, "Who'll be in the café?"

"Rene."

There were no further questions.

AT THE CHAMPS-ÉLYSÉES CAFÉ, some folks were entering with briefcases; others inside lit cigarettes and sipped coffee. I found a table in the center and ordered a cappuccino and a croissant.

Rene, my primary back-up, was seated on the rear left, smoking, demitasse cup on the side. Surveillance teams were in their designated spots outside.

The café was in constant motion: the cash register ringing as people came and went, taking baguettes to go or sipping coffee while perusing the *Herald de Paris*. A woman fitting Ebi's physical description entered, looking around. She unbuttoned her wool coat, revealing a blue blouse and brown pants.

I rose, waving her to me. "Ebi!"

She brought the cold with her. "*Bonjour*, Lisa." She smiled, set her coat behind her chair, and sat.

"*Café? Croissant?*" I offered.

"*Oui.*"

"*Garcon?*" I called out.

Order placed, we began a casual conversation. After the

waiter brought her order, she said, "*Tout bien ferme. Je reveler en bain.*"

"*Mangez-vous premier.*"

Three quarters of the way through, she asked, "*Partir present?*"

"*Vous premier. Vous moda,* uh. . . ." I tugged at different clothing to imply she had to shed some.

She nodded.

"*En cinq minutes, je partir. Je ne penser bon deux partir a bain,*" I added.

"*Ce bon.*"

She rose to enter the bathroom, and a few minutes later, I did also. There were two small stalls; Ebi was in one, door open, shirt above her waist. No one was in the other.

"*Voir?*" she asked.

I tugged at the brick of fine white powder secured around her body by a girdle and a layer of tape. "*Excellent.*"

She smiled, lowering her shirt.

"*Je partir á hotel,* room number *quatre, zéro, six.*" I pointed to the place next door and used my fingers to confirm the numbers. "*Moi* get dollars *pour vous. En cinq minutes,* follow me." I used my hands to signal the French words I didn't know. "Knock *deux, et je ouvrir.*"

"*C'est une bonne idée.*"

"*Merci.*"

"*De rien.*"

We returned to the table and finished our croissant.

"*Voulez-vous partir?*" she asked.

I looked around the café; Rene was still in the corner, an ashtray full of smoked cigarettes before him, as he puffed on another.

"*Attends* until *je partir*. Then, *vous partir*," I said, and I rose, leaving francs to cover the bill on the table, and exited, noticing Rene had stayed behind. After a few steps, I removed my hat and scratched my head.

Seconds later, a car pulled up alongside me, right rear passenger door open. I entered and was whisked away, just as planned.

The French police arrested Ebi at the door of my hotel room. They searched the room, finding nothing except the shirt I had purposely left behind. Scouring the lobby, they approached the front desk clerk to ask who was in my room.

The person went through the registration book. "*Mademoiselle Lisa Bravo, Monsieur.*"

"*Tout identification?*"

"*Non.*"

The French cop was frustrated. "What did she look like?"

"She had very distinctive features."

"American?"

"*Non.* Sri-Lankan." Of all the nationalities I have been compared to, Sri Lankan has never been one. I found it amusing that my social chameleon skills had endured abroad.

During the debriefing, it was confirmed that France would not allow the drugs to leave the country. Bobby's words from years before echoed in my mind: *The most important part of the job is to go home.*

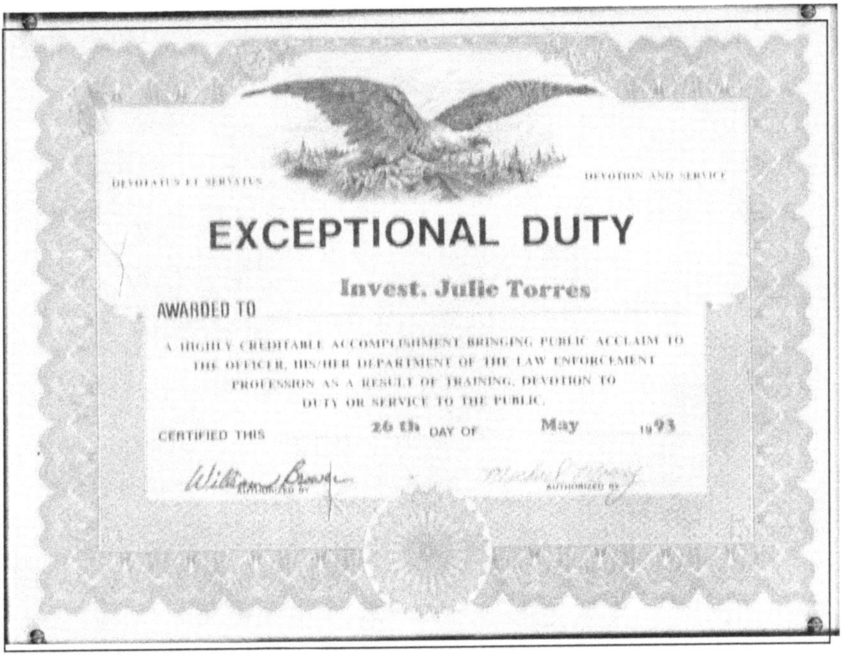

Lakewood Police Department Special Operations Unit award

With some of the guys in Squad B

Jerry Burgos, one of my former partners

On the first case Jerry and I started together, which he finished on his own

Passaic County Prosecutor Ronald Fava and Captain Vinny Moschetta swearing me in

With Prosecutor Fava

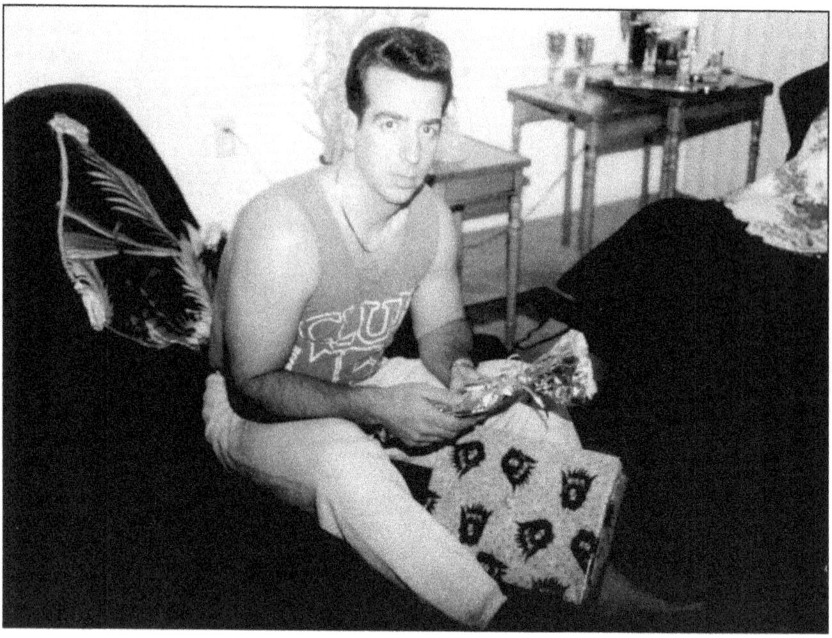

After my brother got out of jail, December 1995

One of my undercover looks

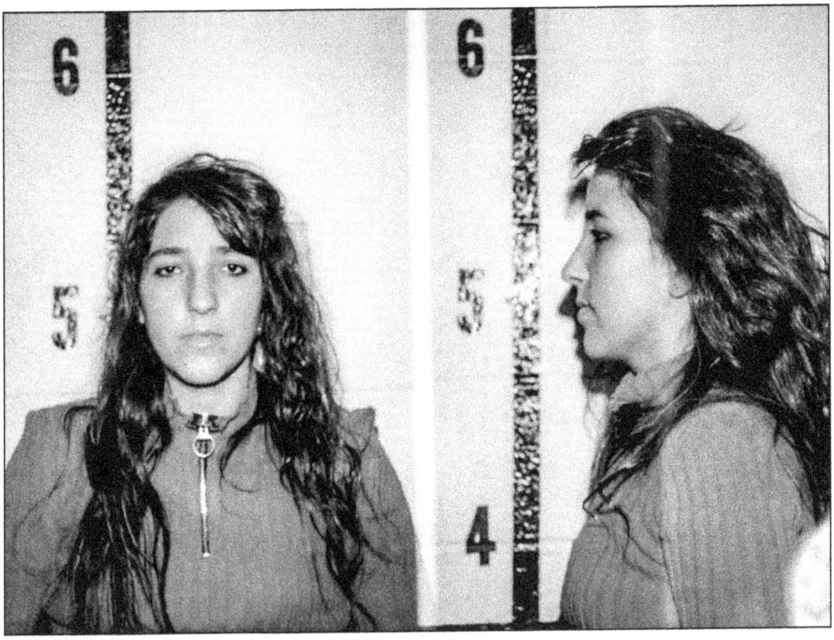

Another look

A third look

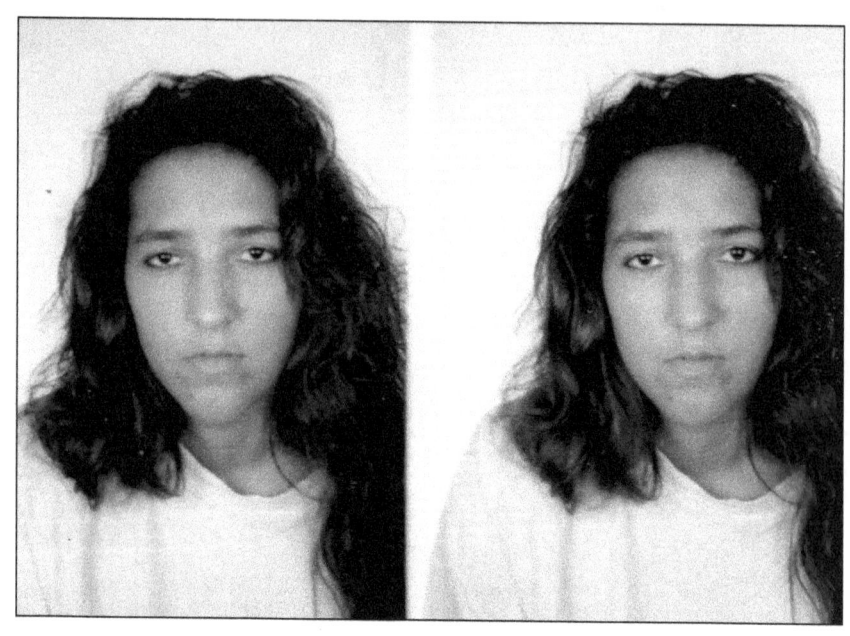

A fourth look

With Mom at my niece Nickie's party, the day I confronted my rapist

My former partner Robert Prause, aka Mr. Russo

With my former partner Brent Edwards at DEA

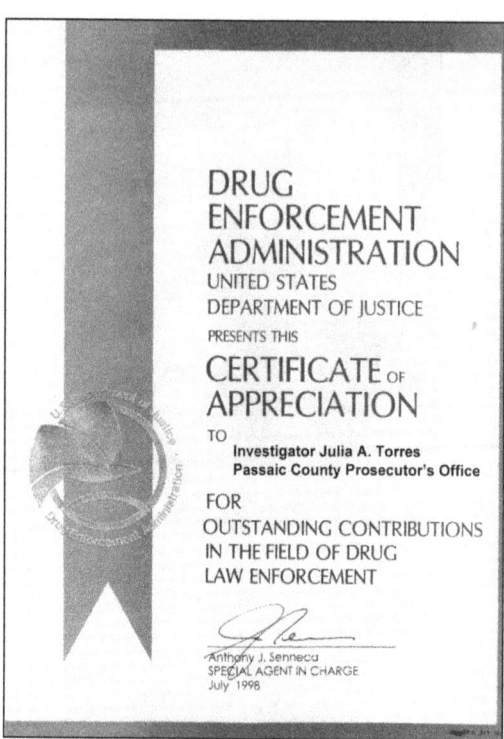

DEA award

West New York Police Department sergeant promotion of former partner Nitin Daniels (fourth from left, front row), the night my husband punched me

During the best time of my marriage, when I was pregnant

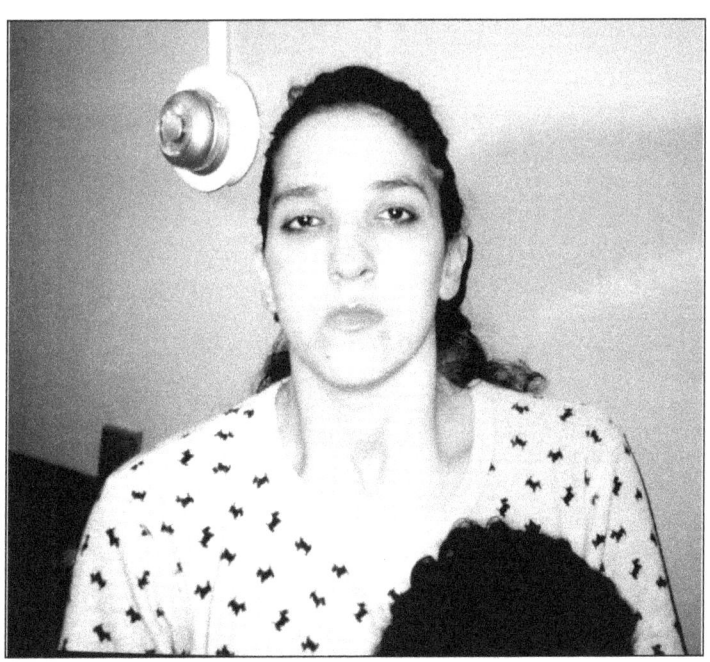

With my daughter at the North Bergen Police Department the night I filed my complaint

The State of New Jersey

POLICE CASE NO. 99067278
PAGE 1 OF 1
5-1999-000901-0908

COURT: NORTH BERGEN TWP, 4233 KENNEDY BLVD, NORTH BERGEN NJ 07047, 201-392-2088

Address: NORTH BERGEN NJ 07047
SS No.: 00-00-0000

COMPLAINT - SUMMONS

Complainant Name: JULIA A TORRES

Upon oath says that, to the best of his (her) knowledge, information and belief, the named defendant on or about the 09 day of 11, 19 99, in NORTH BERGEN TWP, County of _____ N.J

did WITHIN THE JURISDICTION OF THIS COURT, COMMIT ASSAULT BY ATTEMPTING TO CAUSE BODILY INJURY TO JULIA A TORRES BY STRIKING THE VICTIM IN THE FACE AFTER HAVING A VERBAL DISPUTE WITH HER ABOUT HER BEING OUT, IN VIOLATION OF NJSA 2C:12-1A(1).

PROBABLE CAUSE IS FOUND FOR THE ISSUANCE OF THIS COMPLAINT BY HEATHER LUZZI-HERNANDEZ, COURT ADMINISTRATOR BY A FILED NORTH BERGEN POLICE REPORT.

Charge Number: 2C:12-1A(1)

Subscribed and sworn to before me this 10 day of November, 19 99.

YOU ARE HEREBY SUMMONED TO APPEAR BEFORE THIS COURT TO ANSWER THIS COMPLAINT. IF YOU FAIL TO APPEAR ON THE DATE AND AT THE TIME STATED, A WARRANT WILL BE ISSUED FOR YOUR ARREST.

DATE SUMMONS ISSUED: 11/10/1999
DATE TO APPEAR: 11/17/1999
TIME: 09:00 AM

Simple assault charge I filed against my husband

With my brother and sister when we came from Cuba, 1970

My sister Marlene, 1993

My mother and me, 1995

My nephew Adrian and me, 1994

13

Prelude to Strike One

RETURNING HOME FROM PARIS meant consulting an immigration attorney, who gave me positive news: Narciso would be in the United States on a K-1 fiancé petition six months from completing the required paperwork. Once done, Congressman Robert Menendez would send a diplomatic pouch to the Cuban Interest Section.

In August 1997, four months after Narciso and I submitted all the forms, Mom and I boarded a flight to Cuba for Narciso's interview in Havana. The brief air plane ride from Miami was over in less than an hour, landing us at the Jose Marti International Airport.

A crowd of natives was waiting outside in the hot breeze and humid air as friends, lovers, and relatives cleared customs. Cubans rushed to greet their loved ones, shouting in glee, exchanging warm embraces, tears streaming.

Narciso spotted me. "Julia!" Muscular arms carried me, twirling me around, and full lips planted a welcome kiss on mine.

"This is my mom, Daisy," I said once my feet were on the ground.

Mom wasn't impressed, I could see. She must've seen something I, caught up in enchantment, hadn't. Narciso's immediate family—parents and three siblings—had a history of stable marriages, though, and I had convinced myself that it'd be a good indication for ours. I conveniently disregarded the significance of a previous tumultuous relationship.

On the afternoon of the interview date a few days later, Mom waited in the outside rotunda while Narciso supplied answers regarding my personal interests; I followed.

Behind one of the glass windows sat an older, white American woman in an air-conditioned room. She was direct. "Miss Torres, do you want to get married?"

"Yes."

Lines formed above her nose. "You haven't been forced?"

"No."

"Have you been offered money?"

"No." She made notations on a sheet of lined paper.

"Have you been intimate?"

"Yes."

"When will you marry?"

"When he gets to Florida."

An employee in an army-green uniform paced back and forth behind the interviewees, jingling a set of keys in one of her hands. The interviewer asked, "Will you be there to greet him?"

"Yes. My mom, too. She's here now."

She smiled. "Have you invited friends and family to the wedding?"

"No. Ma'am, with Cuba, you never know what'll happen. I didn't want people losing money in case the dates changed, so I only told my brother and my best friend."

"That was very conscientious of you."

I shrugged.

She leaned forward, asking conspiratorially, "Miss Torres, do you suspect Mr. Nadal of any communist activity?"

"No."

"Do you have any reason to believe he has any *socialist* views?"

"No."

"Is he now, or has he ever been, a member of any communist organization?"

"No."

"Miss Torres, do you have a top-secret security clearance?"

"I don't know what type of security clearance I have."

She nodded. "All right. You'll have approximately three hours before a decision is rendered. There's enough time for lunch. Please wait in the rotunda until Mr. Nadal's name is called. At that time, he can approach one of the teller windows. Thank you for being present. Good luck." She rose.

Palates sated, butterflies contained, the three of us strolled in silence down the *malecon*, sparkling ocean water summoning natives to a life offering freedom beyond the horizon. "It's gonna be fine," I whispered to Narciso, aware of his agitation.

He sighed, "I hope so."

Back at the interest section, some hopefuls paced as others

sat, chewing their nails. A voice blared over speakers about an hour later: "Narciso Nadal, please approach window three."

He looked at me and took a deep breath. "Okay. Let's see."

"You're gonna get it."

He marched away and stood still in front of a window, back to me and Mom. Then he turned, looking dizzy, and headed in our direction. He stopped in front of us, raised his Cuban passport, and said in surprise, "I can't believe it. This is the best day of my life." He showed us the stamped visa.

"See?" I beamed, smiling broadly, hugging him. Mom followed, glad someone else was going to leave that miserly existence.

Our return trip a few days later was filled with excitement and anticipation. I bade Mom farewell in West Palm Beach and proceeded back home, where it was business as usual until Narciso's arrival.

The immigration attorney had been correct about the six-month mark. Loud voices, laughter, and nervous energy could barely be contained on October 3, 1997, outside the Havana arrival gate in the Miami International Airport. Mom, dressed in an ivory dress and heels, contrasted well with my short black fitted sheath, with pumps to match.

Appearing at the end of a long line of passengers, Narciso, clad in khaki slacks, a long-sleeved button-down shirt, and dress shoes, was carrying a small duffel bag. He was scanning the reception group when Mom yelled, "Narciso!"

Both of us stared at one another in awe before we hugged. "Wow, I can't believe you're here," I said.

"Me neither. It feels like a dream."

"Congratulations, Narciso. Welcome to the *Yuma*," said Mom.

Three days later, on October 6, Pastor Ariel Ortiz, of Mom's church, married us barefoot on a Lake Worth beach, surrounded by a small group of family and friends. A reception followed, after which we went to Sanibel Island for our honeymoon.

Soon enough, we returned home where he started to become acclimated to life in the United States. The whirlwind had died down. I questioned myself a few mornings later, when I woke to see a big man occupying most of my bed. *What have I done?* Marriage was supposed to be forever.

My stomach knotted. I had abandoned my independence for a life with someone I did not even know. It was obvious that I had acted impulsively, but had I missed any warning clues?

Then a phone call I made to Narciso the previous December came to mind. A woman had answered, but that alone hadn't been surprising; most Cubans didn't have telephones, and they'd use their neighbors', as Narciso did. "Narciso, please," I had said.

There had been a pause. "This is Marilyn. Who's this?"

"Julia."

"Are you the one that's been calling Narciso?"

"Yes. Why?"

"I'm his live-in girlfriend."

He *had* been living with someone, just as I'd suspected. "I'm sorry, ma'am. I didn't know."

"It's okay. I always knew he'd leave Cuba. He has bigger aspirations. I just wanted to know the truth."

An approaching male voice had been audible in the background.

"...Here he is," she had finally said.

"Julia, I knew it'd come to this. I'm sorry. We're not married, we just live together. I'll understand if you don't want to go through with it, since I've been untruthful."

"Give me a few days to think about it."

Do I call it off? I had wondered once I hung up. The irony of that situation was that I had asked God to give me a sign if that marriage wasn't right for me, yet I hadn't seen it for what it was—God showing me the way out. Instead, I'd leaned on my own understanding, assuming that anyone in his shoes would've done the same. Days later, I called him to say that I had understood, but he had to find another place to live.

He had.

Weeks passed, and one night before bedtime, as we removed throw pillows from the bed, Narciso asked, "What's this about a rape?"

Surprised, I looked across at him, white lace pillow in my hand. "What are you talking about?"

"You were raped."

The statement felt like a slap.

"Is that true?" he asked, tone accusatory.

"Who told you that?"

He scoffed. "Your brother."

I felt betrayed. "...When?"

"Yesterday, when I was at his office."

"Just like that, he said it? What were the two of you talking about before that?"

"He was giving me advice on how to handle you."

"*Handle* me?"

"Yeah. He said, 'Be careful, Julia's got a tough character. You gotta keep her in line.'"

"What exactly did he say?"

"He said, 'My sister thinks she's a man. She went to war, became a cop. And look what happened to her—she got raped.'"

I said nothing.

"So? Is it true? Somebody raped you?"

In shock, I said, "Yes. Why are you asking me like that?"

"I didn't know if your brother was lying or not."

The pillow served as my crutch; I held onto it for dear life. "He's not gonna make up something like that."

"You never told me. Why?"

Numb with grief, I answered, "The right time hadn't come up."

"So I gotta hear it from your brother?"

My shoulders slumped. "You weren't supposed to." Tears streaming down my face, I sat on the bed, hugging the pillow, head downcast.

He came over slowly and embraced me, but his hug felt perfunctory. "I'm sorry," he added.

It would've been better if he'd remained silent. It was a stark difference from my response to the story Narciso had told me. He'd been living with his aunt and uncle in Havana since the age of twelve, when he'd won a scholarship. Their drunken stupors would become physically violent, with Narciso being thrown out of their house and forced to sleep on a park bench, something he asserted his own parents, who lived hours away in the country, didn't know. I hadn't questioned the validity of it but accepted it as truth, offering consolation.

Now, I wanted to curl up in bed and cry alone. Instead, I accepted his arms—at least they were strong—and fell asleep, mentally and emotionally drained.

That incident further increased my doubts, causing me to question the sensitivity of the man I'd married. It led me to question my brother's motives, too, when he claimed not to recall making that admission.

BY DECEMBER, THINGS HAD IMPROVED, bringing with them a sudden surprise. Before going to work one day, I looked in the mirror. "I'm pregnant," I said to Narciso, who had come out of the shower, towel around his waist. "Look." I pointed at the mirror. "My waist's bigger."

"Maybe you just gained weight."

"No. That's not food. I'll pick up a pregnancy test on the way home. Gotta go. I'm running late."

First thing the next morning, I said, "I'm going to the bathroom." We watched the windows in the plastic tester; two vertical lines were clear. "Told you I was pregnant."

"Congratulations." He smiled.

"You, too." Hugs and kisses followed before I headed out.

As much as I loved undercover work, soon I'd have to reconsider it. Though I hoped to stay on the cases I had been working on, I knew it wouldn't be possible, especially on the one where I was acting as a mule.

A meeting with that target was scheduled for late January; he'd be funding my travel to Ecuador. It'd be the last undercover job I'd do before going on light duty, and the case I'd suggest another task force officer complete.

It was a wise decision; agents and officers who traveled overseas were gone three weeks. I couldn't imagine how distraught I'd be if I miscarried again, or how I'd explain it to Narciso. It was the one investigation I had filled him in on somewhat, due to the circumstances.

The happiest time of my marriage was from the doctor's official confirmation through the first week of January 1999, and I could say I loved him then. I felt that God had purposed a child through us due to all the fated events before and during my trip to Cuba.

That September, we moved to a condo I was thinking of purchasing—the three-bedroom, two-bath unit downstairs. Around eleven p.m. on the eighteenth, I nudged a sleeping Narciso. "It's time."

In a Meadowlands Hospital birthing room, a heart monitor was hooked up to me. I called my friend Maria, who was the live-in-girlfriend of Brent Edwards, a DEA Special Agent and one of my partners at HIDTA.

She appeared quickly and took immediate action, rubbing my swollen feet with lotion while I took pleasure in hearing the baby's steady heartbeat.

TWENTY-THREE HOURS AFTER MY ADMISSION, the rapid heartbeat slowed.

I looked up at Maria. "Why's it slowing down?"

She fidgeted with her hands. "I don't know."

"What's going on?" Narciso asked, alarmed.

The doctor appeared out of nowhere, peered at the monitor, and left, a grave expression on her face.

My worry increased when she returned with a form.

"Julia, sign here." Her tone was professional, curt.

I stared into her big brown eyes. "What's it for?"

"An emergency C-section. We have to do it now."

My baby! We're gonna die. I became agitated.

"Julia." Maria came closer to me. "You have to relax. The baby'll feel your nervousness. You don't want the baby to be born nervous."

I took a deep breath and signed the paper. "Okay."

Someone wheeled me into the OR with Narciso and Maria in tow.

From there, it all happened fast. An uplifting song played over the speakers.

"Listen, Papi." Standing behind me, I looked up at Narciso.

He smiled, "'*Hakuna Matata*,' from the *Lion King*. That's great."

"Yes. It means no worries for the rest of your days. The baby's gonna be fine."

Minutes later, I heard a doll-like cry and sighed in relief. Our daughter was perfectly healthy.

September 1998 became January 1999, and I was back at work from maternity leave. I can't pinpoint the precise moment things in my marriage began to change—what was said, not said; done, not done—only the day. Yet isn't that how hostility often begins?

January 8, Elvis Presley's birthday, was the beginning of the end. While the baby slept, Narciso had reprimanded me and gripped my arm with force.

"Let it be the first and last time you put your hands on me," I'd said firmly as we stood in front of the refrigerator.

He'd let go. However, he must've chosen to forget the reasons I had given him for soliciting a divorce, ones he had agreed with: "I won't put up with infidelity, violence, or addiction."

A black-and-blue thumbprint appeared on my arm the next day. He remained silent when I had shown it to him. The silence seemed to have affirmed that our marriage had taken a sharp turn for the worse. Then came January 22.

Julia Torres

14

Walking on Eggshells

To my far right, Nina was swaying in her swing, listening to lullabies, while I washed dishes in my robe, and Narciso worked out in the weight room. The clanging of weights stopped. I thought nothing of it when he crossed behind me from my left to sit on the futon.

"I'm hungry. What are you going to make?" he asked, the antagonism in his tone clear.

Hm. Where's this going?

The water continued to flow as I peered at him out of the corner of my eye. His hands were on his waist. *Twice defiant.*

Careful to avoid an argument, I replied, "I'm not hungry." *He's the chef—since when did cooking become a chore?*

"If I don't eat, nobody eats," he said.

What?

He rose, opened the refrigerator door, and removed everything from inside it. After dropping all the food and drinks into large plastic Toys-R-Us shopping bags, he opened the front door and put them in the hallway.

He sat down again, face challenging.

I marched over. "*You* may not eat, and *I* may not eat, but the *baby* will eat."

Narciso glared at me. "If you open that door, I will strike you," I heard him threaten as I headed to it.

I was not going to back down. I retrieved Nina's Similac containers, bottles, and water, and replaced them in the refrigerator. I glanced at Nina to see if she'd sensed any tension, but it seemed she hadn't. My lovely four-month-old, her head full of dark hair, remained wide awake as I returned to the sink.

He remained still, quiet, appearing to be laden with thought.

My stomach churned as he passed behind me moments later on his way back to resume his workout. I thought the worst was over when I heard the clatter of metal, until, without making any sound, he grabbed me from behind.

Gripping my throat and the back of my neck, he dragged me to the weight room and thrust me onto the bench. His grip did not loosen when he barked, "From this moment on, you will act like my wife by cooking and cleaning!"

The rage in his eyes was lethal. Fixed stare, contracted pupils—I saw what was coming. I smelled his sweat.

My heart pounded. My stomach tightened. I knew that if he sensed my fear it'd empower him, feed into his ego, and surely cause my death.

Nina was crying loudly in the next room. *I have to get out of this.* I strained to say, "I c-can't b-*breathe.*"

Nina yelled.

I gotta save her.

To appease him, I pleaded, struggling to say, "I'm sorry."

Robotically, he released his grip, stood up, and headed toward our bedroom.

I rose, shaken, rushed to Nina, and lifted her out of the swing. *How did it happen? Why didn't I see it coming?*

Narciso re-entered the kitchen, carrying my extra handgun in his hands. "Take this. I don't know what I may do next time," he said without a care.

He left the room and entered the master bath. I put the revolver in my robe pocket, remaining calm for Nina, soothing her with whispers.

When the shower started to run, my survival instincts kicked in. Putting Nina down briefly, I grabbed my camera from my purse and took pictures of my neck in front of the bathroom mirror, near the kitchen.

Once I had, I hurried upstairs to tell the neighbors—my baby-sitter and her husband—what had occurred. I knocked quickly.

Cathy opened the door. The smile she greeted me with faded when I put my finger to my lips. "*Shh.*"

I opened my robe to show her the marks on my neck and breastbone area. "Narciso's in the shower. He just did this to me."

Eyes widening, she gasped, bringing her hand to her mouth. Her husband Pastor must've heard her because he came to the door. They exchanged looks and she pointed at my injuries, horrified. His eyes softened, and he shook his head. "*Nena*, he's no good."

"I have to get back before he's done. I just want you to be my first witnesses."

"Of course," said Pastor. Cathy still hadn't uttered a word.

I rushed downstairs with the understanding that I was building a case. The shower was still running.

Before returning to the sink, I moved Nina's swing closer to me, speaking to her as I did, and replayed the lullaby music. I continued with the dishes, which in reality hadn't been many, but memories of my first love, Rudy, watching me do my chores during childhood must've been in my subconscious. They'd provided me solace at that moment.

A while later, Narciso returned to the living room, turning on the television as if nothing had happened.

It was nine o'clock. I was expecting a visit from one of my partners at HIDTA, Eddie *Suave* Torres—who'd gotten his nickname when a fellow trooper pulled over someone who'd asked for Trooper *Rico Suave*. He couldn't get there soon enough.

Then the phone rang. It was Maria, Nina's godmother. Her familiar voice was soothing through the handset. "Hello, dear."

I almost cried with relief, "Yeah...sure, apple juice."

She got the hint. "Is everything okay?"

"No, just apple juice." I trusted she'd understand.

The sound of the doorbell minutes later was music to my ears. There she was, juice in hand, when I opened the door carrying Nina. She looked at the bags on the floor in wide-eyed apprehension. It was difficult to keep a pretense when they stared up at me. "Hey, *chica*, thanks. Come in," I said.

She greeted Narciso, but his eyes didn't shift from the television.

"Come on. I have to change Nina." In the bedroom, I told her what had happened, making her a third witness.

The bell rang again. Suave's voice carried through the apartment when Narciso, muttering a brief hello, let him in and directed him to the bedroom.

My first law enforcement witness became curious when he saw Maria and me whispering. I looked up at him, opening my robe to reveal my neck. "He choked me."

"Ugh," he said, grinning in discomfort.

"*Suave*, I know the law, but I need to hear it from you. What happens if I report this now?" I asked.

"It's an automatic lock-up. You have visible injuries," he replied matter-of-factly.

The tension thickened as his words made the reality of the situation sink in. We all knew that standard procedure required a police officer to notify his or her immediate supervisor upon involvement in a domestic violence incident.

"I'm not ready to do that yet," I told them.

They held their breath. Lines of concern marked their foreheads; they grimaced and exchanged glances, seeming uncertain.

I reached into my pocket, removing the revolver. "Maria, tell Brent to lock this up at home. Narciso gave it to me and said to take it, that he didn't know what he'd do next time."

She said nothing, but I saw the concern in her eyes.

"Follow her in case she gets pulled over for some reason," I said to Suave.

"Okay. Where's your duty weapon?"

"In my gun locker at DEA." I had begun to keep it there after January 8, but not my revolver.

"All right. Call me or Brent if anything," he said, knowing that my mind was made up, trusting that I'd made the right decision.

"I will." With Nina asleep in my arms, they followed me to the door, giving Narciso a brief good-bye, pretending as if nothing had transpired.

I wondered what the remainder of the evening would bring as I laid the baby in her crib and prepared for bed.

We slept apart that night—not that it mattered. As physically appealing as my husband was, I had lost the desire for intimacy the moment he'd first shown aggression, the night he grabbed my arm. I didn't care whom he had sex with as long as it wasn't me. However, wanting an explanation, I approached him a few hours later in the dark living room.

He was lying on his side, on the futon, facing the wall. I stood by it. "Narciso?"

But before I could speak further, without moving from his position, he insisted, "I'm not an abusive person. I don't know why I did that. Maybe we should separate."

It was not what I had expected to hear. I was in a quandary: Was he bluffing? Did I want that? Exhausted, disconnected, I left to the bedroom.

The following day, I went to work and headed straight to my computer, where I had previously begun a written account, knowing the nature of domestic violence: I'd need irrefutable evidence to obtain a restraining order and be awarded sole custody. It appeared my marriage would end in divorce; I'd have to protect Nina by ensuring my role as her custodial parent.

When I returned home that evening from the babysitter's, and after putting Nina to bed, Narciso glanced at me before he entered the shower. "Don't think I didn't want to see you hurt—I did," he confessed, emotionless. He closed the door. Is this how psychological abuse begins, I wondered.

Later that night, his attitude changed again as he lay down next to me in bed. "I felt so bad for what I did that I wished a truck would have hit me while I was driving. I'm proud of you for defending Nina."

I did not respond to any of his comments. It was not amusing to listen to such contradictory statements. I hoped for the best, expected the worst, and maintained my guard.

That February, I learned how deeply I had been sucked into oblivion. It was disheartening that I had gone back on my word.

After putting the baby to sleep, I was reading *Ragtime* by E.L. Doctorow when Narciso's pager buzzed while he was in the shower. I picked it up—*50538*—and stared at it, knowing that secret code. During my single days, I'd sent the Spanish translation for kisses to a boyfriend or two.

Instincts kicked in: I wrote down all the numbers and times on a notepad, put the beeper back on the table, and resumed reading.

The door to the bathroom opened. "Someone paged you," I said, looking up from my book, pretending to have been reading it.

"Who?"

"I don't know. It was bothering me, so I stopped it."

He shrugged, purposely not heading to it.

I got up. "I'll tell you the number."

Standing with cotton swabs in his hand, he glanced my way, trying not to look suspicious.

"Oh, look. They must've forgotten some numbers," I said, walking toward him, placing the pager in front of his face.

"What's the number?" he asked, cleaning one ear.

"Five-oh-five-three-eight. See? They forgot two."

"Maybe it's a wrong number."

I started flipping the pager around. "Well, look at that. It says BESOS. What wrong number would that be?"

"Let me see." He took it from my hand and peered at it, clicking to see the other numbers. "Is this pager gonna give me a problem?" he asked rhetorically, studying me. Without saying anything another word, he threw it against the wall, where it shattered. "There. Now there's no problem."

I grinned. "I already know the numbers."

He threw the swabs in the trash and returned to the bathroom. When he came out, I feigned sleep, but he knew I didn't fall asleep fast. "Don't worry, Julia. I'm not gonna touch you."

Good. The fact that he had a mistress angered me. What nerve, I thought. It was bad enough that he was abusive, but a cheat, too—yet who was I kidding? It was the crude profile of the domestic violence abuser—charming and chivalrous to the world outside, but a terror behind closed doors—and I had fallen for it.

Wanting to know about the affair, I did my homework, finding out where the woman lived and worked. I called both places to speak with her, then I drove to them. Though I was there, not to cast blame, but to get specifics, she wasn't interested in talking to me, so I stopped trying.

THE SIGNS WERE ALL APPARENT; things were going from bad to worse—and then one evening soon after his mistress wouldn't meet me, I made a grave mistake, betraying my beliefs. "Narciso?"

He looked up from the wrestling program he'd been watching.

"What?"

"I'm gonna take half the blame for your infidelity. I haven't been a wife to you in that respect. If you end it with the lady and try to make this work for Nina's sake, I'll resume the role of your wife." I had said the unthinkable.

"Okay." It was the first time I'd seen him smile in months. Perhaps he'd thought he'd broken me.

Although I hadn't been thinking clearly on an emotional level, financially I was crystal clear. Having decided not to purchase the larger condo downstairs, we returned upstairs.

Frank and his girlfriend, Terry, visited us a few weeks after, but neither of them had had any inkling of the tumultuous marriage we had been having. Aside from my neighbors, who'd moved to Puerto Rico that previous December, Maria, Brent, and *Suave*, no one knew.

On that visit, however, Frank and Terry would leave with the knowledge that my marriage would end, and not well. Seated across from each other in the living room, our conversation had led to the subject of child support.

For no apparent reason, and without being asked for an opinion, Narciso remarked, "If I have to pay your sister child support, I'll resolve it by throwing her down the stairs."

You could hear a pin drop. My brother gaped, and Terry's eyes displayed anger and shock.

Unfazed by his remark, I looked at Narciso and calmly replied, "I'm glad you said that in front of them. You have just given me two witnesses." He did not reply, but shortly after, Frank and Terry went home, and Narciso jumped in the shower.

THAT APRIL, MARIA CAME TO PICK UP me and Nina to take us to a children's party. Narciso didn't reciprocate her greeting. Instead, he said, "Maria, Julia can go if she wants to, but I don't want Nina to go."

"But why not? She'll have fun."

"No." He left the room and lay down on the floor beside Nina's crib while she remained in it, watching the mobile spin.

"You go. I don't want to leave without her," I said to her. She left with a worried expression but returned hours later, when he'd gone.

I seized the opportunity to leave with Nina.

After the party, I went to see our pastor, explained what had happened, and asked him to go speak with Narciso. In the interim, I went to Maria's house, waiting for time to pass until Brent drove us home.

He carried Nina up the stairs, handgun at his side. Narciso noticed the weapon when I unlocked the front door. Brent left soon after, and the evening passed quietly.

The following day, Narciso said, "The pastor spoke to me last night. Everything would've been fine if you hadn't come home with Brent. If he thinks I'm afraid of his gun, I'll show him, DEA or not."

Coward, I thought. Why didn't he say that to *him*?

My feelings ranged from shame and guilt to disbelief and humiliation. His manipulative tactics were pretty effective.

Aside from those grueling emotions, I soon sensed fear, never imagining I'd find it in my own home. *What'll happen to Nina if he does something to me?* Had I been single, I would've fired my weapon if and when the situation arose, but a gunshot in our small apartment could have caused damage to Nina's ears.

I pondered how I could be a cop *and* a victim. Then again, why should my job make a difference? Surely, it'd already helped me establish probable cause. *How much more would I need?*

It was unfortunate that, despite the violence, my marriage continued for sentimental reasons. Certain that children brought up with both parents had an edge in life over than those without, I mistakenly assumed she'd be better off with her dad around when, in actuality, she was better off without him.

The logical woman I had once been had been wiped away; I didn't know myself anymore. I was indecisive—to the point I thought getting a divorce would disobey God—and avoided burdening others with worry.

If I'd voiced my concerns, although some would not have wanted to be involved, others would have allowed me to see his hostility for what it was—domestic violence. Knowing something had to change, I again spoke with my pastor, who advised, "Sometimes it's better to get a divorce."

Having witnessed first-hand the mind's diminished capacity to reason, I didn't know what to expect, but a safe way out was my only hope.

15

Homicide Suspects

THE UNDERSIGNED, WHILE ACTING *in an undercover capacity* . . . . As I was sitting behind the computer at my desk, my telephone rang early one evening just as I had begun a DEA 6 Report of Investigation. I picked up the phone. "Hello?"

"Julia, it's Vinny." Captain Moschetta's smooth voice came through on the other end.

"Yes, Captain. How are you?"

"Good. How's the baby?"

A framed photograph of Nina asleep, swaddled in a hospital blanket, stared up at me. "She's great, Captain."

"That's good to hear. I'm calling because there's a job I need you to do tomorrow night. You'll be working with Josie, Sofia, and another female cop from Clifton."

"Okay. . . ."

"I'll give you a quick brief. Two male suspects—"

"Here you go, Ju—"

One of the guys from a different HIDTA group had come to return the stapler he'd borrowed. I swiveled in my chair, indicating it was okay that he'd interrupted, and took it from him, nodding.

"—of a homicide haven't been seen since the night of the incident," Moschetta continued. "Since they work as escorts in Secrets Agency, Sofia called this morning to solicit them for an alleged bachelorette party tomorrow night. Please be at the office at five p.m. for the briefing. You'll get the rest of the information then."

"Okay, Captain."

Immediately after hanging up, I called Josie, the forty-year-old Puerto-Rican woman whom I'd worked with in the street squad. "It's Julia. Can you talk?"

"Hold on, I just got in." Keys jingling, steps echoed as she moved through the apartment. "Okay. *Nena,* it was a long day. Phew! I'm so tired. We were getting ready for tomorrow's job."

"That's what I was calling about. The captain just called. I'm supposed to do a job with you and Sofia. What do you know about it?" I leaned forward.

"Well, two black guys are wanted for questioning on the murder of a Spanish guy at a bar. They're male escorts, but they haven't been seen together since the murder, so Sofia called their escort service yesterday to hire them for a bachelorette party. I don't know all the details, but it's a big job. The office has been working on closing Secrets for a while because they employ minors. Everything's gonna be taken down tomorrow, so there are gonna be lots of cops at the briefing."

"What's our role?"

"We get them on prostitution. They'll arrest them, and then try to flip them on the homicide."

"Okay. I'll meet you at your house before the briefing to get our stories straight."

There was no way I'd be the bachelorette, I thought. I could just imagine that case going to trial, my husband sitting on one of the benches, listening as I testified about dancing in a hotel room with escorts who were homicide suspects. No, that would not go well at all. As it was, he'd have a hard time accepting that I'd be leaving Nina, at five months, in his care, to return from work late, wearing a short dress, make-up, and heels.

After work, I picked up Nina at the sitter's and went home.

Narciso arrived earlier than usual from work. "How's the baby?" he asked, his good mood obvious.

"Good. She's bathed, fed, and I just put her to bed," I said, thankful for the honeymoon phase in the sad yet common reality of domestic violence.

He walked into her room and whispered good-night. "You want me to cook something?" he asked on his return.

"That'd be great. How was work?"

He grabbed a frying pan from one of the cabinets and laid thawed, seasoned chicken inside it. "Good. I finished my truck route early, and the boss told me to go home. How about you?"

"I'll do the rice," I suggested, making it by sight as he'd taught me, and not by measuring as was my custom. "Work was busy as usual. I need you to pick up Nina at the sitter's tomorrow. I'll bring her in the morning, but I gotta work late."

He looked up from the vegetables he'd added. "How late?"

"I don't know."

"You don't *know*?" He raised his eyebrows in exaggeration.

"No. We never know when a job's gonna end."

He rolled his eyes.

"Narciso, it's my job. It's what I do."

"I know." He frowned. "I wish you were a normal woman."

"I *am* a normal woman."

"No, you're not." He flipped the chicken over. "A normal woman is a secretary or a teacher. You're a cop, and not even one that gives tickets, but an undercover one at that."

I shrugged. "I love what I do."

"I wish you didn't." Five minutes passed in silence, until he said, "I don't get it, and I wish you didn't do it. It's not a job for a woman, just like I told Mimi." He sneered.

"It's what I did when you met me, and it's what helped get you here." The bell from the rice cooker signaled it was cooked. I added a little olive oil and stirred the rice.

"...So how late *will* you be?"

"I don't know, but I'd love to eat. It smells yummy."

After dinner, I washed the dishes, and we readied for bed without further discussion about the next night's assignment.

Long, bouncy hair, earth-toned make-up, red lipstick—I slipped into a short, sleeveless print dress, put on heels, and left for Josie's at three p.m., grabbing a coat on the way out.

"Hey, girl, we match," I said when she opened the door to her cozy apartment in a short black dress, holding a curling iron.

She smiled. "I'll be in the bedroom. Gotta finish my hair. Get something to drink if you want."

"Okay." I grabbed a tall glass from the cabinet, poured water from a jug in the fridge, and headed to Josie's bedroom. She was sitting in front of her vanity, curls cascading loosely with each turn of the iron.

"Your hair looks great!" I exclaimed.

"You didn't do this?"

"Nah. I don't own one. I could never get that thing right. And it pulls my hair."

She laughed. "So what do you do?"

"I brush it upside down, put a little hair spray, flip over, and hair spray some more."

"That's it?"

"Yeah. You know, in the army I learned the value of KISS."

Through the mirror's reflection, she tilted her head.

"Keep It Simple, Stupid."

She cracked up. "Ouch," she said, sucking the tip of her thumb, slightly burnt by the curling iron.

"See?" I chortled.

"Okay, I'm done." She put her vanity in order.

"You look *mahvelous*," I said, using Billy Crystal's famous line.

"Thanks. You, too." She lifted a small box from the vanity.

"What's that?"

"A phony engagement ring. I figured one of us could wear it and pretend to be the bachelorette."

"That's a great idea, Josie. You're always good at paying attention to detail."

Extending it to me, she asked, "You wanna wear it?"

"No way." I shook my hands over each other. "My husband would never understand that. You know him."

"Yeah. No problem. I'm not married. I'll do it."

Although we got to the office early, a slew of cops was already there and suited up: bullet-resistant vests, handcuffs over belts, holstered guns, and radios on hips. We walked through the crowd, greeting those we recognized, nodding at the others.

The third cop who was going on the job with us, Sofia, a light-skinned, half-black, half-American Indian, was standing near the water cooler, sipping from a paper cup, wearing a red dress and heels.

"Hey, ladies," she said in her soft, sultry voice. "Nice to get a chance to work together."

"Yeah it is," we said.

"Where's the other girl?" I asked.

"I think that's her over there." Sofia indicated a white woman with short, very light blonde hair and blue eyes.

I shook my head. "She doesn't fit in with us." The fourth woman was wearing khakis, a hunter green polo shirt, and penny loafers.

"That's what I thought," she said.

"And she didn't do her hair or make-up," added Josie.

I asked Sofia, "Where's Ang?" She was an investigator who worked at the office.

"She's on vacation."

"Well, that girl's not going," I said.

Josie nodded.

"I know what you mean," said Sofia.

"Has the captain seen her?" I asked.

"I don't know," she said after tossing her cup in the garbage.

"I'm gonna go talk to him." I marched straight to his office, past squelching radios and cops drinking coffee.

"Captain?" I stepped through the open entrance.

He looked up from the papers on the desk. "Yes, Julia?"

"Did you see the fourth cop?"

"Yes."

"She's not going with us."

Putting down the pen he'd been holding, he replied, "No, she's not."

I paused in front of his desk. "I have some questions."

"What are they?"

"You want the suspects to discuss prostitution services, prices, and once it's done we give the hit signal?"

"Yes."

I nodded. "Who has the audio and visual?"

He leaned back in his chair, interlocking his fingers across his chest. "Tauris will be monitoring the audio in the room next door. Once he hears the hit signal, he'll call it out to the other two teams. His team will go through the adjoining door. A second team will be in the parking lot, and they'll be coming in through the sliding glass doors. Another team will be coming in from the hallway, through the front door."

"Who's got the eyeball?"

He shook his head. "There isn't any."

"Why not?"

"The cameras are being used on the other arrests."

"You should've told me. I could've checked something out from DEA."

"It'll be all right."

"Captain, how are they gonna hear us if the music's blasting?"

"You'll figure it out."

Not appreciating his response but knowing the issue was moot, I simply nodded, knowing that I would but wondering how I'd get it done. "Where's the alcohol gonna be?"

"You're not getting any alcohol."

"Why not?" I asked, raising my hands.

"The assistant prosecutor says there can't be any. If this case goes to trial, it'll be difficult to explain to a jury why cops were drinking."

"It's a *bachelorette party*," I said in frustration.

"The defense would argue that there was an influence of alcohol."

"They can give us a Breathalyzer after the take-down," I offered.

"The A/P said it'd be more trouble than what it's worth."

"How are we gonna explain *not* having it? It doesn't make any *sense*."

"You'll figure it out."

Exasperated, I turned and left his office. The women saw me coming.

"I don't like it." I filled a cup of water and took a sip. "We're not getting alcohol."

Josie's eyes widened.

"Why not?" asked Sofia.

"The A/P doesn't want the defense to make an issue out

of cops drinking alcohol."

"You're kidding." Sofia tilted her head.

"I wish." Resigned, I added, "We're gonna have to say we're waiting for a friend who's bringing the alcohol when she gets off work."

Concern was evident in their expressions.

"But that's not all." After relaying the discussion with the captain about the absence of visuals, I concluded, "I'd take my gun if I were you. I'm bringing mine."

They agreed.

"Let's talk to Tauris since he's our primary," suggested Sofia. She looked for him among the men. "There he is. . . Tauris," she called out. "Can you please come over here?"

He did. "Hello, ladies. Julie, it's been a long time."

"Yes, it has. Good to see you." I smiled, not having seen him since Wake-Up.

"Likewise." He directed his next words to us. "My team's got your audio tonight."

"What's the game plan?" asked Sofia.

"We will be in the room adjoining yours. We need three things done." Tauris began to explain, looking at each of us as he did. "One of you has to make sure that the connecting door is unlocked, or we'll have to break it when we hit. The sliding glass doors also have to be unlocked for the team in the lot, for the same reason. Someone will have to open the front door to let in the third team that'll be coming from the hallway. They'll be plenty of cops there for the three of you. They *are* homicide suspects, after all."

He turned to me. "What's your hit signal gonna be?"

The fourth woman had looked like she was from the Midwest, and an idea occurred to me. "I'll ask the dancer if he can do a rodeo dance."

"Okay, so, 'rodeo dance'?"

"Yeah."

"Okay. I'm fine with that. I'm not gonna worry. I'm familiar with your work."

"Thank you."

He nodded. "All right, it'll all happen at the same time once we get the hit signal. Vinny says the Clifton cop isn't going."

"No," we all agreed.

"Okay. How about she knocks on the front door? We won't have to break it down, and if one of the targets happens to look through the peephole, he won't see a man. Will that work?"

We agreed.

He concluded, "I'll drive you ladies to the hotel after the briefing."

"Okay, everybody, listen up." The captain had emerged from his office. "We have a lot of take-downs going on this evening. By now, you should have spoken with your team leaders and know your designated roles, hit signals, danger signals, and local hospitals."

Someone's pager went off. "Sorry, Captain," said the muscular buzz-cut six-foot owner.

He nodded. "All pagers on silent, please. . . . It is important that everything gets done without incident. Wait for your signal to move out. Do *not* get ahead of yourselves. Make sure you're not in a crossfire. Those of you who are working with Tauris, let me see a show of hands."

More than a dozen hands rose. The captain continued, "There are three teams, for obvious reasons. The suspects are presumed to have committed a murder and have been evading. Consider them armed and dangerous. Please take all necessary precautions. Julia, Sofia, and Josie—" he pointed in our direction "—are the undercovers in this investigation, not the targets. Take a good look at them so you don't arrest them. Are there any questions?"

Some shouted, "No, sir"; others shook their heads.

"Okay. Remember, safety first. Move out."

Julia Torres

16

Three Call Boys

TAURIS TURNED TO US from the driver's seat at the far end of the parking lot. "You're already checked in. Here's the key—it's room 121. Good luck."

We stepped out of the car, eyes and ears alert but appearing relaxed on the outside, ready to party. Speaking loudly, laughing, the three of us headed inside, heels clicking on pavement, tile floor, and carpet.

We scanned our room to ensure nothing was out of place. Josie checked the lamp on the nightstand between two full beds. It wasn't a typical hotel lamp, nor did it match the other one on the dresser across from it. She peered under the lampshade; a small wire was sticking out near the light bulb. "Guys, look," she said, ushering us over.

Josie opened the drawer beneath it, discovering the rectangular silver audio device that would permit us to be heard. She gasped.

"Oh, my," said Sofia.

I smirked. "Oh, shit."

"I'll put my purse in this drawer," Josie volunteered.

"Great idea!" said Sofia. "I'll put mine in the open area underneath. If one of them opens the drawer and tries to pick up the bag, I'll tell them hands off. Guys don't usually go in a woman's purse, anyway."

"Okay. I'll stay sitting here and cover this area. I'll rumple the bed a little," Josie offered, pulling down the covers, throwing the pillows aside.

"All right. I'll take this bed here and do the same," said Sofia.

"And I'll sit on that corner chair by the doors," I told them. "I'm gonna go make the bathroom look used."

Once done, I unlocked the sliding glass doors behind me, and the adjoining one to my right. Seated on the comfortable pub chair, I placed my handbag, which contained my Glock, beside me.

We had clear vantage points of the room and each other. While waiting, we talked about nothing in particular.

About twenty minutes later, there were short, quick taps on the door. Sofia rose. "I'll answer it."

She had a hand on the knob, the other on the doorframe. "Who are you?"

"Kenny." Her question, and the muffled male voice of an unknown sub, made Josie and me exchange glances. "Kelvin and Edwen told me to come here for a party."

"Oh, well, come on in. You're in the right place." She let in the six-foot white guy, lacing her hand around his muscular arm as she walked beside him. "Hey, ladies, look what we've got here," she called out.

They stopped at the foot of the first bed. "This is Kenny. He was told to come along." In his late twenties, Kenny had raw, rough-around-the-edges good looks, the kind thugs in movies draw people to: thick dark hair pushed back, intense dark blue eyes, full mouth under a small, straight nose.

He remained standing, nodding at Josie and me, greeting us with a brusque hello, shuffling his feet.

"Hello, I'm Josie. Sit down." She pointed to the bed.

He sat on the corner, edgy, palms flat on either side of him.

"Hi, Kenny, I'm Julia. When are the other guys coming?" I asked.

"Soon," he said, glancing around the room, eyes shifting to and fro. Without preface, he jumped to his sneakered feet and rushed to the bathroom, leaving the door ajar. Click went the medicine cabinet as it was opened and closed, followed by the swish of the shower curtain being pulled to a side.

The three of us looked at each other, exchanging shrugs and inquisitive looks.

From the bed, Sofia asked, "Hey, Kenny, what are you looking for?"

"Just making sure everything's cool," he said. He left the bathroom and paused near the television on the dresser, giving the room a once-over.

"Sit down. Relax. You're making us nervous," said Sofia.

"Yeah, really. What's up?" I asked.

"Sorry," he said, sitting down on the same spot again, his back to the door, palms under his thighs.

Minutes later, there was another knock. Sofia headed

over. "Hi, I'm Sofia. What's your name?"

Mumbling came through, to which she remarked, "Oh, good, you've got the music. Come on in. Kenny's already here."

A five-foot-eight, medium-complexioned black guy entered carrying a big silver boom box on his shoulder.

Closing the door, Sofia followed him in. "Josie, Edwen over here has brought your music," she said.

"All right!" she exclaimed.

Edwen and Kenny exchanged nods.

"Finally!" I said to the slim radio man, who looked to be in his early twenties. "Put it on the dresser. That's Josie—she's the bachelorette." I pointed to her. "I'm Julia."

He smiled. He wasn't as fidgety as Kenny, but rather cautious. He set the radio on the dresser, directly to the right of the adjoining door.

"When's the dancer getting here?" asked Sofia.

"Soon."

"We wanna see him first. We might not like him," I said.

"Yeah, that's right!" said Josie, shouting from the bed.

Sofia seconded it, adding, "What's he look like?"

"Trust me," said Edwen, nodding, "you'll like him."

He looked around casually, and for some reason, the adjoining door caught his attention. He grabbed the deadbolt and discovered it was unlocked.

Reading suspicion in his eyes, I gasped, "Oh, no!" I rose from my chair and locked it, wondering how I'd undo it for the hit team later.

There was another tap on the door. "All right!" said Sofia, strolling to it excitedly. "We're in business."

Kelvin, a bald, dark-skinned black guy in a long-sleeved, form-fitting shirt, dress pants, and shoes entered the room. Josie, Sofia, and I began making catcalls at his very athletic form.

"Damn, Skippy. Can I be the bachelorette?" I raised a hand.

"I know, right," agreed Sofia.

Edwen turned to me. "I told you."

"Can we start the party before our friend gets here with the alcohol?" I asked him.

"Where is she?"

"She's on her way from work," Josie interjected.

He shrugged. "Do you want to?"

Sofia said, "Sure, but we'd like to work out the money first."

"Okay. What do you want done?" asked Edwen.

"We're ladies. We'd like to hear what you'll do to us," Sofia hinted.

Edwen, Kenny, and Kelvin exchanged glances. "We'll do it all," Edwen said.

"To all of us?" I asked.

"Yeah," said Kenny. "All of you get done."

"How much?" asked Josie.

I interjected, "She's the bachelorette, remember. Don't be greedy."

Edwen laughed. "Three hundred."

"Three hundred? For what?" I asked, indignant.

"Yeah. That's a whole lot," added Sofia.

"It's four of you each getting dick from us for two hundred, and we're going down on you for one hundred," Edwen explained.

"Two-fifty," suggested Josie. "Come on, you're getting fine babes here."

"That's right, honey," agreed Kelvin.

"Okay with you, Kenny?" asked Edwen.

"Yeah. I'm down."

"All right. Two-fifty."

"Turn it on!" shouted Sofia.

Music blasted through the speakers.

"Go, Josie, go, Josie!" Sofia and I cheered for her as she sashayed towards Kelvin, who was calling her over, and already dancing between the foot of the two beds.

Sofia took Edwen's hand, leading him to the space between the dresser and the bed closest to the front entrance. They began to dance.

That left me. Kenny was still seated on the edge of the bed, eyes animated as he watched the two couples. I had to dance with him, but I also had to give the hit signal and unlock the door. An idea occurred to me.

I hurried to the telephone between the beds, crossing in front of Kenny, saying out loud, "I gotta call Molly to see what's taking so long."

I picked up the phone and dialed Tauris' number. "Hey, girl!" I yelled over the music. "When are you getting here?"

Knowing they were waiting for the hit signal, I called out to Edwen, "Hey, go lower the music. I can't hear."

He motioned to Sofia that he'd return and headed to the radio.

"What'd you say?" I directed my question to our pretend friend. Phone cradled in my ear, I asked Kelvin, "She wants to know if you can do a rodeo dance."

"A rodeo dance?" he asked, flashing a big smile full of pearly white teeth.

"Yeah."

"Yee-*haw!*" he shouted, raising an arm over his head, mimicking twirling a lasso.

From that moment, things happened at super-sonic speed. I hung up the phone, ran to unlock the adjoining door, and was caught between the initial entry team and the second team; I was knocked down. A tap on the front door, opened by Sofia, revealed the hallway team. It was over in minutes.

Tauris shuffled Josie, Sofia, and me, handbags over our shoulders, into the adjoining room, but before crossing through, I locked eyes with the music man, who was being handcuffed. Shock, anger, and vengeance registered on his face.

Back at the office for a quick debriefing, we stood before the captain's desk. "Good job," he said. "All one of you has to do now is the investigation report."

We nodded and left his office.

"Listen, guys," I said to Josie and Sofia, "I can't do it. It's late. I gotta go home."

"Don't worry, Julia. We'll take care of it," said Sofia.

On my way home, the night replayed in my head, and with it the certainty that, as much as I loved the thrill of undercover work, it had to end. I had a new responsibility now: Nina. Many things could've gone wrong, but God had taken care of us.

17

Battered No More

AT 2:30 A.M., I PARKED the new DEA mini-van outside my home, heart heavy, mind overly consumed by the thoughts I had entertained on that desolate drive. Under clear skies, my footsteps echoed in the cool, comforting breeze; perhaps it was the calm before the storm.

Downtrodden, understanding that the time to bid farewell to the work I had loved was approaching, I climbed the steps to my condo, my tread heavy.

The familiar Baldwin key slipped in easily. I turned the knob—and entered an unsettling stillness. Narciso was awake. Seated on the bed, he held a sleeping Nina in his arms.

He looked over. "Is *this* the time a married woman comes home?" he barked.

I was mentally tired. The last thing I wanted to hear was a reprimand, though it hadn't been unexpected either. "I *told* you I was working late. I was the first one to go home."

"This can't go on like this. It's the marriage or the job."

Alas, the ultimatum. "Well, you know the answer to that. It puts the bread on the table."

He nodded, and I turned, heading towards the shower. By the time I was done, Nina was in her crib and Narciso was asleep. I sighed, wondering when and how it'd end. I welcomed sleep.

THE MONTHS MOVED ALONG, but I dreaded going home after picking up Nina at the sitter's. I'd stay there for a bit, trying to decompress from a hard day's work. Nana must've attributed my tension to my job; little did she know that, the minute I left her place, the unpredictable was highly probable in mine.

My state of being changed: morale, a convoluted mess; weight decreased; fashion flair insignificant. The latter had been precipitated by a mini-skirt I'd put on months before. It had brought Narciso to block the front door.

"You're not going to work like that," he'd ordered, hands on hips.

"Why not? What's the big deal? It's not short."

"How do I not know you're not cheating on me with one of the men? You have a gym. You could shower there."

I'd grinned. "Narciso, I don't have to go to work to cheat on you. Men are everywhere. That's not me."

"I don't care. I have the day off. Either you change, or you don't go." He hadn't budged. Not wanting to be stuck with him all day, I changed, and left.

My behavior fluctuated between being cautious about what I said to avoid an altercation and trying to appear stress-free for Nina. It was taking its toll. It was no way to live, but I couldn't see the light.

At bedtime on Sunday, November 7, 1999, the marriage that had begun as an enchanting adventure and had been morphing into a horrific reality exposed its crude talons when Narciso lay down next to me. Instinctively, I lifted my arm and rested it overhead, near my ear, covering my neck.

Though he'd turned to sleep on his side, away from me, I attributed my involuntary reaction to the January 22 choking incident, concluding that I was subconsciously protecting myself. It had been the point of no return.

When his breathing grew labored, I knew he'd fallen asleep. I pleaded before closing my eyes that night: *Show me the way out, Lord. Show me the way out.*

I called my brother from DEA the next morning. "Hello?"

His familiar tone was refreshing. It was nice to know some things had remained the same. "Frank?"

"Yeah. What's up?"

"I want you and Terry to come over this weekend. I don't wanna be married anymore. I need you guys to be there when I tell Narciso."

"I *knew* something was up," he said, before adding, "We'll be there."

That weekend's visit never happened, but the following night something else did.

Daniels, a HIDTA colleague who worked for the West New York Police Department, was having his official promotion to sergeant at the city hall on Tuesday, November 9. Afterwards, Narciso, Nina, and I would be attending his celebration dinner.

Sometime that day, when I headed to my desk from the

wire room, I responded to Narciso's page.

"Julia?" he answered, voice low.

"Yes. You paged?"

"I don't feel well. I'm not going to your friend's thing tonight."

"What's wrong?"

"I've got a bad headache. You go with the baby."

"Okay. Page me if anything comes up." I didn't believe him and wasn't surprised he'd called to cancel; he was not a fan of my career or my partners. I hung up relieved that I wouldn't have to put up a pretense in front of the guys.

Around ten-thirty p.m. that night, I unlocked the front door to our apartment, carrying Nina, who'd fallen asleep. The moment I entered, the thickness in the air suggested something dreadful—*The shit's gonna hit the fan tonight.*

Narciso was lying on the futon in sweats and a t-shirt, hands interlocked over his waist, watching the television with a fixed stare. He didn't look up.

In order to alleviate the tension, I asked, "How do you feel?"

He remained silent, not shifting his attention. The situation just escalated another notch, I thought.

It was time to feed Nina. After removing her overcoat, I laid her on the futon, went to put on my pajamas, and opened the refrigerator. There was only one four-ounce bottle of milk. It upset me.

I turned to Narciso. "How come there's no more milk?"

"Why didn't *you* get it?" he snapped.

"You were home all day," I replied. He'd been out of work, receiving worker's compensation, since August.

"Why didn't you fuckin' *get* it? You and your fuckin' job. That's all you're fuckin' good for. . .fuckin' *cops!* What kind of fuckin' woman are you?" he shouted.

"I'll go get it," I said, knowing things would spin out of control if I didn't leave soon.

Ignoring his rant, I put on my jacket but decided to wait until she had finished her milk and fallen asleep for the night before leaving. After slipping the Similac into my pocket to warm up once she was in her crib, I headed toward Nina, who had awakened, brown eyes questioning. Perhaps she'd sensed something.

Whispering sweet words, I lifted her off the futon, and was about to carry her into her bedroom.

And then he was standing before me, hands out. "I'll go buy it," he said.

I wondered what he was up to and hoped he couldn't read the suspicion in my eyes.

"Give me the baby," he demanded.

Fearing he'd take her, as he'd once told one of my aunts he would, I said, "I have to change her."

"*Give* me the *baby!*" Without saying another word, he took her from me, placed her on the futon, turned around, and punched me on the bridge of my nose with a closed fist.

I did what I never do in a chaotic situation; I screamed once as I fell. *Did anyone hear?* My head hit the hardwood floor with a loud thump. I was reminded of a boxing match. *I am not going to be the boxer who gets knocked out.*

My training kicked in: Stay calm, stay alive.

I tried to get up but couldn't. He was restraining me—one hand firmly on my jaw, the other on my arm.

Still I refused to panic; there had to be a way out.

Nina cried loudly. She began crawling toward me on the futon. Her eyes were fearful, worried. Big teardrops fell down her face.

Get up. Protect her.

Again, I tried to rise, but there was no budging. He had moved his grip from my jaw to my other arm. I was pinned.

Two hundred and forty pounds of muscle draped over me. I couldn't even bend my knees to kick.

The odds were not in my favor—at five-foot-six, by that time I had lost fifteen pounds and was weighing a hundred and twenty. I was not operating under the same conditions as when I had wrestled my buddy Burns in the desert during the Gulf War, both feet on the ground, space to my advantage. Nor was Narciso slow; aside from having been a bodybuilder and wrestler, he had also been a kick boxer.

He stared at me, consumed by hatred. I'd seen the devil in his eyes. My death would follow.

However, my baby's fear compelled me. I had been unable to console her, but I had to save her. Staring at the demon Narciso had become, I knew I had to say something to make it out alive with Nina. I snarled, "You *hit* me in front of the baby."

And it was like turning off a switch. He flinched and snapped out of it, releasing his grip. Robotically, he rose, put a jacket on, and left.

I moved fast. Peering through the rear window of our apartment, I noticed our SUV was gone. The immediate area showed no signs of him hovering.

After bundling up Nina, leaving the television on, I hurried outside and carted her up the long hill, looking around for any sign of him, afraid he might be lurking between buildings or in a random driveway.

The cold wind blew against me, making my trek on that long block more difficult. I sheltered her, hugging her tightly. She must've sensed my swiftness required silence; I couldn't hear a peep.

Finally, I made it to my mini-van, unlocked it, and put her in the car seat.

A police car sped down my block as I was rushing to the driver's side. My heart was racing.

Another patrol vehicle followed. Behind the wheel, I started the engine.

A trail vehicle came along. I took off after it as fast as I could.

The North Bergen Police car neared the bottom of the hill. I high-beamed and honked at it until the officer stopped. He climbed out of it and approached my window.

"What's—"

"I'm on the job. I was in a domestic. I'm following you to the police department to file a complaint."

"Calm down. What happened?" he asked.

Hurriedly, I answered, "I *am* calm. I don't have time for this. I'll tell you at there."

He strolled back to his car, too slowly for my taste, and I followed. En route, I called Frank and asked him to meet me at the station so he could pick up the baby, knowing the paperwork would require time.

Seeing the police department building was a comfort. I knew we were safe because I was with my own. The officer directed me to a room in the rear.

Disheveled, in my jacket and thermal pajamas, I marched quickly down a long bright hallway, carrying Nina, who was wide awake. I could only imagine what she was thinking.

I sighed at the sight of the officer at the end of the corridor.

"Ronnie," I said, letting out a breath, my eyes and face red.

"Hey, Julie," he smiled warmly. Noticing my appearance, he added, "Come here, honey, let me take some pictures."

"I don't want to put Nina down," I told him.

"It's okay. Stand there with her and just hold her a little lower." He indicated to a plain wall.

I did.

"Look straight, sweetie." Click went the camera. "To the right...to the left.... Okay, that's it." He put the camera on the desk next to him and added, "It's gonna be okay. Let me take you to the sergeant." Placing a hand gently behind me, he led us to an area where desks were surrounded by cubicles.

"Hey, Sergeant Valdora, this is Julie. We used to work together in Hudson."

He glanced up from a conversation he had been having with another cop, who looked up too and excused himself.

Ronnie resumed, "I already took the pictures. The officer went home—it was a shift change."

Leaning against a desk, the uniformed salt-and-pepper-haired sergeant in his late forties nodded.

Ronnie turned to me. "He'll take care of you now, honey."

18

Presenting My Case

"YOU NEED THIS LIKE you need a hole in the head, right?" Sergeant Valdora asked.

I grinned. "Yeah."

"You wanna call your captain now?"

"Yes."

Still carrying Nina, I followed him to a phone on a corner desk.

"Hello?" It was my new captain's strong, pleasant voice.

"Captain Failla, it's Julia Torres. Sorry to wake you."

He cleared his throat. "No problem. You all right?"

"Yeah, I'm okay. I'm just calling to let you know that I was in a domestic. I'm here at the North Bergen Police Department, getting ready to file a complaint."

"Okay, thank you for calling. Take the day off tomorrow.

Do what you gotta do. Call me if you need anything."

"Thank you, Captain."

Frank had shown up during that time, and after whispering to Nina that she'd be fine, I handed him her bottle, and he took her with him.

About five minutes later, Mom paged me. Narciso must've called her, I thought. I returned her page.

"Aurorita?" Her tone was clear, alert, and in need of answers.

"Yeah."

"What happened?" she demanded.

I was on the defensive. "What do you mean?"

"Why'd you leave the house?"

"Narciso said that?"

"Yes. He said he went to buy milk after you argued, and when he returned home you were gone."

"Really? Is that what he said?" I asked, mocking. "He didn't tell you that he punched me and I fell, right?"

She gasped. "No."

"Of course not."

"What a cynic," said Mom.

"Yeah, and right away you believed him." I reminded her.

"Well, he said—"

"Ma, I can't talk now. I'm at the police department."

"Where's your gun?" Valdora asked once the conversation ended.

"In my gun locker at work." I explained.

"How far do you wanna take this?" he asked, big brown eyes empathetic.

"All the way."

He nodded.

I asked, "Can I charge him with Agg Assault on a Police Officer?"

"No, you weren't performing your duties," he replied matter-of-factly.

"But he knows I'm a cop."

"You weren't acting in an official capacity."

"Too bad." I believe the law should be modified to include a provision that, if a civilian assaults someone they know to be law enforcement, the charge of Aggravated Assault can be applied.

"Yeah."

"So what *can* we charge him with?" I asked.

"Simple Assault, and we can call the on-call judge for a TRO."

"Okay. Let's do it." I signed the complaint and received my Temporary Restraining Order; in ten days, I'd have to go before another judge to request a Final Restraining Order, which was given.

"Okay, what's this guy look like?" asked Valdora.

I took a photo out of my wallet. "Send the biggest guys you have. He's a body-builder, kick-boxer, and wrestler."

He drifted off, photograph in hand.

Ten minutes later, three big officers stood before me. "Will they do?" asked the sergeant.

I sighed, "Yes." The smallest cop, at five-ten, appeared as solid as a brick house. The other two were giants.

"You can follow them in your car," said Valdora. "Good luck."

"Thanks for all your help, Sergeant."

At the apartment, the officers advised me to wait outside on the bottom of the steps. The three of them went upstairs. In the still of the night, I wondered how it'd pan out.

Not too long after, the smallest officer came out. "He's calm," he said, standing before me.

"Calm?" I asked in disbelief.

"Yeah."

Something's wrong," I replied. "Where's the rage?"

"Abusive men turn into cowards once the police are involved," he explained.

Instantly, I recalled Narciso's behavior the night Brent drove me home, but unlike the cop, I wasn't convinced. Something was off.

Ten minutes later, the other two cops left the house with Narciso walking before them, but he wasn't in handcuffs.

At the foot of the steps, he turned to me, tone innocent. "What's happening?"

"Hey!" said one of the cops, "you can't talk to her. We just served you with a restraining order. Get lost."

He did.

Narciso was not arrested but told to leave the premises, and I did not think to question the officers. I was too tired, and glad it was over.

"We're done here. Where will you be staying?" the eldest of the three asked.

"At my brother's place."

"Do you want us to follow you?"

"Yes, please."

Outside Frank's house, I entered the small foyer and rang his bell. Through the glass entrance, I saw him coming down the stairs. He opened the heavy door. "Narciso was here."

"When?"

"When you were at the police station."

"And?"

"I told him he better be calm, 'cause the police were going to get him."

I was flabbergasted. "What'd you tell him that for?"

"Come on, I know how you cops are."

"What's that supposed to mean?"

He said nothing. Steps creaked now and then on our ascent to the second floor.

"No wonder he was calm. You shouldn't have done that, Frank. The cops didn't see his true colors. Why would you give information to the enemy?"

"Enemy? This isn't the *army*, Julia."

"He *punched* me. He *is* the enemy. . . . I can't believe you did that."

We didn't discuss it again. I felt that my brother had betrayed me twice—disclosing my rape to Narciso, and now the police's arrival—but I had enough to deal with, rather than inquire on the reasons why he'd told him.

"Nina's asleep," said Frank when we reached the entrance door of his apartment.

At least he'd said something positive. "Oh, good. Did she have a hard time falling asleep?"

"A little. Terry warmed up the milk and rocked her to sleep."

I readied myself for bed and slept on the couch beside Nina, whose cheeks were pink from the heat. Run-down, I was out in minutes.

THE BELL RANG THE NEXT MORNING. My brother went to answer it and came upstairs. "Julia, it's Narciso. He wants to talk to you."

"There's a restraining order."

He shrugged, "Well, figure out what you're gonna do. I don't want that fuckin' guy there all day."

"Come with me so I have a witness," I said.

He was standing in the foyer, in front of the mailboxes. "We have a restraining order," I warned.

"I know that."

"That means you're supposed to be one hundred feet away from me."

"Julia, don't you think this is enough? I was out like a vagabond last night."

How typical of Narciso I thought, to play the victim. "Enough? You punched me."

"Where am I supposed to go? I don't have any money."

"I'll give my brother sixty dollars. Find a place." I turned and left.

Narciso violated the Final Restraining Order by calling me, paging me, leaving letters on my doorstep, and frequenting places I went to. I was tired of fighting; the whole ordeal was exhausting, and I wanted to put it behind me. It wasn't until one afternoon a short while later that I filed a complaint for a Violation of a Restraining Order.

My friend Betty and I had gone to the North Bergen Post Office and were headed to my parked SUV. Across the street, on the Union City side, stood Narciso. He headed my way.

Hurriedly, I entered the vehicle, but when I started the ignition, he was at my driver's side. He began pounding hard on the window.

I rolled it down so it wouldn't break but kept my cell phone visible. "What do you want?"

"I'm not happy with Maria and Brent."

Narciso had complied with the court's supervised visitation order, but because he lived in a boarding house for men, he had to visit Nina at Brent and Maria's house. Brent would remain in the room during Narciso's visit. "Tell the court," I said.

He demanded, "You tell them."

"No, I'm happy with them." I put the gear in drive.

He reached in through my window and grabbed the steering wheel.

I put the car in park, picked up my cell phone, and dialed the number for the North Bergen Police.

"Who are you calling? The police?"

"Yes."

"That's how you resolve everything, right?"

"Yes."

He let go of the wheel and left.

Coward. I ended the call before it was answered.

Betty, who had been silent, finally spoke. "Julia, I've never seen that side of him. I didn't know he was like that."

"You're not the only one."

"You have to go to the police. I was terrified sitting here. I can't believe you were so calm. I thought he was going to break your window. He reminded me of my ex-boyfriend in Uruguay. He was like that, and the only way it ended was when I told the police. You have to go. He's not gonna stop until you stop him. That's what the cops are for."

"You're right. Will you be my witness?"

"Yes, of course. I saw the whole thing. I'm so sorry this happened to you. That man is crazy."

I filed my complaint, but again, Narciso was never arrested. He was never home when the police attempted to effect his arrest.

A few of the guys at work had volunteered to ensure it was done, but I felt that if God wanted him behind bars, it'd happen. I thought that perhaps the situation would be more dangerous for Nina and me if Narciso went to jail and then got released on bail. I wasn't willing to find out and risk her life in the process.

The court date was often adjourned, tactics used by defense attorneys to tire victims, leading them to drop the charges. I was no different. In the end, I settled for a lesser charge—provided he left me alone.

After it was all over, I spoke with Mom candidly about my marriage. She advised me to get a divorce and communicated the news to the pastor who had married us. His advice was the same. I was relieved, especially before God.

I met with an attorney and filed for divorce, having kept Mom's long-ago advice: *Don't ever stay married for the children. Kids grow up and leave the house to make their own lives. Then you're old and stuck with a spouse you don't even like as a person. It's not worth it. If you're not in love, or your marriage isn't working, get out of it.*

FROM THE MOMENT OF MY INITIAL domestic violence complaint until the day of my divorce, I received unconditional support from my partners. They'd shared their thoughts of how well I had handled things and hoped others would do the same. These righteous men voiced their opinions firmly: Some wanted immediate justice; others accepted my decision; all remained ready to take action if needed. Their encouraging words helped pull me through a very difficult time. I was thankful beyond measure and honored to have worked with them.

Six months later, my divorce was finalized. My attorney, after looking at my notes and the forty-three witnesses I had gathered, had remarked, "Julia, this was more than enough information. You made a strong case and did my job for me." The judge awarded me sole custody. I exhaled.

19

Blessing in Disguise

IN JUNE 2000, MY ASSIGNMENT WITH DEA ENDED, and I returned to the Passaic County Prosecutor's Office one rainy morning to begin working in the Trial Team at the main office. I headed up the steps of the marble building, in a skirt suit and heels, handbag over shoulder, umbrella overhead, joining others who pushed through revolving doors.

I flashed my badge for identification to the sheriff's officer who stood behind a metal detector, bypassing the long line, and caught an elevator. Chatter filled the ride to the seventh floor, where I stood behind an older, distinguished black woman in brown dress slacks and a mustard blouse, a paisley kerchief around her neck.

We entered the same vast glass room, where I tapped on the door to Captain Bakalow's office, and she headed to a desk with a nameplate that read: *Carmetta Lewis, Domestic Violence*

Counselor. A bulky white man in his fifties looked up from a newspaper. "Yes, may I help you?"

"Good morning sir, I'm Julia Torres. I've been assigned here."

He rose. "Oh, yes. Come on in." We exchanged handshakes. "This isn't the street, but you'll learn a lot here. Put your things on the empty desk by the window—that'll be yours—and follow me to meet who you'll be working with."

The captain led me to a corner office down the hallway, where he cleared his throat before we entered. "Excuse me, gentleman, I'd like you to meet my new investigator, Julia Torres. She'll be working for you."

"Hello, Julia. I'm Chief Assistant Prosecutor John Cosme. It's nice to meet you." He buttoned his tailored suit before extending his hand.

"Likewise," I said, shaking it, noticing his elegant cuff links.

"And I'm Assistant Prosecutor Paul DeGroot. Good to meet you." They were a complementary contrast: John wore glasses and was small; Paul, in a gray suit and paisley tie, stood over six feet tall and did not use eyeglasses. Both exuded confidence.

"Okay. I'm done here," said Barkalow, who left.

John continued, "Have a seat. Were you reassigned from Narcotics?"

"DEA."

"Very good." Rain trickled down the large windowpane behind John as he leaned back in his chair. "Do you know what you'll be doing here in the trial team?"

"No, I don't."

"You will be the trial investigator for me and Paul. Your duties will be diverse and will entail things such as completing witness lists, obtaining evidence, preparing testimony, and selecting juries. There will be very little street work. If there is any, it will consist of interviewing victims, witnesses, defendants, and perhaps looking at crime scenes."

Paul grinned. "I'm sure it won't be anything like what you've been used to, but here you'll get to see how the judicial process works."

"That's correct," added John. "This is where your cases come after you have completed your investigation. At what level have you testified in court?"

"Local, state, and federal. Both grand jury and trial."

"Great. Well, I wish you luck. You'll enjoy working here." The rain had already stopped when he and Paul rose.

Preparing cases for trial was similar to grand jury work, and I quickly became acclimated to my duties.

One afternoon, Carmetta, the DV counselor, and I were both in our small lunch room. The microwave beeped. "That smells good. What is it?" she asked as I sat down across from her.

"Thanks. Ground beef—or as we call it, *picadillo*."

"Is it a Cuban dish?"

"Yes. What's yours? It smells delicious."

"Jamaican chicken and rice. Would you like some?" she asked in her British-accented English.

"Sure. Have some of mine, too," I offered.

After placing a little on each plate, I added, "I love homemade meals."

Astute brown eyes smiled behind elegant prescription

glasses. "So do I. Do you enjoy cooking?"

"It depends."

"On what?"

"Whether or not I'm ordered to."

She began her assessment naturally. "Does your husband order you?"

"I'm divorced." I raised my left hand, pointing to my naked wedding finger with the other.

"Was that one of the reasons?"

"Not exactly. My marriage ended in domestic violence."

"I'm sorry to hear that. It never is easy."

"Thank you. No, it's not. Your mind plays head games."

"How do you mean?"

There, between forkfuls of international food, Carmetta and I spoke of the nature of domestic violence. Concern written across her face, she said, "Be thankful you got out alive."

"I am. But why doesn't a victim realize the best thing to do is to get help right away?"

"Signs aren't often clear during courting. Then, you hope for a change. One has to understand the profile of an abuser to see through their charades, and when emotions are involved, judgment can be clouded."

I nodded. "My brother says, 'You can't see the picture when you're in the frame.'"

Tilting her head, she remarked, "Yes, that's right. Don't beat yourself on the head thinking about what you could have or should have done. They are narcissistic individuals with charismatic personalities, unsuspected by others most of the time."

"Why are they like that?"

"It's what they've known. Generally speaking, though there are exceptions, they were victimized somehow, and it caused them to create an image of themselves because they did not like who they were. They learned to love it. Their ruse is difficult to see because they appear caring and chivalrous to others, but people who do not know how to love are incapable of loving."

"That's sad."

"For those of us who've experienced love, yes, but hurt people hurt people. I usually ask what held the person back from leaving. What was your reason?"

"Growing up without a dad. I knew I should've left, but like you said, I hoped for a change. It wasn't the lost love that I cried over. That began to end when he first showed me violence." A memory came to me; I stared off into space, closed my eyes, and sighed. When I opened them, I noticed she hadn't moved. I appreciated her stillness.

I added, "Carmetta, It's a funny thing about love—it happens more than once but never the same way twice.... I loved two men before I got married, but what I felt for my ex wasn't anywhere close. Don't get me wrong, I remember loving him at one point, but the bad moments outweighed the good."

"Yes, love is always different." She gazed at me with the eyes of a woman who has known its depth, then asked with tenderness, "What were your tears for?"

"The loss of what I wanted as a child: a family."

"I understand. It's the mourning of our expectations. We enter marriage full of hopes and dreams, which is fine, but sometimes we don't consider what our spouses are able to give, only what we'd like to have." She had finished her lunch and replaced the lid on her Tupperware. "There is nothing wrong with expecting more, as long as it's something we discuss with our partner beforehand. Couples may then reconsider marrying when they see their desires can't be met."

"That's a definite way to avoid a failed marriage. Carmetta, overall, in your experience, do abusers ever change?"

"I don't want to say no, because then it will mean there's no hope for anyone, but I would have to say it doesn't occur often. Many times, they will swear on their children's graves that they will, begging and pleading on hands and knees for another opportunity, and they are given it. But, after awhile, it escalates into a worse incident than the one before."

"What do you recommend to a victim before they make that mistake?"

"I tell them not to make a decision based on emotion, and suggest they find a safe place for themselves and their children. I also advise them to speak to someone neutral who will give them sound advice, like their priest or pastor. If they are in this country illegally, I explain Clinton's Violence Against Women Act, passed during his presidency, that protects victims from deportation. Many are coerced to remain in an abusive relationship because the abuser threatens to call Immigration. Sadly, the victim remains, not knowing the law that protects them. No woman or man needs to put up with any abuse. You did the right thing, Julia. Don't doubt yourself. Your daughter could've been hurt eventually. It happens."

She'd stood up. The screech of the chair had underscored her final words.

"Thank you for your honesty, Carmetta."

"You're welcome. I can't afford not to be."

Two months later, on August 11, 2000, a compelling devotion I read in the Oswald Chambers book Drew, a DEA agent, had given me, indirectly pointed Nina and me in a new direction: "It is no use saying you cannot go; this experience must come, and you must go."

Previously, I'd been deliberating relocating to Florida, where my mom and Marlene were living. Recently divorced and now a single parent, I thought it'd be best for Nina to be near family. However, I wondered where I'd find employment and residence. Yet when I read further: "You have a strong disinclination to take the initiative and trust in God," and, "Determine to trust in God," I knew we'd go—but did not know when.

Things have a way of developing by themselves when we leave them alone, though, just as what we say often becomes a self-fulfilled prophecy. It'd been apparent that December, when Barry Woods, one of my partners, and I returned to the office after locating a witness.

We were hanging our coats on a rack; without consciously thinking of my words, I declared, "This is my last winter in Jersey."

"Where are you going?" He placed his scarf over his wool coat.

"Florida."

Eyes narrowing, he asked, "Aren't you going to retire here?"

"No." I tossed my gloves on my desk. "I never saw myself doing twenty-five years."

"Why not?"

I shrugged. "I don't know. I just had that feeling."

Curiosity in his dark blue eyes, he asked, "What will you do?"

"I have no idea." There was no master plan in my mind, simply the knowledge that we'd relocate without any effort on my end.

TIME PASSED UNEVENTFULLY until the following February, when something strange began to happen. At my desk, working on a case file, I suddenly had difficulty writing in bold print. There was no dexterity in my hands or strength to grip the pen.

After a few minutes, I tried again and was able to hold the pen, but my writing was very slow and difficult. I looked at what I had written, head tilted, mind boggling. The print was that of a kindergartener. *What's going on?*

Worse followed; my mouth felt as if a dentist had pinched my gums with Novocain. I glanced at Carmetta's desk, relieved to find her sitting behind it, telephone in the crook of her neck.

I rose slowly, carrying the paper in my hand. "Carmetta?" I asked when she had hung up.

"Yes?"

"Look at this." I handed her the lined yellow sheet.

"Who wrote this?"

"I did."

She flipped it over, trying to find an explanation. "What happened?"

"I don't know. It just happened. And another thing—my mouth feels like I was at the dentist."

Her eyes widened. "Where?"

"Here." I touched the right side of my jaw.

She removed her glasses. "Julia, make an appointment to see a neurologist when you get home today. Don't delay."

Although those symptoms didn't last much longer, they made me reflect. Staring at the childlike print, memories returned: numbness and tingling on my hands and feet followed by a stiffness in my left leg when I was in the Gulf; my left leg feeling like lead as I ran up the stairs in Hudson before executing a search warrant; chasing a subject with a partner across a Paterson street and involuntarily running sideways; taking step classes at a gym and losing coordination; suddenly dancing with two left feet and falling if I didn't sit down.

It seemed there were more than plenty of instances. I made an appointment with the neurologist who'd taken care of me when the undercover vehicle I was in was struck by a bus on my side during a buy-bust operation in Hudson. I had gone from a walker to a cane, until I could run at 8.0 on a treadmill, and had returned to work.

I hoped to get a concrete answer.

IN HER JERSEY CITY OFFICE, after explaining my symptoms, she said, "Julia, aside from the accident with the bus, you've been involved in multiple motor vehicle accidents while working. As a result, you have fifty percent permanent nerve damage."

"No, doctor. This isn't *nerve* damage. It's something else."

She shook her head.

I left her office in frustration, wondering why she thought she knew my body better than I did.

Work resumed without any further occurrences for a few weeks, but one evening in late February, while driving home, I was unable to brake. Realizing it was something grave, I called a friend to drive me to the Christ Hospital Emergency Room.

Once there, I was admitted and made three telephone calls: to my sitter, who agreed to stay with Nina until I returned; to Barkalow, to explain any future absences; and to my mom.

The next two weeks at Christ brought a battery of tests: spinal tap, myelogram, CAT scan, and brain MRI. After that, the doctor discharged me, pending results.

Once home, I paid the taxi driver and rushed up the stairs to see my princess. I couldn't open the door quick enough when the sounds of hurried little footsteps met me. "Nina!"

"Momma!" It was all I needed to hear to make my eyes tear.

A few hours later, Mom called when Nina was taking her nap. "What'd the doctor say?"

"Nothing. She doesn't know what it is. She's waiting for test results."

Silence.

"It's okay, Ma."

"What do you mean? Do you know what it is?"

Not knowing what propelled me to utter what I would, I began, "Ma, I think it's multiple sclerosis."

"How'd you figure that?"

"I didn't. It's like God told me."

"But what is MS?"

"I don't really know, only that it's an illness I did a walk for years ago."

"Don't wish an illness upon yourself."

"I'm not, Ma. I think for some reason He wants me to leave New Jersey. God knows how much I love being a cop, and the only way I'd leave my job is if I can't do it anymore."

"Where are you getting that information?"

"Nowhere. It's like I know it. I think God's preparing me for it before I hear it."

"But why?"

"I don't know, but don't worry, it'll be gone in two years. He just wants me to be in Florida for some reason. Ma, I know it doesn't sound logical, but I don't know what else to say."

The confusion on her end of the line was palpable; I could see why. My words hadn't made any sense to me either, but they seemed a given. I couldn't rationalize the quiet certainty of what I knew, but without a doubt, it was the diagnosis God had revealed to me.

"Okay," said Mom in resignation. "Call me when you hear from the doctor."

ON MARCH 12, 2001, I sat against the wall in a small patient room and glanced at medical terms on posters displaying the brain and spine of the human anatomy. On a counter, were glass jars of cotton balls and Q-tips.

Across from me, the doctor, in her white coat, pen in one hand, removed two x-rays from a manila envelope. Turning on the light box switches, she placed a film on each box and pointed to some white spots on a film of my brain. "These are lesions. You have MS," she said, without preface.

Not knowing what it meant to have 'lesions' but not surprised by her diagnosis, I asked, "What are my options?"

She looked confused. "You have MS."

"I know. I heard you the first time." My response perplexed her further. Her big brown eyes shifted, her eyebrows remained arched, and the crease above her nose deepened. "Doctor, I already knew this. God let me know. He didn't physically tell me—it was more like an intuition. I think He wanted to prepare me for the diagnosis beforehand."

She was quiet. It was apparent that my faith-based explanation was insufficient for her. She began, "There are three MS treatments available at the moment, called ABC drugs—Avonex, Betaseron, and Copaxone. Based on your MS being Relapsing-Remitting, I think Copaxone would be good for you. It's a once-a-day subcutaneous injection. Betaseron is also subcutaneous, but every other day. Avonex is a weekly intra-muscular injection. You can decide which is best for you and call my office with your decision." She handed me packets addressing each.

"Doctor, I'm gonna move to Florida, so I'll start the treatment there, but I'll do the Avonex even though it's in the muscle. I'll inject myself, and if I can't, I'll get someone to do it, but once a week is enough of a reminder that I'm not a hundred percent. I'm not gonna be a slave to this, and an injection every day or every other day is just that. Thank you."

I left her office comforted, not by her diagnosis, but by God's divine intervention.

At home, I called Mom, who was amazed that what I'd previously told her was correct. Afterward, I dialed Personnel to request a retirement date of May 1, having the feeling I'd be approved by then. The lady I spoke with wasn't as confident and listed July 1 instead. It was no surprise to me that she telephoned me in mid-April, astonished that my retirement had been approved.

IN RETROSPECT, RETIRING WAS UNNECESSARY; my Instructor Training Certification from the New Jersey State Police, and certification from the Defense Language Institute in Washington, D.C., enabled me to teach at the police academy, but I hadn't thought out my decision. I was simply being driven.

Wanting a fresh start, I dropped the FRO, sold my two condos, called a moving company to transport my furniture to a storage facility in Florida, and drove southbound on Route 95 on May 1, wondering what God had in store for us. It was sad to leave behind my career, the great guys I'd worked with, and New Jersey, the state that would remain *home*, but I sensed that God was telling me to trust that it was time to move on.

20

Many Scars

WALKING UP THE PATH TO OUR HOME in West Palm Beach, Florida, that June, palm trees, heat, and humidity surrounded me and Nina when I slipped the key into the lock. The arresting lake view from the sliding glass living-room doors spread perfect stillness beyond the yard's freshly mown grass, the hammock between two tall coconut trees, and Nina's doll house.

She dashed to her miniature version of our residence, a five-and-a-half-foot peach house with a white veranda, hanging plant on one end, mailbox on the other. Inside it, toys, play furniture, and a kitchen set kept her imagination busy while I dialed Burns' number from my office overlooking a calm, suburban two-way street.

"Hey, Buddy, I retired," I announced while keeping an eye on Nina. My dear buddy—Lester Burns—who'd been my best friend in the Gulf, had remained in touch with me. We had hurdled unnecessary obstacles overseas, not succumbing to antagonism, proving the essence of battle camaraderie. Now, he'd be instrumental in my life once again.

Incredulity came through the North Carolina end of the telephone line. "...Retired? Why?"

"I was diagnosed with MS."

"Julia," he immediately said, "go to the VA hospital right away. You got sick because we were in the Gulf."

"You think so?" The doubt in my voice was obvious.

"Yes. Remember, you got out. I didn't. I saw troops get sick. Some died from strange stuff." He let it sit for effect.

My head spun. *Sick?* "Strange how?"

"Shaves just fell out and died one day, Bean got some stuff in his blood, Fords had a heart attack...I forget the rest. It's part of that whatchacall Gulf War Syndrome—nobody can tell what it is. You need to go to the VA. You took those pills. Go file a C & P."

"What's that?"

The only contact I had had with the VA when I came home in 1991 was adding my name to the Gulf War Registry. Being in the East Orange facility was depressing enough; I hadn't wanted to go back. Its dark, crowded halls felt oppressive, seeing ungrateful workers snap at comrades unsettling. Perhaps conditions would be better in Florida, I thought; after all, ten years had passed.

"A Compensation and Pension. The military is responsible for bringing you back home the same way you left. *Are you the same, Julia?*"

I paused, glancing out the window as the loud rumble of

Harleys announced the arrival of Harry, my next-door neighbor, and Kevin from down the block. "No." I shook my head at the framed accolades that surrounded me, disappointed that my adventures had ended at the drop of a hat.

"Julia, go to the Disabled American Veterans tomorrow. They'll help you," Burns advised, worry dominating his tone.

"Buddy, *you're* okay, right?"

"So far."

I let out a breath. "Good. No sense in both of us being sick."

MY ODYSSEY BEGAN AT THAT POINT. For about three years, I dealt with incessant paperwork, medical check-ups, and the "hurry up and wait" routine the military was famous for, not to mention ignorant employees who thought they were doing veterans a favor, or worse, that we were trying to get over on them, as if a vet chose to be sick. Twice, my claim was denied.

The first time it happened, I made an appointment to see my DAV rep. "Tony!" I yelled on the main floor of the West Palm Beach VA, holding paperwork in my hands, stomping toward Pegg's office.

He opened his door and came down the corridor, calling, "Julia?"

"Yes."

He read the anger on my face. "What's wrong?"

"That ignorant jerk-off in the desk pods said that just because my orders say I served in the Gulf doesn't mean I *served* in the Gulf."

"Don't worry about him. He doesn't know what he's talking about. Come here. Let me see what's going on."

I followed his long strides with my VA-issued cane, blowing off steam as I went. "This is why vets get their claims denied. They have morons like that reviewing them."

"That's why there are people like me who make sure they're taken care of," he replied.

"I was just trying to get an ID before seeing you. I needed to show my DD-214."

In his small office, motivating slogans hung on the walls. On his desk a small radio was playing music low. Neat piles of cases, some thicker than others, lay to the left of books on top of thick binders.

"We'll do it after this. It's not a big deal. Let me see what St. Pete sent you." I took a seat across from his desk, and he went through the papers I handed him. "It says here you didn't submit paperwork reflecting symptoms during your seven-year presumptive period."

"I didn't know such a thing *existed*, or else I would've sent it. I included copies from my diagnosis onward."

"So you have symptoms that fit that time frame?"

"Yes." I leaned forward. "You mind if I shut the door all the way? There's too much noise out there."

"No. Go ahead."

Doorknob in hand, I gazed at the usual line of disabled veterans in wheelchairs, with amputations, oxygen tanks, canes, or walkers. I rolled my eyes and let out a breath as a television blared from a carpeted waiting room not too far off. Knowing, resigned eyes peered at my irritated, inexperienced expression, offering empathy. I grinned sheepishly, closing the door slowly. "Anyway, I have lots of medical reports, even my redeployment physical from the Gulf."

"Great. What other overseas stuff?"

"I have the form that says I took over twenty-one PBs, but on that same form we were told to check off *No* on the question about NBC exposure. Tony, we were *exposed*. There were alarms. We masked. None of us was delusional."

"Those PBs were bad news. I know you were gassed, Julia. You don't have to make a believer out of me."

"Thanks. I appreciate it." VA personnel did not often commit to an opinion, but representatives who worked on cases often went the extra mile to help a fellow veteran. Tony was one of them. "When I came back, I went to my home unit and asked to copy my entire medical file. I wanted to see what the nine inoculations we got before deploying were, but they weren't there. Someone said they weren't in any Gulf service member's files. I researched that info and learned they had all disappeared. Is that true?"

"I heard that, too. Julia, I don't know what the shots consisted of, and we may never know." With a note of camaraderie, he offered, "Let me see how I can help you with what I *do* know. Do you have other evidence, aside from the Gulf?"

"Yes. I have medical records from a motor vehicle accident in '92 when I was on the job that left me temporarily paralyzed for twelve days. My doctor thought it was nerve damage and didn't check for MS. It was my left leg back then, now it's my right."

"Okay. Get it all together, and we'll overnight the paperwork to St. Pete."

The second denial came a few months later, making me livid but Tony even madder.

In his office, I handed him the package as he sat on his chair. "This is ridiculous. The evidence is right here, and they don't even have it noted!" His blue eyes darkened as the papers in his hand shook. "This isn't even my claim, and I'm mad." He threw it on the desk, put his elbows on it, and asked, "Julia, do you wanna go to Washington?"

"I'll go to Oshkosh if I have to," I said, seated beside him in the cool air-conditioning, disregarding the Florida sunshine coming through the window. Exposure to the sunny, humid weather was often debilitating. I had explained it on my last C & P exam: "...my abdomen swells, I get fatigued, and sometimes my speech slurs."

"What do you do when you're outdoors?" the doctor, an older Filipino woman with glasses, had asked.

"I pace myself, go inside a store, find a place to sit, cool down, and then go back out."

"How does going from hot to cold affect you?"

"It makes me wanna pee. When I go and I've already washed my hands to leave, I gotta go again."

She had nodded. "Do you ever feel completely voided?"

"Not usually."

"What do you when you're out?"

"Find out where the nearest bathroom is. . . . I get that, I've learned to deal with it, but why does my stomach swell? It looks like I'm three months pregnant sometimes, and the funny thing is, when I cool down in the a/c or go in cold water, it flattens again."

"I don't know. I don't hear that often."

"But what can it be connected to?"

"Perhaps the fact that heat expands."

"How about the speech slurring?"

"The central nervous system works slower in the heat in everyone. When someone has lesions, or many scars, like you do, they interfere with the functions of the nervous system."

"Like a short circuit?"

Head askew, squinting, she had replied, "I suppose that's a good way to explain it in layman's terms."

"So it's like the message to walk, talk, write, whatever, doesn't flow smoothly because of the scars?"

"Yes. You should exercise. You'll feel less fatigue and have better balance," she'd suggested.

"I do weight training."

She had nodded. "That's good. It'll help strengthen your muscles, which may be weakened by the MS. It also helps with stress and depression, which are common symptoms. Perhaps joining an MS group will be beneficial to you, if you suffer from either."

"No, I already tried that group thing. I don't like pity parties, and that's all it was."

She'd raised her eyebrows. "Do you want to try another group?"

"No. I try to stay positive on my own. God won't give me anything I can't handle."

"How are your feet?" she'd asked.

"I have foot drop on the right. Sometimes I can't pick it up, so I trip. And both my feet have numbness and tingling, and feel like they're on fire."

She had said nothing but noted it in the case file.

Neurologists wouldn't precisely explain my symptoms; instead they'd provide a simple definition of multiple sclerosis, an unpredictable disease, adding that I should consider myself lucky it wasn't worse.

I asked Tony, "How soon will I go to DC?"

"First, I'll try to get you a telephonic hearing or an interview at the regional office in St. Pete."

MONTHS PASSED BEFORE I WAS SCHEDULED an appointment with a Washington, DC, representative in St. Petersburg. Mom and I headed out at the crack of dawn to be there by eight a.m., allowing an hour for any incidental road occurrences.

We pulled up in front of glass lobby doors, where wheelchairs were folded alongside a large half-moon wooden desk. It was odd that no one was there, but I was thankful; perhaps we wouldn't have to wait long. "Ma, get me a wheelchair. Most VA places have very long hallways. It'll be faster."

She parked in a disabled spot, hooking the decal onto the rearview mirror, and left, returning with one. She wheeled me through the automatic doors and the vast foyer, onto an elevator, and down a long hallway to our second floor destination.

A tall, young, clean-shaven man in his early twenties was standing in front of an unmanned desk in casual business attire, holding a few case files and a thick binder. "Sergeant Torres?" he asked.

"Yes."

"Kory Schmitt. It's a pleasure to meet you. Thank you for your service," he said, extending his hand.

"Nice to meet you. You're welcome."

He resumed, "You're early, and so are we. A veterans law judge from the Board of Veterans' Appeals is waiting in the interview room. I'll take you in in fifteen minutes if you'd like."

"That'd be great. Thank you."

He turned, heading down another hallway.

The barren room, still air, and PTSD poster of a helmeted soldier, foliage sticking out of slits on his cover, hollow look in his eyes, were more than I wanted to see. The once-healthy soldier, like me, had become afflicted with Post-Traumatic Stress Disorder. Listed in bold print—flashbacks, nightmares, hopelessness, irritability, self-destruction—a few elements shouted out boldly.

It had been difficult having to regurgitate my experiences with a mental health counselor at the VA, but Tony had insisted that it get done for my C & P. Nightmares had returned, their graphic nature increased. Poignant images of a young girl being raped by a man who turned out to be a gorilla were heinous. A seemingly beautiful, palatial home lured me, only to find, once inside, a cold morgue, torsos hanging on chrome shepherd hooks, bodies on steel examining tables, all left haphazardly by a medical examiner nowhere to be found. Fearing those nightmares would be repeated, I had called to cancel any future visits.

The air in the room shifted, becoming lighter; I glanced to my far left. Schmitt was returning, file in hand. "He's ready for you, Sergeant Torres. Your mom can wait here."

He escorted me into a conference room with a long oval table in the center. An older black gentleman with soft, smart eyes behind rimless oval glasses, sat behind it, holding a pen in his right hand. "Good morning, Sergeant Torres. I am Abraham Bond. I will be hearing your request for a compensation and pension. Do you require some time to begin, or are you ready?"

"I'm ready, sir."

"Very well, then. I have reviewed your case file and would like to ask you a few questions. At any time from the moment you completed your tour in the Gulf, did you detail to anyone the symptoms you were having?"

"No, sir."

"Did you keep in touch with anyone from the Gulf that you shared this with?"

"I told Sergeant Burns I was diagnosed with MS."

"Is he here?"

"No, sir."

"Mr. Schmitt says your mother is present."

"Yes, sir, she is."

"Let's bring her in. Perhaps she can testify to something." He set his pen on the desk.

We waited in silence until Schmitt returned with Mom.

"Good morning, Mrs. Torres. Have a seat. I am Abraham Bond. I'd like to ask you a few questions." She nodded. "Can you please tell me how your daughter's health has changed since she returned from the Gulf?"

"Oh, my goodness. My daughter love sports. She exercise, she dance, she runs. She always do things no one else can do and win lots of time. In the army, she was the best at many things. In police, she do dangerous things good. She's not afraid. I say, 'Aurorita, why you do that?' and she say, 'Because I love it, Ma.' I don't understand her because I worry, you know."

He smiled. "Can she do any of those things you speak of now?"

Mom shook her head. "No. She can't run. She can't dance like she did or move fast. You know, it's sad for me. When she come back, she wanted to be alone. And she couldn't sleep. I asked her, 'You okay, Aurorita?' and all the time she said yes. My daughter doesn't complain. She was never the same since she return, and she didn't have to go." Her tone shifted to anger, and she continued, "She volunteered, and she didn't tell me. Her colonel told me. I said, 'What?' He said, 'Mrs. Torres, you should be proud of your daughter, she was the only one to volunteer.' All those men didn't go. She's a woman—I don't understand. When she come back, I ask her why she did that. She said she wanted to. I don't know. That's for men. And now, look. She's not the same." Mom started to cry.

Bond grabbed the box of tissues on the table and handed it to her. "Thank you, Mrs. Torres. I apologize for making you cry." He turned to Schmitt. "Will you please escort Mrs. Torres outside and get her some water? We are done."

Once the door had closed, Abraham asked, "Sergeant Torres, is there anything you want to say?"

"Yes, sir."

The door clicked open. Schmitt entered and returned to his seat.

"I volunteered for this war and left my house in perfect health. When I led platoon runs, some of the men would ask me to slow down. Now, I can't even run the length of this office. I had a successful career as a cop. There was nowhere for me to go but up, and that had to end. I loved what I did, but I couldn't risk a partner getting hurt because I was unable to respond in time or couldn't squeeze a trigger. . . . Someone has to be held accountable for my condition. I shouldn't have to be here, begging you to give me something that's rightfully mine. There is no reason for any vet to have to do that. It's shameful. We shouldn't have to endure an inquisition to receive what we have earned, and other veterans should not have to be the ones to tell us what we are entitled to. A list of state and federal benefits should be provided to every returning veteran, because we served our country when others did not."

"Thank you. I will return to Washington and recommend that your C & P be granted."

I shook my head. "Sir, does that mean someone has to approve it? I don't want to have to continue waiting."

"You won't have to wait. When I make a request, the request is granted. You will have your C & P. Thank you for your service."

"Thank you, sir."

Schmitt wheeled me to my mom, and we left. The ride home in the beaming sun was without chatter; I maxed the air conditioner and Mom put on her cardigan. Her favorite Spanish radio station played ballads while I drove to West Palm, mindful of the soothing beats, calmed by the voices. The trip had been exhausting; my mind was tired.

At Mom's about four hours later, I slept.

WHILE I WAITED FOR ST. PETE'S LETTER, I worked out regularly. Staying fit was no longer something I could enjoy at leisure, but a necessity. With the uncertainties of MS, I began to learn to appreciate the simple things I had taken advantage of—walking, dancing, high heels, tanning—they all took on different meanings.

Almost four months after my interview, I received a

manila envelope from the Board of Veterans' Appeals. I said a silent prayer before reading it.

> *It is at least as likely as not that the veteran's multiple sclerosis began during service or was manifested to a compensable degree within seven years of discharge from service.*

I cried with relief.

Mom had entered the living room, where I was sitting on the couch. "What's wrong?"

I handed her the papers.

"*Gloria a Dios*," she declared.

Being awarded a one-hundred-percent service connection meant I'd receive monetary benefits and tax-exemption on my primary residence. As a single parent and sole provider for Nina, this outcome would prove invaluable; God had taken care of me once again and provided helpers along the way. Had it not been for Burns, former Marine Ray Grande, Tony Pegg from the Disabled Veterans of America, and Dave Weinstein from the Paralyzed Veterans of America, I may not have continued with such zeal.

Once again, camaraderie had prevailed. However, I knew it'd be up to God to make my running dreams come true and one day annihilate MS, the enemy. My faith was in Him, not the medication that, at best, attempted to slow down the progression of the disease but brought horrific side effects. There by the grace of God, I live in confidence, knowing that He continues to have my back.

Julia Torres

21

Altered Consciousness

IN-TRO-SPEC-TION: Having nothing but time on my hands after officially retiring in July 2001, I began to think, considering the areas I had valued too much or too little, paying closer attention to the people I had hurt. An illness can do that sometimes, and it's not necessarily a bad thing but a type of inner healing, crushing to the ego yet crucial for growth.

George was the first person who entered my mind. I wanted to apologize for the wrong I had done. It had been fourteen years since I returned from the army's *AIT*, Advanced Individual Training, with a presumed fiancé; I needed to explain myself.

Knowing he had achieved what he had wanted—to be a corrections officer—I called the sheriff's department where he worked. A man with a Northeast accent reminded me of my old partners—deep voice, no-nonsense tone, heavy breath. I smiled, missing their crass humor, sensible approach to civilian outbursts, and ability to make quick assessments in dangerous circumstances. "George Marin, please."

"He's not in today. Would you like to leave a message?"

"Yes, please. Tell him Julia Torres called. I'll give you my number."

"Hold on." I heard the shuffling of paper. "Okay."

The next morning around ten o'clock, the phone on my nightstand rang just after a raccoon in the backyard had led me to close my sliding glass bedroom door. It must've been rabid, I'd thought; they didn't normally come out in broad daylight. "Hello?"

"Jewels, you're a witch."

I'd have recognized his gruff voice anywhere. I laughed, pushing aside the netting from my four-poster French bed, and sat down. "Why?"

"I was just thinking about you and wondering where you were and I said, 'Man, knowing Jewels, she could be anywhere.' I just walked in the office, and my sergeant said I had a message on my desk. It was you. I couldn't believe it. I laughed out loud. It had a 561 area code. That's Florida, right?"

"Yeah, I moved to West Palm a few months ago."

He chuckled. "You never did stay still."

"You know me."

"Yeah, I do. So what's up, Jewels?" The screech of a chair let me know he'd sat.

"I'll be flying to Jersey at the end of October, and I'd love to see you."

"Okay. Take my cell. Call me when you're in town."

I wrote the number on a piece of paper. "Got it. See you

then."

"Jewels, it was great to hear your voice." I could sense his smile on the other end.

"Yours, too." I hung up, visions flashing slowly in the distance, a carousel of pleasant memories, musical voices, shrieks, laughter; and the course of events leading to its end, moving up and down, suspended at times, turning my stomach into knots while I waited for the final drop. Finally, I could provide him with the explanation he deserved.

That Fall, a couple of days after landing in Newark, I called him. The beloved familiar trumps guesswork, and old habits emerge at the sound of a voice. "Hey, it's me. You busy?"

"No. When'd you get in?" he asked.

"Two days ago. Can we meet tomorrow?"

"Sure. Where?"

"Well, I'll be in Union City, if you don't mind picking me up. How 'bout Baja's?"

"In Hoboken?"

"Yeah." After agreeing on a time and place, we hung up.

AT FIVE O'CLOCK, I WAS STANDING by the glass doors inside a friend's business when a Ford F150 pulled up horizontally behind other cars in the lot I was facing. The driver turned to look in my direction, and then waved. It was George.

I raised an arm, waving in exaggerated glee, shouting as if he'd hear me, and opened the door.

He climbed out, shaking his head, laughing.

Before I knew it, he stood facing me in jeans, a t-shirt and sneakers, same amazing smile. For a few seconds, we grinned broadly, then hugged, arms lingering around each other. The comfort of the known, a hold that still contained love, an expression that in the silence spoke—at long last I felt it and knew he had also.

We separated at the same time. He smiled. "Ready?"

"Yup."

He opened the door for me.

As he was walking around the front of the vehicle, he suddenly stopped. Smile faded, jaw tense, he pointed at me, put his fists together, indicated a breaking motion, and signaled to his heart. The message had been clear: You broke my heart. I felt like a total deadbeat, but how do you turn back time?

The inexperience of youth has a tendency to spread—traumatic incidents that principally affect us kick up dust from the ground that lands on others. He grinned and entered the car. Once inside, he looked over at me, saying what had been on his mind all those years. "You left me for Elvis Presley."

His hurt was obvious still. I widened my eyes to prevent tears from spilling. "No. I didn't," I said slowly, softly.

"Yeah, well." He shrugged, and we drove away.

"You look great," I offered, trying to alter the disheartening mood.

"No, Jewels. I'm old. *You* look great!"

I laughed, "Stop. You're just a year older."

"You know, on the way here, I asked myself how you'd look. I remember your mom was a little chubby, and I wondered if you were, too. Then I said, 'No way, not Jewels. She always took care of herself.'"

"Thank you. I try." I looked down at the fitted denim

jumpsuit I was wearing. Despite my physical challenges, I made efforts to stay in shape.

We parked outside Baja's and got a corner table in the front, away from the bar. It was noisy, packed. Friday Happy Hours often were. He leaned across the table. "Jewels, it's great to see you."

"You too, George. It feels just like yesterday."

"Yeah, but that's us. I'm not surprised."

A waitress came over with chips, salsa, and menus, and took our drink order, ready to leave speedily for the next table. "Hold on," I said. "I'd rather order now. I know what I want."

We placed our orders before she hastened away.

George lowered his voice. "By the way, Jewels, I saw your brother in county. I kept an eye on him before he went to Northern State."

"I heard. Thank you."

"Did he do all right over there?" he asked, concerned.

"Yeah, he did. He was spoiled. You know Mom."

He nodded, adding, "You know, I was walking around the cell block and did a double-take when I saw him. I called him out and took him in a private room, you know, so the inmates wouldn't know."

"I understand."

"And I said, 'Coñó, Frank, what the hell you doing here?' I asked him about you, your mom."

I nodded. "He told Mom about you in one of her visits. She was really happy you were there. . . . So tell me about you."

"Well, kiddo, what can I tell you? I'm married, have two

girls, two and four, and, you know where I work. How 'bout you?"

"Divorced, one daughter, three, retired with MS."

"You all right?"

"Yeah, I'm fine. God doesn't allow anything I can't handle. It was compliments of Uncle Sam, by the way."

He nodded. "Jewels, I almost got deployed. We were ready to go and then they called it off."

"Good. . . . I'm glad you got your girls—that's what you always wanted. I still remember that little girl who lived beneath your mom's apartment. You loved her."

He smiled, "You remembered. Yeah, Marilyn. She was so cute. She's in her twenties now."

"Wow, time sure does fly."

"Yeah, it does. Who would've thought, me and you here, having dinner at a Mexican place, just like—"

"Caramba's," I interrupted. "I haven't forgotten."

He smiled. "You know, Jewels, you and my best friend's wife are the only two women I've ever opened up to."

Drinks—tequila sunrise, and beer—and a combination platter of wings, potato skins, and *taquitos* arrived. We dug in, more with eagerness than hunger. "Sammy, right?"

"Yeah. He still jokes about that night we picked you and Marissa up. I said to him, 'I don't care if she's wearing a leather skirt, I'm not giving in.' He said, 'Yeah right, George.' And then the two of you walk out of her house to get in the car, and I said, 'Oh, shit, that bitch!' and he just cracked up. He knew I was done."

I laughed. "Yeah, I remember that night. You were trying to be a big shot, like you didn't care if I was giving you attitude. But, that night was great. George, we could always talk about anything."

"Yeah, we still can."

While we were recounting great memories, most of which he recalled in minute detail, our waitress arrived, entrees in hand: yellow rice, chicken, *pico de gallo*, and guacamole on the side. "No, Jewels, you're wrong. It was in Atlantic City, for my twenty-first birthday." He turned to the twenty-something girl who was serving us. "She wants to argue with me about the first time we made love."

I chuckled at his brazenness, something I always loved. The girl blushed. "Oh," she managed to say as she removed the small empty plates from our table.

"It's okay." I said to her. "We go way back."

"Yeah, high school," added George.

She looked relieved. "Oh, how cool, you're still together."

"No, she lives in Florida. I'm married, and my wife doesn't know I'm here."

She looked displeased by his last remark.

"We just met for dinner," I said.

"Waitress!" A person at a table on the far right yelled over the clanging of dishes and the shattering of a glass onto the floor. It was the perfect excuse for her to leave.

"You made her very uncomfortable," I said, chuckling.

He shrugged. Through bites of chicken and sips of drinks, we were back in time, together again; it was magnificent. The air was imbued with the love we had shared, reminding us it still remained. But along with that was the mature knowledge that, as much as we wanted to, we could not turn back the clock.

"Jewels, tell your mom I'm sorry. I didn't mean to rush out of her house, pissed."

I tilted my head. "What are you talking about?"

He began to explain what had happened the ill-fated summer day in 1987 when he went to see Mom.

The bell had rung that Saturday afternoon when Mom finished cleaning, mop drying in a bucket on an empty corner in the outside hallway. She'd glanced down the corridor, beaming at the sight of George standing behind the glass-and-wooden door, ready to be buzzed in.

Rushing to greet him, she had grabbed the old doorknob and pulled open the heavy door, elated. "*Mi niño!*"

But George had not been his usual chipper self. Mom stopped short, knowing not to ask questions. Instead she said, "Come in."

Behind her, heavy footsteps echoed.

"Sit down. Do you want espresso?"

"No, Daisy. Thank you." He'd sat at the kitchen table with a pained expression in his eyes. He had caught the lingering smells of freshly mopped floors and air freshener, which would have appealed to many, but not to George, whose heart was heavy.

Mom had sat across from him, waiting.

Finally, he'd said, "Daisy, I heard Julia's getting married. Is it true?"

It had broken Mom's heart to see his turmoil, deeply hurt but with a determination to know the truth. She wouldn't have lied, yet she knew it'd cause him pain. "Oh, George," she had begun, using her hands as she spoke, "you know how Julia is. That's just a crazy idea of hers. You know she always gets them."

Silence. Then he had asked, "What's this guy look like?"

"Like Elvis Presley.... Just forget it. She will." She had seen his reluctance, heard his stillness; fearing he wouldn't take her advice, she had tried again. "Don't worry about it. Let time pass. You'll see, it'll all be over before you know it."

Having heard the news he didn't want to hear, George's dignity had asserted itself. He'd stood up quickly, chair screeching on the floor. "No, Daisy. I can't forget it." He had stormed out of the house.

Mom had been upset.

It made sense; that must've been the day she asked me why I had hurt him. "She never told me," I offered.

"She probably didn't think it'd make a difference. Julia was just being Julia."

"What's that supposed to mean?"

"You were just being yourself. When you said you were gonna do something, you did it. I always admired that about you."

"You should've come after me."

"No, Jewels. You left me, remember?"

"George, that's your pride talking. You should've asked me what was going on. I wouldn't have been able to lie to you. You would've seen through it.... But maybe it's just as well."

"What do you mean?"

"I probably would've said some awful things to make you leave me anyway. I wasn't right, George." The chicken had lost its flavor.

"I wasn't right either, Jewels. It wasn't easy for me." The hurt in his eyes was clear, and then came the anger. "I should've kicked his ass."

"It wasn't his fault. He had nothing to do with it." A few years later on Facebook, I reached out to Dakota, apologizing and explaining my behavior, but he never replied.

"What do you mean?"

"I asked *him* to marry *me*. I wasn't gonna do it. I just needed to find a way to break up with you without having to face you."

"So you played with his feelings, too."

"I didn't play with anybody, George."

Lines formed on the bridge of his nose, his mouth tightened. "But why split us up? We got along great."

"I wasn't ready to get married. You asked me to be the mother of your children."

He shook his head, frustrated. "Jewels, I didn't mean get married right away."

"But you got married at twenty-three. That would've made me twenty-two—it was too young. I had a life to live. A marriage would've held me back. My focus would've been primarily on you as my husband, like it's supposed to be."

"That's right," he snapped. "So you lived your life."

"You did, too."

"No, Jewels. I just lived." There was a long pause before he added, "You went through all that trouble to break up with me, when all you had to do was tell me how you felt." He shook his head.

He wasn't getting it because I had been omitting a huge chunk, simply scratching the surface, but that restaurant wasn't the right place to talk. "I'm sorry, George. Really sorry. We would've been great together."

"I always told you that. Me and you, Jewels." He let out a

breath. "We would've been great. You taught me how to love."

I had my hand around my drink, was about to lift it. I stared at him. What he'd said was profound: I had taught him something I hadn't thought myself capable of. Rather than being upset with me, he was being forgiving—a portrayal of the depth of his love. I almost cried. "George, can we leave and go for a walk?"

After settling the bill, we crossed Washington Avenue, strolling along River Street. "Some Hoboken, huh?" I asked.

"Yeah. It's incredible."

"Remember when the viaduct was all broken down? Me, Marissa, and Lola would walk across it after school, stepping over small cracks, jumping over big ones, and look at it now. In college, I read an essay on gentrification in Hoboken. I felt good and bad about it at the same time."

A young professional with a Louis Vuitton backpack came by pushing a blue-and-white Peg Perego stroller in the opposite direction. We moved to the side, and I resumed, "The streets look great, sidewalk restaurants are awesome, but the rents are so high that it pushes out the original residents. Where do they go after thirty or forty years, you know? It's sad. It's cool that it looks like a mini Village, but it's mostly yuppies now. That's not Hoboken."

"I agree, Jewels. Remember how many fights there used to be here, and after the football games, too?"

"I remember. We couldn't cheer the entire game; we had to board the buses before the fourth quarter ended. The coach was always concerned one of us would get caught in a scuffle."

"Yeah. That's right."

"Can we sit?" I asked, spotting a bench in the park across the street.

"Sure." A car honked as we were about to step off the curb.

There, on the black metal bench, joggers on the street, teenagers striding along, I told him everything. He was quiet but attentive. The hurt I saw pained me; his anguish was heartfelt, intense, as he'd always been. To make matters worse, his deep brown eyes changed, crumpled, as sequences played out in his film reel, vivid scenes of atrocious events, unimaginable, unexpected. It unnerved him.

It was heartbreaking to sense his sorrow, to feel the controlled emotion in his fixed stare. As he listened, I almost lost control of the tears that had welled up in my eyes, for him, for me, for the us we had lost. Discreetly, I widened them, understanding very well that, once a teardrop fell, they'd all come running. If he saw me cry, it'd break his heart. I could not bear to do that to him again.

Once done, I sighed and read him. My behavior had finally made sense. I asked, "What would you have done if I'd told you back then?"

He just shook his head. "I don't know, Jewels. I don't know."

We strolled back to the car, arms interlocked. I suppose both of us needed that comfort. The night was cool, refreshing; I rolled down the window, allowing the breeze to carry off tattered thoughts.

The radio was low, and I turned it up when I heard '80s music. "Wow!" I exclaimed. "Mighty Real. I saw Sylvester live in Studio. He was great, man. We had the best music. I know every generation says that, but we really did."

He glanced at me and smiled. "We did, Jewels."

George dropped me off at a friend's house that night; he stepped out of the truck and opened my door.

When I stood before him, I searched his eyes. "What, George?"

"I'm sorry."

"Me, too."

"Don't think about Judas anymore. He's a loser. Look at how much you've done. You can do anything."

I shook my head.

"I wish I could be cruel, Jewels. . .but I can't live without my girls."

"I would never ask you to do that. You love your daughters. I love mine, too, and I love God. I know how much you wanted to have girls—I have one, too. It'd be like I was doing it to her, also. I wouldn't hurt any of them. You're a great man, George."

"No, Jewels, don't say that. I'm just a man. Will you do something for me?"

"Of course."

"If you get married again, will you let me know before you do?"

"I will."

"Jewels, I care about my wife, she's the mother of my children, but. . . ."

I knew what would follow was something I'd need to absorb more than everything else. "Yes?"

"I will love you 'til death." He leaned over and enveloped me in his arms.

22

In My Father's House

BACK IN WEST PALM, I changed into a bikini, grabbed the portable telephone and refreshments for each of us, and entered the Jacuzzi in the covered patio section. Starting the jets but not the warm temperature, I relaxed in cool water, watching Nina grab plastic tea cups from a table through the curtained windows of her doll house.

Within the hour, the phone rang. "Hello?"

"Aurorita, your sister—" Mom broke down crying.

I turned off the jets, waiting for the ebb and flow of her sobs to diminish the rumbling sorrow. Modern technology is too precise for pain.

When she paused, I asked, "What's going on?"

"They diagnosed her with brain cancer," she exclaimed. Howls followed.

". . .Ma, where are you?"

Her screeching at last controlled, she said, "At work."

"Why don't you have someone drive you home?"

"No, Aurorita. I need to stay here. I have to be distracted. I just called to tell you."

I glanced up at the clear blue sky. Was the sun blaspheming life or bestowing grace? "Where's Marlene now?"

"Home with her husband."

"How's she taking it?"

"She's okay. She has faith in God."

"Ma, I'm gonna get ready and go over there with Nina. We'll spend the night. Make sure you can drive. If not, call me."

NINA MOVED HER FEET to harmonized toddler music as she looked out the window at the cars and stores on Military Trail on the way to her aunt's condo. In my air-conditioned BMW 328i, I considered my sister's initial diagnosis four years before, when she called me with the dreadful news. "Julia, I went to see the doctor about the lump I found on my breast. He said I have stage two cancer."

"What can be done?" Tears had started rolling down my face, but I'd had to remain strong for her.

"Chemo."

"How 'bout a mastectomy? It's not a vital organ, Marlene. Get rid of both and get a bigger size," I'd said.

"No. He said I'll still be in the same boat either way. I got a second opinion."

On that car ride, I concluded that my sister's illness had been the reason for my early retirement. It all made sense.

The breast cancer my sister had been diagnosed with in

February 1997 had never gone into remission, though she'd fervently exposed herself to chemotherapy, radiation, and surgery. What had looked like a pimple in January 1998 had led to the diagnosis of cancer on the right side of her forehead. From there, the summer of 1999 had brought with it cancer in the femur and, in the spring of 2000, in the neck.

With every incision, Marlene had lost some quality of life—cognition, speech, rational thought—but it had not stopped her from believing God would heal her. However, as her family, seeing her condition worsen, we hadn't been as confident.

Throughout the years, Marlene had much support of family, friends, and church members. In her home, she had her husband and Caridad, a live-in nurse. On Saturday mornings, when Marlene's home care left, Mom would go to her house to resume as caregiver until the nurse returned on Sunday.

Though I was discovering the challenges of being a single parent with MS, I'd put my needs on the back burner and focused on providing assistance to my family. Marlene's cancer wasn't getting any better and, after hearing dire news from her doctor, I felt she'd want to know her prognosis, but Mom and Frank didn't want to be the ones to tell her the truth.

It wasn't until a small group Bible study lesson concluded one afternoon that Cindy, one of the women, hugged me. That was when I found the strength to speak with Marlene.

Cindy's warm embrace brought me to tears. The women stopped gathering their items to leave. "Something told me, 'Go hug Julia,'" Cindy explained.

"Sit down, Julia," said Tara, her big blue eyes full of concern. "You can't leave here like this. What's going on?"

"My sister's gonna die, and nobody wants to tell her," I blurted, relieved.

"Will *you*?"

"Yes. She'd want to know."

"Okay. Tell her when you get home. We'll be praying for you." She glanced at the three women by her side.

"Go in peace. God will help you find the words," one said.

I drove from Boynton Beach with confidence, knowing my sisters in Christ were interceding for me. At Marlene's, I tapped on the door and was met by Caridad. "Is Marlene awake?"

"Yes. She's in the living room, watching television."

She was on her favorite recliner, upholstered with a fabric of tropical birds, cup of water on her right. I paused to look at her: wisps of hair here and there, full pink cherub cheeks, prescription glasses over big brown eyes.

"Hey, Marlene," I said cheerfully. "You look like an angel."

She looked over and smiled. Her eyes lit up, one more than the other. The brain tumor had compressed an eye, causing it to open only slightly.

"I just left Bible study. There was this song I never heard of. It was beautiful. Can I sing it to you?"

She nodded, not caring that I couldn't sing. Though she was unable to speak aside from a yes or no now and then, her facial expressions spoke a thousand words.

"Isn't it awesome?" I asked when I was done.

"Yeah, yeah." Her right index finger went up, making her point.

"I knew you'd like it. It's called 'This Is The Air I

Breathe.'"

Knowing the women were praying that very moment made the difficult subject less sore. "Is Annette coming today?" I asked.

"No." Annette was a hospice nurse. She admired my sister's faith in God and her not succumbing to adopting a poor spirit.

The family had been provided a booklet detailing the dying process of a cancer patient. One of the points made was the common reluctance of the patient to let go, possibly out of concern for others. It suggested that someone speak with them to release them, relaying news that the family would be fine.

And so I began to speak of an obscene topic in soft speech and tender words. "Marlene, I went to see Doctor Farkas in his office the other day."

Her brows rose.

"Do you want me to tell you what we talked about?"
She nodded.

"Okay. I asked him how your condition was." I spoke slowly, pausing between my sentences, checking her reactions. "He said it was not going to improve."

Expectant, waiting for information, her puppy dog eyes softened.

"Remember when he said that your quality of life decreased after every operation?"

Indeed, it had been unbearable to watch. Its effects varied. Some, including Mom and Frank, became tight-lipped, carrying with them an air of purposeful ignorance, not acknowledging her reduced state. The ever-faithful prayed, hoping for a miracle, trying not to see with their human eyes what they'd perceive as demise. Others were forthright, firmly committing not to visit, expressing the impact of seeing her decline. That attitude was hardest for Mom to comprehend, though I explained that not everyone's coping mechanism allowed them to endure the grossly evident process of dying.

I'd told Marlene how I felt, impotent at being unable to do anything for her. Despite the fact that we hadn't always gotten along, I'd declared that we were supposed to grow old together, and it wasn't right that we wouldn't. She'd replied with a simple okay, one that although I'd said it was not, I'd had no choice but to accept.

She nodded once more.

"He reminded me of it again." Seated behind his grand mahogany desk, medical books on the shelves behind him, the wise brain surgeon, white coat over shirt and tie, had spoken with ease. In that warm office, the desk full of files and reports, sunlight muted by the extra-protection windows, what some might have considered as callous and cruel was nothing more than a timid humility called forth by the woes of life, and necessary for survival.

I leaned towards her, adding, "Don't worry about us. Mom will be fine. She has lots of people here that love her."

Her eyes digested my words.

"And Frank always lands on his feet. He yells, but that's just to scare people," I chuckled.

So did she.

"You know me and Nina are moving back to Jersey this summer, so she can do kindergarten up there, but we'll be back." She knew I wouldn't leave Mom alone.

"Marlene, Oscar will be all right. Eventually, he'll remarry because that's part of life, and that's what you'd want anyway."

The faint smile on her lips was bittersweet. She knew. Letting go *was* the toughest thing to do.

With great love, I went on, "This is no way to live. You've always been so vibrant, looking to do something or go somewhere." Memories of fun, crazy times spent together flashed through my mind. "We love you. You'll always be in our hearts and minds."

Though she made no sound, she nodded, seeming at peace that someone had taken the time to speak with her candidly.

Thankful that that moment had been prayed over, I leaned over and kissed my sister's forehead. She wrapped her arms around me, and we hugged with the calm resignation that our lives together would soon come to an end.

That July 2003, after my house was sold, we returned to Jersey and moved to Lodi, where Nina began kindergarten.

ON OCTOBER 14, MOM CALLED.

"Aurorita?" Her tone was low, heavy.

"What's wrong, Ma?"

"I'm on the train to Miami. Marlene is *malita*." If Mom said she was not well, it meant she was grave, but Mom wouldn't say that my sister had developed a fever, complicating her illness further.

"You going to the Leon's house?" I asked. Oscar and Marlene had moved into his parents' four-bedroom home in Miami when her condition worsened.

"Yes."

"Is the nurse there?"

"Yes." Mom's normally strong voice had become a whimper.

"I'll call her."

I did.

"It's Julia, Marlene's sister. What's going on?" I asked the hospice nurse.

She replied, "If you want to see your sister alive, you should come here immediately."

I hung up and called Frank. "It's time," I said.

He knew what that meant.

"I'll call the airlines. You call Tio. I'll meet you at his place with Nina, and we'll go to the airport from there."

The irony of life: It was the first time the four of us had ever been on a plane together. We toil, living separate from loved ones, gathering at weddings and funerals, making well-intentioned promises to get together more often, only to find ourselves in the same state years later.

Past a sleeping Nina, staring out the rectangular window, the giant cotton balls in the sky lost their childlike appeal; the brightness of the sun had vanished. We were descending into a pivotal moment; our immediate family would soon learn how the death of a sibling affected it.

We headed to Miami in silent dread. Hospice nurses had been working around the clock, and the morphine dripped. What was normally a pleasant visit with bountiful Cuban food, a light ambience, and stories to share had become a wasteland.

Trepidation increased with every step we took until we entered the bedroom where Marlene lay on her hospital bed. The odor wasn't as bad as what it represented.

Mom rose to greet us from the chair at Marlene's bedside. My sister looked up, knowing our presence meant something was amiss. We took turns kissing her and remained standing around the bed. She gazed at us individually, smiling, her eyes lingering.

I said, "We weren't that bad, huh?"

She shook her head.

"Look, Marlene," said Frank, who pointed at the baseball cap on his head. It read *Union City*. "Five-finger discount."

She smiled, realizing it probably had been.

It was time for her to rest, so we returned to the living room, where Oscar's mom assigned rooms for all of us. We settled in for the night, mentally exhausted, welcoming sleep.

The next morning, Eddie, Frank's childhood friend whom we considered family, arrived, followed by Tio Miguelito, Abuelo Celio's son from his second marriage. Waiting for someone to die is horrid; every day is marked by edginess, the wonder of when it will be, how it will happen, and the hope to be present when it does.

No grave change occurred for three days. The family was seated in the living room, listening to the news on the television, sound low. Tio and Frank were on recliners, Eddie and Miguel on a sofa, and I was sitting next to Nina on a kitchen stool. She was having a ham-and-cheese sandwich, juice on one side, Jell-O on the other.

While Marlene slept, her in-laws napped in a neighboring room, and Mom rested in the bedroom closest to my sister. When she was asleep, the hospice nurse would sometimes go to the kitchen and have an espresso, a conversation, or both.

Mercy was on duty that night. She poured some coffee

into a demitasse cup and had gone to sit in the dining room when Tio said, "I have to go back to work soon."

"Me, too," said Eddie. "I'm actually leaving in a couple of days. It was the only time I could take off from work."

"I understand," added Frank. "I have a business, too."

Miguel shrugged. "Me too, but luckily I have an employee that I left in charge."

"*Sobrina*—" Tio indirectly hinted at what everyone wanted to know but didn't want to ask. The nurse had said Marlene's death was imminent, and now the question remained.

I said, "I'll go ask."

Past the refrigerator with doctor's appointments clipped onto magnets and a pot full of black beans on the stove, I approached the nurse, who was seated at the head of the table. "Mercy?"

The familiar scent of Bustelo was pleasing, but not what I was about to say. "We, uh, we were told to hurry here. The men have to return to their businesses. I don't mean to be uncaring, but do you have any idea when it'll happen?"

Every word I had uttered seemed sinister.

Her face softened. "I understand. It'll happen this weekend." I relayed the information.

On October 18, 2003, I entered the Leons' house with a cake I'd bought for Marlene's fortieth birthday, which would be November 30. The men were enjoying a personal break, watching the Marlins playing the Yankees; it was the first time Florida would win a World Series.

I placed the 4 and 0 candles near the words *Happy Birthday Marlene*, and asked Mom to tell her we had a surprise. She returned, wheeling Marlene, and stopped beside the kitchen table.

Moments later, all of us surrounded my sister, lit candles glowing, clapping while singing her the birthday song, love in our eyes. Mom and I helped her blow out the candles, and we were all delighted when she ate a small piece.

The irony of forty was that, years earlier, Marlene had told Oscar that she felt she wouldn't live to see her fortieth birthday. I wondered if she had recalled her words then.

That night, and the next, moved along.

On October 20, 2003, at about 2:30 a.m., Mom woke me. "Go calm your sister. She's struggling in her sleep." The midnight shift nurse hadn't shown up, and we were taking turns watching her. Luckily, Caridad, Marlene's live-in nurse, had come to stay with us two days before. Her shift was after mine, which began when Mom's ended.

When I entered her room, the hospice booklet information about a patient's struggle before death came to mind. Marlene was groaning in pain.

I neared the bed, whispering, encouraging her. ". . . Marlene, don't struggle. People wanna go where you're going. You made it."

Her eyes were closed, her moans decreasing.

I continued, "There's nothing for you here. . . . You're more there than here. Remember Jesus' promise in the Bible, He's preparing a room for you in His Father's house. You may be decorating in heaven." I smiled. My sister had loved designing homes.

"Speak to God through your mind. Ask Him to forgive you, even for the things you can't recall. Tell Him you're committing your spirit to Him."

"Yes, yes," she repeated.

"Don't be afraid. Jesus will be with you. You'll see Abuela up there. Tell her I said hello. Marlene, we all love you." Her breathing had calmed; her moans had ceased. Then, she fell asleep.

Later that morning, Mom, Tio, Frank, and I were in the room with Marlene; her in-laws were near the kitchen; Eddie had accompanied Oscar to get something to eat for his mom. Mom was speaking softly to Marlene, Frank was seated quietly to Mom's right, and Tio, magazine on his lap, turned pages mindlessly as he sat on a chair at the foot of the bed. I frothed my sister's left leg with lotion.

Mom asked, "Aurorita, do you remember that church song about the fish in the sea?"

Looking up and over, I answered, "Yes."

"That was Frank's favorite," she said, and glanced at him. "Right?"

He nodded.

"Can you sing it?" asked Mom.

I did, and she joined in for a few verses. Afterward, I stopped and hummed while Mom spoke softly to Marlene. It was a tender family moment.

Suddenly, I looked over and saw tears in Frank's eyes. He whispered something unintelligible.

"What did you say?" I asked, leaning towards him.

Slowly, he repeated the words I had missed. "She died. A tear drop fell from her one eye."

I gazed up to heaven, and said, "Thank you, Jesus." It had been a blessing that we had been present with Marlene at the end of her life, just as we had been since the beginning.

There was a sudden shift in the atmosphere; the air was lighter; troubled hearts were lifted. After dabbing lotion on my sister's other leg, I went to the living room to speak with Nina, who'd been watching cartoons, eyes bright, sweet smile on her lips. "Nina, honey?"

She looked over, expectant.

"Tia Marlene went to be with Jesus." We had spoken about her sickness. She knew her aunt would be fine when she was in heaven.

Nina asked, "Can I say good-bye?"

"Sure," I said. That question would've melted an ogre's heart, what followed driven him to tears.

Nina rose, walking bravely down the long hallway to the bedroom. She paused at the entrance, peeked in, head full of bouncy curls, and waved her hand. "Bye." And as easy as that, she went back to her television program. There was much to learn from Nina at that moment; her resilience is something adults don't often give children credit for having.

Things moved quickly from there; Marlene's wishes had been known. We notified close family and friends to attend a small burial on October 23, 2003. Her suffering had ended, and she was living with Jesus in a new healthy spirit.

A few days later, Frank, Nina, and I flew back to Jersey; Tio and Miguelito remained another week with Mom. The twisted cruelty of death is the common knowledge that life goes on. Those left behind pick up the pieces day by day; for some, it is harder than others. Without a doubt, Mom would have traded places with Marlene.

23

Redeemed

NINA HAD HAD HER HEAD START IN KINDERGARTEN, completing it by New Jersey's school age deadlines, not Florida's. It was the reason we had moved back home, but my sister's death returned us to West Palm Beach, where we stayed for the next five years to be near Mom.

Life in Florida consisted of raising my daughter to be a well-rounded woman. She was accepted in the gifted program at school, took swimming and piano lessons, and went to church with me on Sundays.

Aside from the challenges of being a single parent and starting my Avonex treatment for MS, I shopped and worked out to de-stress. Wanting to share my prior training and experience with others, while Nina was in school, I volunteered at the courthouse and a local police department to help victims of crimes.

It wasn't until I saw an article in the newspaper for an audition with a theatre group that I was able to develop the passion for acting I'd always had but never had the time for. Being on stage was similar to doing undercover work—you had to pretend to be somebody else, think quick on your feet, save the others working with you—I loved it. Nina enjoyed it as well, often going backstage during shows, meeting my fellow thespians, and learning the inner workings of an actor's life.

Between shows, I'd drive her to Miami Beach to visit with her dad, just as I'd done during her pre-school years. For her sake, I overlooked the fact that he wouldn't come up on the train, or that he'd only visit if someone drove him or loaned him a vehicle. It was more important for me that she knew her dad was present, and that, in the future, she'd know I had not hindered her relationship with him.

During those visits, I sometimes noticed a change in his behavior. He appeared to have become less self-absorbed and arrogant. But, other times, I wasn't so sure.

However, since retiring had afforded me the opportunity to think in retrospect, I'd become more sensitive to situations and people around me. Although I knew that our marriage had had to end due to its volatility, we had never discussed its failure, and I wanted a clean slate.

In one of his rare visits, while Nina took a nap, I looked at him across the dining room table and asked, "Can we talk?"

"About what?"

"Why our marriage ended."

He grinned. "Julia, the way I came here, it was so unreal. I can't believe it had to end the way it did."

"Yeah, it had an incredible beginning. I'm sorry it didn't

work out, but you left me no choice, Narciso."

"I'm sorry, too, Julia. I never meant to hurt you. I know I was violent. I can't deny it. I wish I hadn't been. There were too many changes too soon. Coming *here* from Cuba, leaving my family and everything I'd known. You know, the U.S. is the ultimate, and you had to teach me everything—I couldn't even set the alarm right."

"Yeah, I remember, but that was a given. You just had to learn it, that's all."

"It was hard, Julia. It's easy for you. You grew up here. I know you said it'd take about five years to adjust, but it was still difficult. And your job wasn't easy for me either."

"But you knew that's what I did, and it helped get you here."

"I know, but knowing it and living it are two different things. You didn't talk to me about it. You'd say, 'If you see me on the street holding hands with someone, don't flip out. I'm working this case where I'm married.'"

"I *was*."

"Yeah, but that's hard to accept."

"That's why I told you beforehand."

"Still, then we had to be careful where we went. Remember that night when we had just sat down to eat, and you said, 'Let's go. Somebody's here'?"

"Yeah, we had Nina with us. Narciso, I told you I did undercover. If a target happened to show up where I was, the last thing I'd want for him to know was that I had a family."

"I know all that now, Julia, but at that time it was all new to me."

"Exactly why I couldn't tell you about my cases. It was

better that way. You didn't understand how I liked what I did, and you definitely wouldn't have understood the details either. You always said being a cop wasn't for women, that you couldn't respect women who did it. You told Mimi, 'If the woman has a vagina, she can't be a cop.'"

"It was too much of an adjustment. Something was bound to happen."

"But not violence. I know what you're trying to say, but your reasons don't justify what you did in any way. There is *never* an excuse for abuse."

"I'm not using them as excuses, Julia. I'm just explaining what I was feeling."

"I understand, but it doesn't come across that way."

"I'm sorry for what I did."

"I'm sorry too, and I forgive you, even though it's not innate in human nature to forgive someone who's harmed you. But I want you to forgive me, too—for not being the kind of woman you expected me to be. You had your views, and I had mine."

"I forgive you, Julia. You weren't easy. The army and your job made you tougher. It's not like I had an ordinary wife. You were tough."

"You keep saying that. I'm not *that* tough, Narciso."

"Not since you've retired. You're tamer. If we would've met now, maybe it would've worked out. It's that environment you were in."

"I'm calmer, not tamer. You speak as if I was an animal. It's okay, though. I'm just glad we're talking again for Nina's sake."

"Yes, me, too."

Later, when Nina was in second grade, we attempted to be

a family again. Perhaps he'd learned good work ethic after five years, and better yet, I thought, maybe he'd assume his role as dad in a loving and responsible manner. I gave him the benefit of the doubt, considering that perhaps time had been the best healer, and that the memory of our domestic violence incidents was erased, but the events hadn't faded.

Though he had been non-violent, the slightest rise in his tone for any reason, or change of gesture, would cause a tightness in my stomach, leading me to hold my breath and shift my eyes. At times, I wondered if he was reading lines from a script, telling me things he'd think I'd want to hear. His words had a falsehood to them, his demeanor hidden, manipulative, his personality a Jekyll and Hyde.

Moreover, Narciso's ability to provide basic needs of love and safety, including financial security as a parent and mate, were highly deficient, if not, non-existent. I was, and am, unable to love or respect a man who is not a caring father, a responsible worker, or a loving partner.

Narciso's past behavior had left deep traces in my subconscious. Indeed, much as with a broken glass that one attempts to piece together, the residual effects of violence seep through the cracks at unexpected moments.

Nina and I moved on without him and planned to remain in Florida until the end of her fifth grade, when we'd decide where to relocate. Due to my MS, the heat and humidity were having adverse effects on my health, and we spoke of moving to a better climate.

LITTLE DID WE KNOW HOW OR WHERE God was guiding us. As a result of my adventures onstage, Nina had acquired an interest in the performing arts and had begun taking acting classes. By the time she had entered fifth grade, it had become her career choice. Los Angeles had been the place she'd yearned to visit after fourth grade, and we were going there for Easter.

About a week before boarding a plane, while having Swedish meatballs and pasta at the dining room table, I asked, "Do you wanna move to Jersey or California?"

"Well," she began, pausing to swallow, "we've already lived in Jersey, and we're gonna be there for high school. Let's go to Cali."

"All right. I'm gonna pray about it and ask God to open the way for us on this trip if that's where He wants us to go."

Things moved along on their own in LA that week: We found Millikan Middle School, Performing Arts Magnet and Science Academy, and inquired into housing. The PA program was very competitive, having in it professional child actors, and as such the audition process was grueling. We concluded that Nina's acceptance into Millikan would be the deal breaker.

Once home, my friend and Nina's drama coach, Sara Premisler, helped her compile an acting, singing, and dancing audition on a CD, and mailed it before the deadline. Soon enough, we heard great news: Six hundred hopefuls were on the PA waiting list, but Nina had been accepted.

That August, we left our furniture with my good friend Floyd Hood, packed our car with clothes, and drove west.

The plans we make, and the life that happens, are sometimes polar opposites that never cease to amaze me. After a spring audition in Studio City, hopeful actors listened as director-producer and casting director James Quattrochi said, "The movie *Donnie Brasco* was based on an FBI investigation."

He had my attention when he mentioned the movie, whose story had absorbed me but whose book had enthralled me. Thinking back to my deep cover job at the Wake-Up Café, though it was no comparison, when questions were being taken, I raised my hand. "Would you be interested in undercover stories from the Northeast?"

James tilted his head. "Would that be you?"

"Yes."

"See me when we're done."

As fellow thespians left, he extended his hand. "Hi. Call me Jamie."

"Okay. Julia Torres."

"What have you got?" His candid style reflected the New Yorker he'd been.

"I was an undercover cop in Jersey for over ten years. I did a deep cover job for about nine months."

"Okay. Here's my personal email. Send me a synopsis."

I went home that night and did as he asked.

A few days later, I got a call. "Julia, it's Jamie. I *love* it. I wanna know your whole life."

"From what age?" I asked.

"Since you were born."

That threw me off. There were two major issues I'd never told Nina about: my rape, and the domestic violence. "Can you give me a few days? I've got a couple of things to think about."

I dialed Mimi, who'd been my police mentor, and asked her opinion. "I think revealing your rape and domestic violence will bring Nina more good than harm. She'll be able to make wiser choices with friends and men. In the end, it'll be a learning experience. *Mamita*, you're gonna be the voice for a lot of women. It's all gonna be good."

Afterward, I called Narciso to explain that I'd be disclosing our DV incidents. "I can't deny what happened, Julia. I've paid for it. I just ask that the two of us be present to tell Nina."

"Of course. I was planning to do that this summer in Florida."

Once their remarks were gathered, I went into the living room to speak with Nina with the understanding that I couldn't begin writing about my rape without telling her. It'd feel like a betrayal on my part.

My precious child was drawing on a sketch pad when I crept forward, trepidation in each step, edginess in my stomach. "Nina?"

"Yes, Mom?" Her lustrous eyes, untainted, wholesome, met mine.

"I'd like to share something with you, but I don't want you to lose respect for me when I tell you."

She put her pencil down. "Okay, Mom."

I took her back to 1985 to help her understand the sequence of events that led to the rocky road I'd trod. It was very difficult to bare my soul to the one person whose opinion mattered most. If her response was negative, I felt it'd throw me into a deeper abyss than the rape had.

As I spoke, I gauged her responses, changing my tone, its pace. Her body language was crystal clear: hurt, empathy, protection. I wanted to reach out and cradle her in my arms, but I refrained, knowing that moment was crucial for us both. It'd show me how she'd respond to another person's traumas, and, it'd help me release the secret that had held me captive. I finished.

Slowly, she began, "Mom, I don't lose respect for you. On the contrary, I have more."

"Why?"

"Because there were so many bad things you could've done with your life—drugs, alcohol, selling your body—and you didn't. You turned it around for good."

I put my arms around her and held her tight. "Thank you, Nina," I whispered. Resting my chin on her shoulder, comforted, relieved. We cried together.

In those minutes, I soared higher than before. The remains I had buried could now be excavated. My chains had been broken. I said, "You know, honey, you've told me something some adults wouldn't say, and you're only eleven years old. God made a good team when he put us together. Now, I can write freely."

"To Jamie, you mean?"

"Yes."

She nodded. "So what are you gonna write him?"

"Well, he called and said he liked the synopsis I sent him. He wants me to write a book about my life, but I couldn't write about it until I told you what I just did."

Nina grimaced, looking uncomfortable, eyes shifting, and suddenly she started to cry. "Mom, I don't want people to think we're weird because of what happened."

"Sweetie, listen to me." I grabbed her hands. "I did nothing wrong. That guy who was supposed to be my friend committed the crime, not me."

"I know, Mom." She added, sniffling, "But people aren't nice sometimes."

"Nina, honey, people are people, we can't control what they say. Some will be nasty, but others won't. Putting this out there will help a lot of people in different ways. It would've helped me back then. This happens to a lot of people, men and women both, more than we know. They have to believe it wasn't their fault and stop blaming themselves. Trust me, this will be good, and we'll be fine." Since she was still a bit apprehensive, I added, "Besides, it won't be coming out right away. Things take time."

"Okay, Mom. But I don't wanna read the book until I'm in college."

"That's fine, honey. You don't have to read it unless you want to, and not until you're ready."

She nodded.

"Thank you, Nina." I kissed her forehead, hugged her once more, and went to my bedroom, where I sat down behind my computer and sent a short email to Jamie. The arduous task of writing my life story had begun.

Things moved along speedily; it was becoming cathartic to let my fingers do the talking. Water, tissues, and a wastebasket were always by my side. Three weeks and sixty-four pages later, I hit *send* and a rough draft of personal accounts went into Jamie's in box.

Having disclosed my most traumatic event, I waited, feeling lighter.

He called. "Julia, I gave this to the people who do the Jason Bourne movies. To me, you're a female Jason Bourne."

"I wouldn't say all that, but thanks."

"Anyway, I see this as a series, a one-week Lifetime movie, or full feature film. There are so many elements in here—love, war, life, death, crime, passion, betrayal—it covers everything movies should have. You're an incredible woman."

"Thank you, Jamie."

"Well," he went on, "your project was turned down because they're currently working on the story of a retired woman cop from New York. Because they started with that one and you were a cop too, they don't want to feature two films that can be similar."

"Okay."

"But Julia, don't sit on this. You got something good here. Get your book done. Let's get your movie made."

"All right. Thanks for your effort, Jamie."

That same month, Sandra Donofrio, an old college friend, called me while Nina was napping. "Hi, Jule." Her pleasant voice was a welcome break from my bright computer screen.

"Hey, Sandi! How you doing?"

She caught me up on her life and afterward, asked, "So what's going on with you on the West Coast? How do you like it?"

"The weather's fabulous. It's much better for me here with the MS. Low humidity, and the sun's not so hot 'cause you get a constant breeze from the Pacific Ocean. It's beautiful. I pull over in my car all the time to take pictures. Even the bad areas aren't so shabby."

"That's great. I'd like to go visit California one day. So what do you do over there?"

"Well, I've got some exciting news."

"Ooh, what?" she asked with anticipation in her voice.

"Can you believe a producer in LA is interested in making a movie about my life? He asked me to write my book first."

"*Sure* I believe it. You've been through some things that can help others. Are you going to include your rape?"

"Yes, I have to. It's a major part of my life." I couldn't believe how easy it was to say.

"Jule, that's so great. Think about all the people you'll help. Maybe some can report the crime to the police if the statute of limitations hasn't expired."

"I hope so. That'd be great!" She was right; the healing of others, and the opportunity to purge myself once and for all, were my driving forces.

"You know, Jule, I wasn't conscious during my rape either, and although I wondered what happened, I knew it in my subconscious." My pretty, dear friend Sandi had been a date rape victim in her early twenties.

Without knowing the details that had been on my mind for such a long time, she went on. "You know what I did the next day?"

"No," I answered, curious.

"I kissed him, Jule."

I held my breath. *Like me.* "Why?" Maybe, I thought, she'd answer my own questions.

"Unknowingly, I was validating the immoral act committed against me by kissing him. If I justified it by replacing it with a hypothetical relationship, I could avoid its reality."

My questions were being answered. Without conscious thought, she had explained my rationale for kissing Judas the following day. The thought that had been corroding my inner being finally made sense. Captive, I continued to listen.

"I even asked him how the sex had been."

Just like me. It was an epiphany.

"The jerk said it had been good. When he said that I'd *screamed* the whole time, I knew he'd raped me, because that's not my style. What an asshole. The whole incident was repulsive, and I knew I'd have to address it sooner or later."

A soft light at the end of the tunnel had begun to emerge, and I said, "I did the same thing, Sand. For a long time, I thought I was losing my mind, and wondered how I could've betrayed myself."

"Don't, Jule. I think it's normal. Think about it. It's our brain's defense mechanism to prevent a victim's emotional harm in order to ensure survival and sanity." She was always good at explaining things, arranging events in their proper categories, defining their ambiguous nature.

I nodded on the other end of the line. "Yes. It makes sense. Thank you so much for clearing that up. I was so confused and felt really bad about it. You're the only person I ever told."

"Well, don't feel bad about it anymore. I think it's a great thing you're doing. It'll help you in the process as well. Write freely. Maybe reading your book will make it easier for others to talk about their experiences and ease their troubles."

"Thanks, Sandi. You're a life saver, really."

After ending the call, I concluded that God would lead me through the writing of my book. A script had begun to unfold, and I was more than willing to be a participant under His direction.

24

Purging Waste

Every page I wrote strengthened me—united scattered fragments, cleared emotional pollution, laid a solid foundation. In time, I no longer blamed myself for what I had or hadn't done, and began to describe my experiences to others who'd had similar ones, affirming how many carry heavy burdens keeping them from loved ones, just as I'd had.

In the summer of 2010, before Nina and I left for our trip to New Jersey, I searched for Anthony and Judas on Facebook, and found the latter. I sent him a private message: *Hi Judas, I'll be in Jersey this July. Please call my cell. It's time we spoke. Julia.*

As expected, he didn't respond.

Our twenty-fifth-year high school reunion was approaching that September; as part of the planning committee, I, Maria Arriola-Fernandez, and Rolando Corujo met for a late lunch at Houlihan's in Weehawken early one evening.

I spotted my former classmates in a booth and waved. "It's almost here," I said, taking a seat.

"We gotta make sure we've covered everything," insisted Mari.

Over nachos, chicken salads, and iced teas, we spoke of the alumni who couldn't make it and others we still hadn't found. "When I get back to Cali, I'll try to find Mandy Fajardo."

Suddenly, Rolando said, "Judas says he's not interested in going."

"Why wouldn't he be?" Mari asked as a young woman with a yellow hobo bag over her shoulder greeted someone at the table to my right.

I ate some salad, curious to hear his reply but pretending not to be.

He sipped his beverage before answering, "I don't know. I'm just relaying the message."

"You're in touch with him?" I asked, trying to appear casual, paying attention to the tone of my voice.

"I see him now and then."

Something about Rolando seemed suspicious—dark eyes inquisitive, words too vague. I wondered what had, and hadn't, been said in their conversation. Hoping he'd follow through if Rolando asked, I said, "Give him my cell and tell him to call me."

"Okay," he said, too nonchalantly.

Our meeting ended once we paid, and we parted ways.

Judas did not contact me.

Two weeks later at Limoncello, an Italian restaurant in North Palm Beach, Florida, as the sun shone bright, I waited in the parking lot with Nina seated in the back. From my radio, Andrea Bocelli's soothing voice sang of love—until the car that pulled alongside us drowned it by trumpets blasting salsa tunes. I looked over. "It had to be you."

"Of course," Narciso said, raising his hands.

We climbed out of our vehicles and headed inside.

A host led us to the dining area, past a display of mouth-watering appetizers. The ambiance was perfect for our pending conversation: walls in rich earth tones lit by sconces between framed artwork.

"*Benvenuto. Buon appetito*," said the good-looking Italian who handed us menus. "Your waiter will be with you shortly."

Amid the scent of garlic, our server arrived with warm sourdough bread and butter florets. "*Buona sera*. Are you ready to order?"

After taking our requests for soft drinks, ravioli *all'aragosta*, salmon *alla griglia*, and *pollo sorrentina*, he left.

"How do you like Cali?" Narciso asked Nina.

"It's good." She grabbed baked bread from the basket, the butter melting on it as she spread it on with her knife.

"Do you like it better than Florida?"

She shrugged and took a bite.

"Your mom says you changed your mind about acting?"

"Yeah, it wasn't what I thought." She began chewing, a clear indication that she didn't want to talk.

Feeling the need to fill the uneasy silence, I said, "Nina, honey, I told your dad about the book."

She looked over at him.

"Yeah," he said. "You ladies are gonna be famous."

I ignored his remark. "He wants to tell you something."

Eyes inquisitive, she held her fork over her plate. "What?"

"Well. . .you know, your mom and I got divorced when you were little? I made errors, and we've talked about them." His indirect approach was making her more uncomfortable. The waiter returned with our dishes at the perfect time.

"This smells delicious," said Narciso, rubbing his hands.

I wished he'd get to the point. Nina ate in silence. I looked across at Narciso, raising my eyebrows to prod him on.

He resumed, "I'm not like that anymore. Your mom forgave me. But it was hard for me, too many changes. I did the best I could, but I made mistakes. It's okay now."

It was enough ambiguity. I changed the topic. "We're moving to a base when we get back. Nina wanted to live on one." The remainder of the meal continued with snippets of general conversation and bridging awkward gaps—Nina not wanting to be there, her dad either trying to ignore her lack of interest or oblivious to it. We finished our dinner and parted ways.

The ride to Mom's was quiet. Nina gazed out the window; slight creases on her forehead confirmed that she was thinking. I said nothing, figuring we'd talk about it the next day.

In the morning, we drove to Sanibel Island, taking Mom with us. We enjoyed the calm, careless feeling of beach living and tried to go there whenever we could.

After settling in, Nina, Mom—whom I used as my cane—and I walked over the driftwood path to the ocean. My daughter dove right into the sparkling water; the sand was full of seashells, seagulls cawing.

A short while later, inner tube around my hips, I entered the water and floated toward Nina. I sighed. "I just love the peace here."

"Yeah, it's nice," she said, looking around in the far distance at a sailboat in the middle of the ocean.

"Can we talk?"

"Sure, Mom."

"Did you understand anything your dad said yesterday?"

"I was doing okay until he started using big Spanish words I didn't know, and then none of it made sense."

"He was just beating around the bush. See, when I told him about the book, we agreed to discuss the reason for our divorce with you, together. But when I saw how uncomfortable and confused you got when he was talking, I changed the topic."

"Thanks, Mom."

"You're welcome." Slowly, I began, "Look, honey...your dad got physical with me three times."

Her eyes widened.

"It's okay now. Since I had a baseball philosophy when it came to relationships—a three-strikes-you're-out policy—the third time, he had to go."

She was absorbing my words.

"I stayed married ten months more than I should have because I always wanted to raise a family with both parents."

She grinned. "Mom, that's more of a reason to get a divorce."

"You're right, and wiser beyond your years. I admire you. Yes, I should've left when it first happened."

She nodded, a serious expression on her face, empathy in her eyes.

"I love you, Nina."

"I love you too, Mom."

"You all right?"

"Yeah, I'm good."

"Any questions?"

"No." She grabbed onto my floatie. "I'm glad you're okay."

Today, communication with Narciso is scarce. His parenting skills and work ethic remain poor, and I remain the sole caregiver, something which, in hindsight, would've ended our marriage anyway. She is no longer the child who doesn't see his true colors, and I no longer the mom who wishes to make excuses for him.

We returned to Fort MacArthur in San Pedro, California, enjoying the beautiful ocean views, a cool breeze in the mornings. It was the perfect atmosphere for writing and for MS; perhaps the two worked in concert, releasing rotting carcasses, replacing them with wholesome flesh. However, I was still on a quest for answers that three people, but mainly one, I thought, could provide. I found Mandy and dialed her number one evening.

She answered on the second ring. "Hello?"

"Mandy?"

"Yes. Who's this?"

"Julia Torres."

"Wow, Julia Torres! What a blast from the past!"

"Yes, it's been a long time. How are you and the family?"

"Good. Everyone's great." Her words seemed perfunctory, scripted, hollow. Then she said, "You know, your grandmother was a special woman. I still remember her. Man, she was something!"

I heard the nostalgia in her voice. "Yes, she was. I still miss her." That's strange—why is she bringing that up now? I sensed that she had mentioned Abuela to keep me from discussing something else. She knew I wouldn't taint her memory by following it with negative talk. Perhaps I was reading too much into it, but when she mentioned having a disabled relative, I didn't want to burden her further. "Well, I'm calling to let you know that we're having our twenty-fifth-year high school reunion this month. You interested in going?"

". . .I don't know, Julia, but I don't think so."

"Well, if you change your mind, just show up that night."

I wondered how the incident so long before had affected her but knew it had remained troubling from the brevity and lack of affect in our conversation.

That night, in our cozy family room, with Nina asleep upstairs, I proceeded to write about what I thought I'd found closure on years before. Yet detailing it, and bringing it back to memory from hidden recesses in my mind, stirred up unexpected emotion.

Shoulders slumped, heaving with the wretchedness I had felt, angrily shouting, "*Why?*" I finally had the breakdown essential for my healing. Years of isolating a pretense, welcoming its bold desire to combust, I sobbed for all the years I hadn't. I fell asleep spent, knowing full well I'd still have to speak to two more people—Anthony and Judas.

By March of 2011, I had written over two hundred pages. Life on base was grand, but I sensed that it was time for us to move back to Jersey, where we'd known all along we'd return for Nina's high school years. Late at night on the 28th, wanting to be sure, I prayed before bedtime: God, give me a sign so clear that I don't have to second guess in any way.

At 5:15 a.m. the next morning, the bell tone on my cell phone rang. Who could it be? I thought, groggy with sleep. Reaching to my nightstand, I looked to see who it was: Lester Burns.

The text read: *Julia please get out of CA this year love you.* Smiling, I shook my head, amazed at God's way of sending me an irrefutable sign.

Ok. Praise God! U answrd last nite's prayr. Call u l8tr, I replied.

Later that morning, I relayed the news to Nina after Burns had explained sensing a prodding to send me that text at that specific time. Nina agreed that it had been our sign.

I was eager to see what God had in store for us, and on July 1, 2011, after ten years of living elsewhere, we drove cross-country.

It was great to be home.

Finding a place to live, having our furniture delivered, and registering Nina for school were simple. While she was in classes, I resumed writing my book and went to a gym to de-stress.

Before you knew it, my daughter had begun her freshman year and, aside from continuing the book, I had begun an Elijah House Inner Healing class at Calvary Temple in Wayne, facilitated by Reverend Dee VerHagen: a course that assisted people with bitter roots, forgiveness, and judgments.

Things rolled along, and I went to see a psychiatrist, something I should've done a long time before. Between talking to her, typing away at old skeletons on my desktop, and meeting in small discussion groups after Elijah classes, God was transforming me into a new person.

I made a final concerted effort to learn the truth. Based on my doctor's recommendation to try to sound cordial, I sent Judas another private message at 1:14 a.m. on October 15, 2012: *Hi Judas, It's been a long time, but I can recall when we were friends. Although things changed, God has a funny way of turning things around. Please know that I hold no ill towards you. If it's okay, I'd like to meet. You can pick the time and place. Call my cell when you can: I'm in Jersey for awhile. I hope to hear from you, honestly. Best to your family, Julia.*

The Facebook messenger noted that it had been seen at 8:56 a.m., on October 15, 2012, but he didn't reply.

A few days later, I called Mandy to give it a final try.

"I was just getting ready to leave," she said, "but I saw a different area code and wondered who it was."

"I won't hold you. Just wanted to say that I'd love to sit down and catch up with you."

"That'd be nice."

Perhaps she was ready to tell me what she knew, but that notion was short-lived. She paused and added, "We don't have to see each other, but you can call me anytime."

My balloon deflated. "Okay. I'll try you another time."

I did. The first two times, I left messages, the third, I did not. It was over.

Having obtained Judas' number, I called him three times the morning of October 18, 2012, from Nina's godmother's business, her godfather beside me. He answered the third call. "Hello?"

"It's Julia," I said.

"Oh." He was guarded.

"Can we meet?"

"I don't think that's a good idea."

"Why not?"

"I have no desire to speak to you. I have nothing to say."

"I have some questions."

"Well, you can ask over the phone but we don't have to meet."

I was surprised. Maybe that means he'll talk, I thought. "Okay. When's a good time? Sounds like you're busy."

"No, I'm not. Right now's fine. What do you want to know?"

"Why did you do what you did?"

"Julia, you know, it's been a long time. I don't have to answer anything." My doctor was right; he was afraid of me. His tone changed entirely—frustration, annoyance, fear.

"Don't you think I have a right to know?"

"I have no desire to speak with you."

"Why not?"

"I don't keep in touch with people from high school. I can't believe you're still calling me with this."

"What are you talking about? It's the first time I've called."

"That was a long time ago. I have no interest in talking to you. I don't want to go there. If you want to continue bringing this up, I have nothing to say."

"Continue? I haven't spoken to you in twenty-five years."

"Well, then, you know, keep it another twenty-five."

"But I have questions only you can answer."

"Well, you know, I have no desire to answer any of them.

Look, I have a family now, and I don't want to stay in touch with anyone from high school."

"We're not staying in touch. Don't you think I deserve to know what happened?"

"I'm hanging up. I don't have anything else to say."

"I guess you haven't addressed it yet."

"Think whatever you want."

"I'm okay with it."

"Good-bye, Julia."

I hung up before he could. Brent, Nina's godfather, patted my back. He'd heard my end of the conversation and figured out who I'd been speaking to. I turned towards him, shaking my head. "I was hoping he'd say something."

"He's not."

"But why? Doesn't what he did bother him?"

"No. Motherfuckers like that don't have remorse."

My cell phone rang. "Hello?"

"Julia, it's Rolando. Judas just called me."

"Oh, that's interesting. We just spoke."

"Yeah, I know. He said you kept calling him."

"I only called him three times. Listen, I don't wanna taint your thoughts with what he said to me, so you speak first."

He began, "Well, after exchanging the obligatory how-you-doings, he proceeded to ask me if I speak to you. I told him that I do but not on a regular basis, and that I bump into your brother once in a while since he lives up the road from me. He asked me if I gave you his number, and I asked why I would give you his number, and I pointed out to him that his number is on Facebook and that anyone there could have given you his number. He sounded anxious, so I asked him what the problem was."

After our 2010 reunion, Rolando, Mari and I had remained in contact. Having disclosed the contents of my book to him, Rolando, had been in a perfect position when Judas called—assessing subtle nuances and behavior without bias.

"And?" I asked.

"He said that you were a psycho. He tells me that you have repeatedly called and harassed him. I ask him, 'About what?' He says, 'It's not important,' that you had accused him of something that dated back to the high school prom, that I could easily figure out what you had accused him of doing, that it was the worst thing a guy could be accused of. So I jokingly asked him if he owed you money or had stolen something from you years back, and he said no. I ask again what it was, and he says I should forget it. That you were a crazy psycho. He says, 'Hey, don't worry about it, it's not important.' I say, 'OK, but if you want to keep your number private, then don't list it on Facebook, you idiot.' My exact words to him. He laughs and says, 'I know. I didn't realize it was there.' That was basically the conversation. We eventually hung up."

"Rolando, I didn't mention the prom. That's guilt speaking. He's just setting up his defense. Typical. Crazy psycho. That's funny and redundant."

"Yeah, I laughed. You're the most sensible woman I know. You know, Julia, I never doubted you. But when he spoke, it was so obvious, he sounded guilty. I mean, he was nervous, he giggled, stammered.... I'd like to call him back, see if he'll admit something."

"Go ahead. He opened up the can of worms."

"I'll call him in a couple of days."

I knew a lie would not live. Rolando didn't wait; he called him within the hour, and afterward, he relayed the dialog to me: "'Judas, you left me very confused about why you called me to talk about Julia. I thought that, if there was an issue between you two, maybe I could patch it up—so I called her after we spoke and asked her what the issue was with you. . .and after asking her many times, she broke down. She told me something very disturbing, and—'

"'What did she say?'

"'She said you raped her after the prom.'

"He says, 'That is a total lie. I was a total gentleman at the prom.'

"'Well, did you go anywhere after?'

"'We ended up down the shore.'

"I ask him, 'Did you rape her, dude?'

"He says, 'No! Of course not! I only kissed her a few times . . . . It was Anthony.'

"'Who's that?'

"'Mandy's date. We were lying in bed side by side. We had been drinking a bit. We could hear Mandy tell him to stop! To get off her! To take his hands off her! It happened for awhile. We went to sleep. We woke up the next day, and we saw Mandy's panties on the floor, torn and bloodied. We knew what had happened. But I never touched Julia. I will not apologize for something I didn't do. I want to put it behind me. Besides, I believe in karma—if I did do something, it'll come back to me. She's crazy, dude. She's been harassing me for years. Now she's calling me at home.'

"So I say, 'Well, and here I thought it was about money or belongings—' playing it stupid. 'I was going to try and patch this up. I would have given her whatever you owed her, so that this feud ended. So that everyone could be cordial again! . . . But I gotta tell you, Judas, these are serious accusations, and I want no part of it. You hear me, Judas? Why did you call me in the first place? This is a matter between you and her. Now you got me involved. So I'm going to tell you *once*. I don't ever want you to call me about this or anything to do with this. . .or I will blow my stack, OK, Judas? You *comprende?*' He says, "Yes, and I'm sorry you got involved.' I say, 'No, Judas, I didn't get involved—you *got* me involved when you called me earlier with accusations that I gave Julia your number. That is fucked up, dude!' Then he says, "Please tell Julia that, if I did something wrong, that God or Karma will get me. . .so I will get mine.' So I said, 'Again, don't *ever* call me about this shit. This is seriously ugly stuff, Judas! I remember you being not so kind to a few girls back in our high school days! . . . I will not be going to any more of your poker games, so don't bother including me in your poker list on Facebook.' He says, "OK. . .sorry again.' I hang up."

I began, "Rolando, it's transference of culpability. That's what he's doing. Look, he *was* a perfect gentleman at the prom, I told you that. The problem was *after*. When I called him, all I asked was, 'Why did you do what you did?' His guilt brought up the prom, and he's blaming Anthony for what he did. If I'd heard Mandy telling him to get off, like he says I did, I would've done something about it, and why didn't he, if that was true? And my bikini wasn't torn or full of blood. It had blood on it. . . . Rolando, he put something in my drink. I felt numb. It hurts when you have sex for the first time, and I didn't feel anything. And I couldn't even speak, or lift a finger."

"Julia, no doubt he drugged you, and I wouldn't be surprised if he did it before. He didn't have a good reputation with women. He was a douche bag."

"I never knew that. We were just friends. He was never nasty with me. I wouldn't have gone with him to the prom otherwise."

"Well, I told him not to talk to me about that matter again."

One more puzzle piece was missing—Anthony. I found him and called. "Hey, it's Julia Torres. You went to the prom with my friend, and we went down the shore after. Can we meet?"

We agreed to meet at TGIF's in Clifton at nine o'clock that Friday. I got there early and sat facing the host stand. About forty minutes later, after I'd eaten a salad, a dark-haired guy, about forty years old, entered. I recognized him right away and waved him over. I rose. "It's been a long time, Anthony. Thanks for meeting me."

"No problem. You look great." We sat down, and when the waitress arrived, he ordered an appetizer and a beer.

After some small talk, he said, "Tell Mandy we didn't have sex."

I peered at him. "What are you talking about?"

"I figured that's why you called." He began to explain. "She thought we had sex, although I told her we didn't. Remember you were consoling her the next day?"

"I was?"

"Yeah. When I came in the room, she was crying, and I heard you tell her, 'Look at your underwear. Is it stained?' She shook her head, and you said, 'You didn't have sex with him.'"

"You know, now that you said that, I *do* remember saying that to her. I had forgotten. But why would you have felt guilty if you didn't do anything?"

"Because she *thought* we had. It wasn't like I didn't try. When I heard you and Judas, I asked her if she wanted to, but she said no."

"What did you hear?" I asked, hoping for some answers.

"The bed."

"Any voices?"

"No."

The waitress arrived with his order, and once she'd departed, I asked, "Were you able to see anything?"

"No, it was dark."

"There was some light coming from the window," I suggested.

"I didn't see anything."

"When did it begin?"

"I don't remember."

"Was it long?"

"I don't know. We were all pretty drunk." He looked confused.

"No, not Judas. I was out after I went to the bathroom. That's why you didn't hear any voices. He raped me."

Anthony was stunned. "Julia, I—I didn't know. I'm so sorry that happened to you. After hearing that, I'm glad I didn't keep insisting. Please, tell her we didn't have sex. . . . Julia, if I had known what was happening to you, I would've stopped it."

"I don't blame you. I was just hoping you knew something."

"Did you try asking Mandy?"

"Yes. She won't return my calls. Judas either."

He grinned. "Of course he won't. But why not her?"

"I don't know. Maybe she feels bad about not stopping it, but I don't blame her. Judas was the bad guy here, no one else. He drugged me."

"You think so?"

"He had to, I was numb. Roofies' side effects fit. Did you see him slip anything into my drink?"

"No."

"I was hoping you did."

"I'm sorry, Julia. I wouldn't have known anything about that drug anyway. It's not something I would've done. My mom would've kicked my ass." Eyes soft, voice clear, he said, "I wish I could've been more help."

"Me, too. By the way, just so you know, he's putting what he did on you."

"Of course."

After settling the bill, he walked me to my Hummer. "Julia, I'm really sorry. Call me whenever you want to talk."

"Thank you, Anthony."

I drove out of that lot, window down, cool breeze in my hair, knowing it was over with him, too.

Julia Torres

25

Alpha and Omega

THIS IS THE CHAPTER WHEN THE WRITING SLOWS DOWN—riding the brakes to scan areas uncovered, reversing for places overlooked, making sure no turns were missed. Having revealed so much of my life, I am no longer crushed or tormented by my past; rather, I feel invigorated, having apologized to some people, accepting and forgiving others—my family, whose views were drastically different from mine, but most of all, myself. Wondering where I go from here leaves me with no trepidation, for I know the possibilities are endless.

The depths of words I had not previously understood, which had brought tears, now ring in my head—"Julie, it's the process of writing the book that's important. This book is for *you* first. Then, others." Glorin had been right.

Glorin Torres-Batistich, my friend and Christian mentor,

and her husband Andrew, were introduced to me through a mutual friend, Perla Regina Espinal. Before "Reg," as I called her, died of breast cancer on October 18, 2010, her hope was that we'd form a bond; we had.

I dialed Glorin. "It's almost done, girl," I said, letting out a deep breath.

"*Hollah hollah!*" she shouted with glee. "How do you feel?"

"Relieved, happy, a little anxious. It's like giving birth, you know. You anticipate the time, try to make sure you have what you need."

"Julie, what are you talking about? God's gonna make sure whatever needs to be there is there. Or haven't you listened to anything?"

"You're right as usual, lest I forget. I should just stop trying to stir the pot, huh?"

"Yep, like the seventeen or twenty-one chapters. I told you you were gonna write books." She was referring to how I'd wanted one of my favorite numbers to be the number of chapters in my book. She'd been correct there as well; it'd turned out to be a total of fifty chapters in two books. "Who's in control?"

"God. No doubt. You know how much this book has changed."

"Yes, I do. You were angry in the Judas parts when you first started it. Cursed a whole lot more, too, especially when you talked about that army captain of yours making things worse for you overseas." On many occasions, my poor friend had heard me curse like the truck driver I had been in the Gulf, but she hadn't complained, knowing God would correct my foul mouth.

"Yep. Guilty."

"Good girl." Her voice softened. "Julie, you've been running from Him, and God is a gentleman—He won't push His way into anybody's life. He's gotta be invited in. He's had a plan for you before your mother had you."

"I know, Glorin. I'm a condom baby, remember? The tip of that Chinese rubber broke off." I chuckled, "Then Mom tried those warm baths to prevent me from being born. Goes to show those old wives' tales are senseless, 'cause here I am. It's just like little me to try to prove people wrong. That's funny. I can see myself thinking, *You can try whatever you want, lady, but I'm gonna be born.* I know I have a mission. Like that verse says, huh? What is it again?"

"Hold on." She called out to her husband Andrew, "Daddy, how's that verse go about God knowing us before the womb?

I could hear Andrew's familiar voice in the background. I admired them; they imparted *agape:* a spiritual, selfless love for humanity, as Jesus revealed. It was a joy to be around them; their love and respect for one another was transparent. It was the kind of relationship I aspired to have in the near future.

"He said...wait, he'll tell you." She handed him the phone.

"Hello, my love, how are you?"

"Good. You?"

"I'm great. It's good to hear your beautiful voice." That was her tender-hearted hubby, quick with kind words. "That verse says, 'I knew you before I formed you in your mother's womb. Before you were born I set you apart.'"

"That's it! Man, you know 'em all. I guess that's why you're a pastor."

He laughed. "My wife always says that. You two are so alike."

"We are. Andrew, I wanna thank you for the love and support you guys gave me during the writing of this book. It helped me become fully delivered, and you were right. God did turn it around for good."

"That's right. Romans 8:28, 'And we know that all things work together for good to them that love God, to them who are called according to His purpose.'" He paused. "Julia, God's plans are to prosper you, not to harm you. He wants to give you hope and a future."

I knew what verse he was referring to and shouted with excitement, "Jeremiah 29:11, my favorite Old Testament verse!"

"Good. Always remember it. He'll use what you've been through to lead others out of the same captivity that he has set you free from. Satan tried to hurt you. There are demonic spirits on Earth trying to keep people in bondage, but that's why Jesus came. What that kid Judas did to you will always be wrong, and those men in the military, too. That wasn't from God. Maybe years from now, they'll ask for your forgiveness, having felt convicted, because it is God's desire that no one perish. We may not know why certain things happen, until we die and it's revealed in heaven, but God is always good."

"I know what you mean, Andrew. I know God didn't make the bad happen to me, and the fact that he didn't stop it doesn't decrease my faith in Him."

"That's good. He blesses the faithful. My family and I love you very much, Julia."

"So do me and Nina."

ONE NIGHT, WANTING ANSWERS, I called Glorin. Leaning against the granite kitchen countertop, I asked, "When am I gonna catch a break?"

She had once said, "You come in peace, or you come in pieces." Being meek, tranquil individuals, Andrew, and our friend Reg had come to God in peace. I and Glorin, fiery by nature, had come in pieces. Lovers and fighters—that's what the four of us were. No wonder I'd had to get knocked around when others, it seemed, had had it easier, but I was tired of being beaten with what appeared to be a battering ram, and becoming upset that I didn't have someone worthwhile in that present stage of my life.

"With what?"

"A good relationship. I see people shacking up so quickly, sometimes just after a break-up, or getting married, having kids, whatever...." I looked out the window over the sink, at nothing in particular, before adding, "And I'm still single. It's frustrating." She was the only person I ever vented with. Accustomed to doling out advice, I had seldom been on the receiving end before Glorin came along.

"Don't go comparing yourself. You're assuming they're happy. A lot of people can't be alone. They don't make wise decisions and get with the first person they meet. Do you settle, Julie?"

"No. You know I don't."

The familiar clanging of metal on metal signaled her culinary preparations. "Then what's the problem? What do you need?"

"It's not about *need*. It's about wanting to have someone to talk to, go out with, travel, you know, and share what I have."

"To get married, too. You're not opposed to that, are you, or if he has children?"

"Not at all."

"All right. God knows the desires of your heart, Julie. He has a special man for you, just like you like 'em."

"Bad ass."

She laughed. "Yeah, if that's what you wanna call him, mighty man of God. You'll have a breakthrough soon."

"Well, I can't wait for this Lone Ranger."

"That's right, honey. And you're his Tonto."

I laughed. "Yeah, I even have my arrows ready."

"Oh, you're too much. Julie, God's been working the kinks out of you."

"I have *that* many?"

"Well, you've been carrying them like they're yours. They belong to Him—'Come to me all who are weary and I will give you rest?'—not you."

I sighed. "It took me a long time to accept that. I'm not gonna lie—at times, I still carry them."

"It's all right. You're still learning. But look at you, God turned bad into good. You're free. He's gonna set others free, too. Dry bones are gonna live again."

"Amen. You sound like your husband. Glorin, you know what I really hope?"

"What, honey?"

"I really hope that these words bring people to God, that they ask Jesus into their heart and let Him guide them. If they see how He turned my life around, they'll know it'll happen to them too, 'cause I'm no different. I want people to know that life is better with Him."

"Julie, the word of God is never void. The other day, John 13:7 came to me, and I know God meant it for you. He wants you to include it in your book. It says, 'Jesus replied, *You do not realize now what I am doing, but later you will understand.*' This is gonna be big, Julie."

"I believe it. You're not the first person that's told me that. I'm looking forward to seeing where God is gonna take this 'cause all along the way, He's introduced me to key people, without me even trying. It's really cool, to just go with the flow."

"That's right, Julie, and think of those buildings that'll come out of this, for runaways, domestic violence victims, rape victims."

"Yeah, they'll be counseled, empowered, learn a trade. That's one of my dreams. That, and helping inner city youth with scholarships."

"It'll happen because you have the right attitude. God will bless that. You're trying to help others. It's not about you."

"No, it's not."

"Julie, have you forgiven Judas?"

"'Cause we're talking about right attitudes, huh? Glorin, I thought about the Elijah House teaching on forgiveness, and how not doing it affects the one who's been hurt. I didn't know if I really had—could've sworn I did, but just to make sure, I asked myself, if I passed him on the side of the road, and he was lying on the ground all bloody and dying, and no one was around, would I help? You know, I'd probably be disgusted at first, but I'd have to stop. Not because I'm a goody-two-shoes, you know that, but because I'm accountable to

God."

"Uh-huh. Go on, I'm listening."

"If I said, 'You're gonna be all right,' just like in the military, my voice might crack. I might wanna puke if I had to touch him to stop the bleeding, and I might think he didn't deserve to live, but God would prevail."

"Why?"

"Because I'd think of Jesus. God sent Him to die for us, and that includes rapists and murderers, as much as I may not agree, 'cause I'm human. But, it's what God's wanted since the beginning of time, to have everybody live in heaven after they died. So yes, I'd save his life. Glorin, I've asked Him for the ability to forgive 'cause it's hard. My CO in the Gulf, too."

"That's good, Julie. God'll keep helping you forgive, and one day, you won't even be feeling those things you said. We forgive through God, and it *is* hard for us, especially in cases like yours, but that's why God wants you to ask for His help because we can't do it on our own."

That conversation ended with hope, and this self-driven individual was eventually transformed, receptive to seek God's will, to find a church home: Abundant Grace Christian Church in Rutherford, New Jersey, pastored by Steve Hannett, where religiosity does not hinder, and Jesus reigns.

Things were finally falling into place, and one sunny afternoon, while I sat on a wooden pew in the back of the church, the pastor announced the start of a leadership series of classes to strengthen and expand the church worldwide. A video depicting overseas missions in impoverished countries was playing overhead. At its end, Pastor Steve concluded, "If anyone is interested in pursuing roles as pastors, missionaries, evangelists, and church planters, or would enjoy learning more about the word of God, please see me after service."

While some members strolled down the empty tree-lined street on that clear spring day, others remained speaking with friends as the pastor's wife put her toddler in a stroller. I approached him at the bottom of the entrance steps. "Pastor?"

"Yes, Julia?"

"I'm a forever student. When you said 'learn more about the word of God,' I thought that was cool. Sometimes I'm in conversations and I can't take it further because I don't know how to answer certain questions or direct them where to look."

He nodded. "Apologetics."

"What's that?"

"Offering a defense. It's what you mentioned, trying to explain something while defending your beliefs."

"I didn't know there was a name for that. Anyway, I heard the word 'missions,' and it got me interested. I've thought about going on missions before. And now that I'm working on a master's in Homeland Security, maybe the two can work together somehow."

His eyes expressed confirmation. "Oh. It's interesting you say that. I've been talking with some people, and that's a strong possibility in the future."

In my Hummer, with Nina riding shotgun while I drove on Route 46, my future appeared very bright. My most adventurous years weren't behind me, after all; I had just scratched the surface. To make a vision a reality, for me, was a matter of claiming it as done, and I could envision this book's contents unfolding into a film, being spoken of in talk shows, and used in colleges and graduate dissertations.

Finally, I welcome the plans that God, not I, has in store for me. The adrenalin rush for the unexpected has started to form, assuring me that my life's direction would once again bring the thrills I thrived on. I can't wait to see when and how the euphoria will beckon me, but I know it'll be phenomenal.

Resources

GOD 24/7 Prayer Line
Cancer Treatment Centers of America 1-800-515-1217
Disabled American Veterans National HQ 1-877-I AM A VET
Narcotics Anonymous World Service 1-813-773-9999
National Center for Missing & Exploited Children 1-800-843-5678
National Center for PTSD 1-802-296-6300
National Domestic Violence Hotline 1-800-799-SAFE
National Multiple Sclerosis Society HQ 1-800-344-4867
National Runaway Safeline 1-800-621-4000
National Sexual Assault Hotline 1-800-656-HOPE
Paralyzed Veterans of America National HQ 1-800-424-8200
VA Benefits 1-800-827-1000
Wounded Warrior Project 1-877-832-6997

About the Author

Julia Torres believes one never stops learning. By the age of twenty-seven, she had obtained a bachelor of arts degree, completed a Teacher Certification program, enlisted in the U.S. Army, become a Persian Gulf War veteran, been awarded various medals, honors, and specialties, received a real estate license, graduated from a police academy, and acquired additional awards and training certificates.

In 2001, after a diagnosis of multiple sclerosis, Torres, then a single parent of a toddler, retired from law enforcement, but that didn't stop her. She devoted her time to raising a strong, confident child, and volunteered at police departments and courthouses, obtaining further training and licensing to assist adults and children, victims of crime. Later, she became involved in an old passion, acting, and attended Bible studies to increase her knowledge in the word of God.

Currently, she obtains her medical care at the East Orange VA, which, she states, has changed for the better since her 1991 encounter. Because MS is a spinal-cord injury, Julia joined the EOVA Thunder Team, participating in the annual National Veterans Wheelchair Games. She feels blessed and honored to train with her extended family—fellow vets, volunteers, and trainer Ralph Jones.

Aside from working on a Masters in Homeland Security, and a Bachelors in Ministry, Julia is preparing the way for her daughter's future in college. She describes that as the greatest challenge with the highest reward. She believes her future husband is right around the corner.

Passaic County Prosecutor's Office
Paterson, New Jersey

POLICE

Julia Torres
County Investigator

Signature — County Prosecutor

**COUNTY OF PASSAIC
PROSECUTOR'S OFFICE**

THIS IS TO CERTIFY THAT JULIA TORRES is attached to this office in the capacity of COUNTY INVESTIGATOR and is granted all privileges and is vested with all authority allowed by law.

County Prosecutor

RETIRED

"For I know the plans I have for you," says the Lord, "plans to prosper you and not to harm you, to give you a future and a hope."
—Jeremiah 29:11

www.ingramcontent.com/pod-product-compliance
Lightning Source LLC
Chambersburg PA
CBHW031313160426
43196CB00007B/519